D1267498

THE REVELS PLAYS

Former editors
Clifford Leech 1958–71
F. David Hoeniger 1970–85

General editors
David Bevington, E. A. J. Honigmann, J. R. Mulryne
and Eugene M. Waith

ENDYMION

John Lyly was undisputed master of the private theatre stage in the 1570s and 1580s, that is, for the acting companies comprised of boy actors performing in indoor select theatres like Blackfriars. Lyly's *Endymion* (1588) represents his famous Euphuistic style at its best and also gives us vintage Lyly as courtier and dramatist.

In this love comedy, Lyly retells an ancient legend of the prolonged sleep of the man with whom the moon (Cynthia) fell in love. The fable is piquantly relevant to Queen Elizabeth and her exasperated if adoring courtiers. This edition makes a new and compelling argument for the relevance of *Endymion* to the threat of the Spanish Armada invasion of 1588 and to the role of the Earl of Oxford in England's politics of that troubled decade. Full commentary is provided for every aspect of the play, including its philosophical allegory about the relation of the moon to mortal life on earth.

David Bevington is Phyllis Fay Horton Professor in the Humanities at the University of Chicago.

THE REVELS PLAYS

THE REVELS PLAYS

ENDYMION

JOHN LYLY

edited by David Bevington

MANCHESTER
UNIVERSITY PRESS

Manchester and New York

*Distributed exclusively in the USA and Canada
by* St. Martin's Press

Introduction, critical apparatus, etc.
© David Bevington 1996

Published by Manchester University Press
Oxford Road, Manchester M13 9NR, UK
and Room 400, 175 Fifth Avenue, New York, NY 10010, USA

Distributed exclusively in the USA and Canada
by St. Martin's Press, Inc., 175 Fifth Avenue, New York,
NY 10010, USA

British Library Cataloguing-in-Publication Data
A catalogue record for this book is available from the British Library

Library of Congress Cataloging-in-Publication Data
Lyly, John, 1554?–1606.
Endymion / John Lyly; edited by David Bevington.
        p.   cm.—(The Revels plays)
        ISBN 0-7190-1551-0
I. Endymion (Greek mythology)—Drama.   I. Bevington, David M.   II.
Title.   III. Series.
PR2302.E6L95   1996
        822'.3—dc20
                                                        95-21690
                                                        CIP

ISBN 0 7190 1551 0 hardback

First published 1996
99 98 97 96   10 9 8 7 6 5 4 3 2 1

Typeset in Hong Kong
by Best-set Typesetter Ltd
Printed in Great Britain
by Biddles Ltd, Guildford and King's Lynn

101196/6750 K8

Contents

TO GEORGE HUNTER

friend, wise editor, fellow-student of John Lyly

General Editors' Preface

Clifford Leech conceived of the Revels Plays as a series in the mid-1950s modelling the project on the New Arden Shakespeare. The aim, as he wrote in 1958, was 'to apply to Shakespeare's predecessors, contemporaries and successors the methods that are now used in Shakespeare editing'. The plays chosen were to include well known works from the early Tudor period to about 1700, as well as others less familiar but of literary and theatrical merit: 'the plays included,' Leech wrote, 'should be such as to deserve and indeed demand performance.' We owe it to Clifford Leech that the idea became reality. He set the high standards of the series, ensuring that editors of individual volumes produced work of lasting merit, equally useful for teachers and students, theatre directors and actors. Clifford Leech remained General Editor until 1971, and was succeeded by F. David Hoeniger, who retired in 1985.

The Revels Plays are now under the direction of four General Editors, David Bevington, E. A. J. Honigmann, J. R. Mulryne and E. M. Waith. Published originally by Methuen, the series is now published by Manchester University Press, embodying essentially the same format, scholarly character, and high editorial standards of the series as first conceived. The General Editors intend to concentrate on plays from the period 1558–1642, and may include a small number of non-dramatic works of interest to students of drama. Some slight changes have been forced by considerations of cost. For example, in editions from 1978, notes to the introduction are placed together at the end, not at the foot of the page. Collation and commentary notes will continue, however, to appear on the relevant pages.

The text of each Revels play, in accordance with established practice in the series, is edited afresh from the original text of best authority (in a few instances, texts), but spelling and punctuation are modernised and speech headings are silently made consistent. Elisions in the original are also silently regularised, except where metre would be affected by the change; since 1968 the '-ed' form is used for non-syllabic terminations in past tenses and past participles ('-'d' earlier), and '-èd' for syllabic ('-ed' earlier). The editor emends, as distinct from modernises, the original only in instances where error is patent, or at least very probable, and correction persuasive. Act divisions are given only if they appear in the original or if the structure of the play clearly points to them. Those act and scene divisions not in the original are provided in small type. Square brackets are also used for any other additions to or changes in the stage directions of the original.

Revels Plays do not provide a variorum collation, but only those variants which require the critical attention of serious textual students. All departures of substance from 'copy-text' are listed, including any relineation and those changes in punctuation which involve to any degree a decision between alternative interpretations; but not such accidentals as turned letters, nor necessary additions to stage directions whose editorial nature is already made clear by the use of brackets. Press corrections in the 'copy-text' are likewise collated. Of later emendations of the text, only those are given which as alternative readings still deserve attention.

One of the hallmarks of the Revels Plays is the thoroughness of their annotations. Besides explaining the meaning of difficult words and passages, the editor provides comments on customs or usage, text or stage-business—indeed, on anything judged pertinent and helpful. Each volume contains an Index to the Commentary, in which particular attention is drawn to meanings for words not listed in *OED*, and (starting in 1996, with this volume) an indexing of proper names and topics in the Introduction and Commentary.

The Introduction to a Revels play assesses the authority of the 'copy-text' on which it is based, and discusses the editorial methods employed in dealing with it; the editor also considers the play's date and (where relevant) sources, together with its place in the work of the author and in the theatre of its time. Stage history is offered, and in the case of a play by an author not previously represented in the series a brief biography is given.

It is our hope that plays edited in this fashion will promote further scholarly and theatrical investigation of one of the richest periods in theatrical history.

DAVID BEVINGTON
E. A. J. HONIGMANN
J. R. MULRYNE
E. M. WAITH

Preface

It has been my honour to collaborate with George Hunter (to whom this volume is dedicated) in editing two plays of John Lyly for Revels, *Campaspe* and *Sappho and Phao*. Although he edited the first and I the second, we compared notes at every stage and shared what wisdom we could bring to bear on our task. My work was greatly enriched by what I learned from that joint enterprise. Our plan is to continue with another volume of two plays, *Gallathea* and *Midas*.

Meantime, while George has been busy with a history of Renaissance drama in the Oxford History of English Literature, I have gone ahead with *Endymion*. The play is one that can suitably be edited in a single volume, I hope, since it is probably more often read than most of Lyly's other plays. I have been eager to get this edition into print partly because I think I have worked out a satisfactory explanation of the play's political and religious allegory in relation to fears of Spanish invasion in early 1588. I have not worked alone, however. George Hunter has contributed his advice as fully to this edition as to other aspects of our collaboration. Eugene Waith has been enormously helpful, as my fellow general editor of the Revels series and as supervisor of this present edition. I am no less grateful for the help and support of our British colleagues who are general editors for Revels, Ernst Honigmann and Ronnie Mulryne. Anita Roy, Matthew Frost, and other members of the staff at the Manchester University Press have offered unfailing assistance. Alan Nelson has read the introduction to this edition and has rescued me from a number of errors.

As in the edition of *Campaspe* and *Sappho and Phao*, spelling and punctuation in this present edition have been modernised. Editorial additions to the original stage directions are in square brackets. Lyly's massed entries of characters in accordance with the continental scheme of scene divisions have been altered to the more familiar convention of indicating when each character seems to enter. Speech headings are regularised, and some standard Elizabethan abbreviations are silently expanded. See 'This Edition' in the joint volume containing *Campaspe* and *Sappho and Phao* for further de-

tails about editorial principles, which apply here as well. Because
that volume also contains a brief biography of Lyly, no brief sketch
of the dramatist's life is presented here.

DAVID BEVINGTON

Abbreviations

ANCIENT TEXTS

Wherever possible, Graeco-Roman texts are cited by the standard reference to book, chapter, and paragraph for prose texts, and by book and line (for Virgil) or by book, poem, and line number (for Horace, Ovid, etc.) The Loeb Classical Library (LCL) offers a convenient edition for many of the following classical authors.

Aelian   Claudius Aelianus, *De Natura Animalium* (*On the Characteristics of Animals*), LCL.
Aeschylus   *The Oresteia*, LCL.
Apollodorus   *The Library*, LCL.
Apollonius Rhodius   *Argonautica*, LCL.
Apuleius   *Metamorphoses* (*The Golden Ass*), LCL.
Aristotle   *Nicomachean Ethics*, LCL.
Aristotle   *The Physics*, LCL.
Cicero   *Works* (*Tusculan Disputations, De Finibus Bonorum et Malorum, de Officiis, Paradoxa Stoicorum*), LCL.
Curtius Rufus   Quintus Curtius, *Works*, LCL.
Hesiod   *The Theogony*. In *The Homeric Hymns and Homerica*, LCL.
Homer   *Iliad*, LCL.
Homer   *Odyssey*, LCL.
Horace   *The Odes and Epodes*, LCL.
Juvenal   *Satires*, LCL.
Lucan   *Pharsalia*, LCL.
Lucian   *Works* (*Deorum Dialogi*), LCL.
Ovid   *Amores*, LCL.
Ovid   *Ars Amatoria*, LCL.
Ovid   *Heroides*, LCL.
Ovid   *Metamorphoses*, LCL.
Ovid   *Tristia*, LCL.
Pausanias   *Description of Greece*, LCL.
Phaedrus   *Babrius and Phaedrus*, LCL.
Plato   *Works* (*Phaedo*), LCL.
Plautus   *Plays*, LCL.
Pliny   Gaius Plinius Secundus, *Natural History*, LCL. References are to book and paragraph.
Plutarch   *Moralia*, LCL.
Terence   *Plays*, LCL.
Theocritus   *The Greek Bucolic Poets*, LCL.
Tibullus   *The Elegies of Albius Tibullus*, ed. Kirby Flower Smith (New York: American Book Co., 1913).
Virgil   *Aeneid*, LCL.

Virgil   *Eclogues*, LCL.
Virgil   *Georgics*, LCL.

OTHER ABBREVIATIONS

Abbott   E. A. Abbott, *A Shakespearian Grammar*, new edn, 1886. References are to numbered paragraphs.

Aesop   *The Fables of Aesop Paraphrased in Verse*, by John Ogilby (London: Thomas Roycroft, 1665).

Altman   Joel Altman, *The Tudor Play of Mind* (Berkeley: University of California Press, 1978).

Baker   George Pierce Baker, ed., *Endymion*, by John Lyly (New York: Henry Holt, 1894).

Bardon Papers   The Bardon Papers: Documents Relating to the Imprisonment and Trial of Mary Queen of Scots, Camden Society Publications, 3rd series, vol. XVII (London: Camden Society, 1909).

Barish   Jonas Barish, 'The Prose Style of John Lyly', *ELH*, XXIII (1956), 14–35.

Bartholomew   (Berthelet) *Batman upon Bartholome, His Book De Proprietatibus Rerum* (London: Thomas East, 1582), published in 1535 by Thomas Berthelet as *Bartholomaeus de Proprietatibus Rerum*. References are to book, chapter, and page.

Baskervill   C. R. Baskervill, Virgil B. Heltzel, and Arthur H. Nethercot, eds, *Endymion*, in *Elizabethan and Stuart Plays* (New York: Holt, 1934), pp. 171 ff.

Bennett   Josephine Waters Bennett, 'Oxford and *Endimion*', *PMLA*, LVII (1942), 354–69.

Berry   Philippa Berry, *Of Chastity and Power: Elizabethan Literature and the Unmarried Queen* (London: Routledge, 1989), pp. 111–33.

Best   Michael R. Best, 'The Staging and Production of the Plays of John Lyly', *Theatre Research*, IX (1968), 104–17.

Bevington   David Bevington, *Tudor Drama and Politics: A Critical Approach to Topical Meaning* (Cambridge, Mass.: Harvard University Press, 1968).

Bible   *The Bible and Holy Scriptures . . .* (Geneva, 1560).

Blount   *Six Court Comedies . . . by . . . John Lilly* (London: printed by William Stansby for Edward Blount, 1632).

Bond   R. Warwick Bond, ed., *The Complete Works of John Lyly*, 3 vols (Oxford, Clarendon Press, 1902).

Boughner   Daniel C. Boughner, 'The Background of Lyly's Tophas', *PMLA*, LIV (1939), 967–73.

Calendar of State Papers   Calendar of State Papers, Domestic Series, of the Reign of Elizabeth, 1581–1590, ed. Robert Lemon (Nendeln, Liechtenstein: Kraus Reprint, 1967).

Cartari   Vincenzo Cartari, *Le Imagini, con la Spositione de i Dei degli Antichi*, trans. into Latin as *Imagines Deorum*, 1556 and subsequent dates.

Chambers   E. K. Chambers, *The Elizabethan Stage*, 4 vols (Oxford: Clarendon Press, 1923).

Chambers, 'Court Performances'   'Court Performances before Queen Elizabeth', *MLR*, I (1906), 1–13.

Chaucer   *The Riverside Chaucer*, 3rd edn, gen. ed. Larry D. Benson (Boston: Houghton Mifflin, 1987).

CL   Comparative Literature.

CompD   Comparative Drama.

Conti   Natale Conti, *Natalis Comitis Mythologiae* (originally published 1551; Venice, 1581).

Daniel   Carter A. Daniel, ed., *The Plays of John Lyly* (Lewisburg, Pa.: Bucknell University Press, 1988).

Croll and Clemons   *Euphues: The Anatomy of Wit; Euphues & His England*, by John Lyly, ed. William Croll and Harry Clemons (London: G. Routledge, New York: Dutton, 1916).

Dent   R. W. Dent, *Proverbial Language in English Drama Exclusive of Shakespeare, 1495–1616* (Berkeley: University of California Press, 1984).

Dilke   Charles Wentworth Dilke, ed., *Old English Plays* (London: for John Martin, 1814), vol II.

DNB   The Dictionary of National Biography, ed. Leslie Stephen and Sidney Lee (Oxford, 1885–1900).

Drayton   *The Works of Michael Drayton*, ed. J. William Hebel, 6 vols (Oxford: for the Shakespeare Head Press by Basil Blackwell, 1961).

Edge, 'A Crux'   Donald Edge, ' "Philadelphi in 'Arays' "—A Crux in Lyly's *Endimion*', *N&Q*, CCXXIII, n.s. XXV (1978), 439–40.

Edge, '*Endimion*'   Donald Edge, 'Lyly's *Endimion*', *Explicator*, XXXIX.3 (1981), 3.

Edge, 'Prosody'   Donald Edge, 'Classical–Comical Prosody and Proportion in John Lyly's *Endimion*', *N&Q*, CCXXIX, n.s. XXXI (1984), 178–9.

Edge, 'Sources'   Donald Edge, 'Lyly–Ovid Parallels: *Endimion*'s Sources', *N&Q*, CCXXIX, n.s. XXXI (1984), 179–80.

ELH   English Literary History (ELH).

ELR   English Literary Renaissance.

EM   English Miscellany.

Erasmus, *Adagia*   In the *Opera Omnia*, ed. J. Leclerc, 10 vols (Leiden, 1703–6). The *Adagia* are also in process of being edited in *The Collected Works of Erasmus* (University of Toronto Press, 1978–).

Erasmus, *Apophthegmata*   In the *Opera Omnia*, ed. J. Leclerc, 10 vols (Leiden, 1703–06).

Erasmus, *Parabolae sive Similia*   In the *Opera Omnia* and in the *Collected Works*, as in the previous two notes.

Fairholt   F. W. Fairholt, ed., *The Dramatic Works of John Lilly* (London, 1858).

Feuillerat, *Documents*   Albert Feuillerat, *Documents Relating to the Office of Revels in the Time of Queen Elizabeth* (Louvain: Uystpruyst, 1908).

Feuillerat, *Lyly*   Albert Feuillerat, *John Lyly: Contribution à l'Histoire de la Renaissance en Angleterre* (Cambridge University Press, 1910, rpt New York: Russell & Russell, 1968).

Fleay   Frederick Gard Fleay, *A Biographical Chronicle of the English Drama, 1559–1642*, 3 vols (London: Reeves & Turner, 1891).

Fulgentius   Fabius Planciades Fulgentius, *Opera*, ed. Rudolf Helm, in the Bibliotheca Teubneriana (Leipzig, 1898); *Fulgentius the Mythographer*, trans. Leslie George Whitehead (Columbus: Ohio State University Press, 1971).

Gannon   C. C. Gannon, 'Lyly's *Endimion*: From Myth to Allegory', *ELR*, VI (1976), 220–43.

Gower   John Gower, *Confessio Amantis*, in *The Complete Works of John Gower*, ed. G. C. Macaulay, 3 vols (Oxford: Clarendon, 1901).

Gray   Henry David Gray, 'A Possible Interpretation of Lyly's *Endimion*', *Anglia*, XXXIX (1916), 181–200.

Greg   W. W. Greg, *A Bibliography of the English Printed Drama to the Restoration*, 4 vols (London, 1939–59).

Halpin   Rev. N. J. Halpin, *Oberon's Vision in 'The Midsummer-Night's Dream', Illustrated by a Comparison with Lylie's 'Endymion'* (London: for the Shakespeare Society, 1842).

Hawes   Stephen Hawes, *The Pastime of Pleasure* (London: for the Percy Society, 1845, from the edition of 1555).

Heywood   John Heywood, *A Dialogue of Proverbs* (London, 1546).

Heywood   John Heywood, *Epigrams* (1546).

Hillebrand   Harold N. Hillebrand, *The Child Actors* (Urbana: University of Illinois Press, 1926).

HLQ   *Huntington Library Quarterly.*

HSL   *Hartford Studies in Literature.*

Hunter   George K. Hunter, *John Lyly: The Humanist as Courtier* (London: Routledge & Kegan Paul, 1962).

Hunter and Bevington   George K. Hunter and David Bevington, eds, *John Lyly: 'Campaspe' and 'Sappho and Phao'* (Manchester University Press, 1991).

Huppé   Bernard F. Huppé, 'Allegory of Love in Lyly's Court Comedies', *ELH*, XIV (1947), 93–113.

Hyginus   *The Myths of Hyginus*, trans. and ed. Mary Grant (Lawrence: University of Kansas Publications, 1960).

Knapp   Robert S. Knapp, 'The Monarchy of Love in Lyly's *Endimion*', *MP*, LXXIII (1975–76), 353–67.

Knight   G. Wilson Knight, 'John Lyly', *RES*, XV (1939), 146–63.

Kyd   *The Works of Thomas Kyd*, ed. Frederick S. Boas (Oxford: Clarendon Press, 1901).

LCL   Loeb Classical Library.

Le Comte   Edward S. Le Comte, *Endymion in England: The Literary History of a Greek Myth* (New York: King's Crown Press, 1944).

Lenz   Carolyn Ruth Swift Lenz, 'The Allegory of Wisdom in Lyly's *Endimion*', *CompD*, X (1976–77), 235–57.

Lilly   William Lilly and John Colet, *A Short Introduction of Grammar* (London, 1577).

Locrine   *The Lamentable Tragedy of Locrine*, ed. Jane Lytton Gooch (New York: Garland, 1981).

Long, 'An Addendum'   Percy W. Long, 'Lyly's *Endimion*: An Addendum', *MP*, VIII (1911), 599–605.

Long, 'Purport'   Percy W. Long, 'The Purport of Lyly's *Endimion*', *PMLA*, XXIV (1909), 164–84.

Lyly   Page and act-scene-line references to *Campaspe* and *Sappho and Phao* are to the Revels editions of those plays by George K. Hunter and David Bevington; references to *Endymion* are to this present volume; references to *Euphues* and other prose works and to other plays are to

the edition of W. Warwick Bond (see 'Bond' above). *Euphues* references
are by volume in Bond's edition, page, and line number on the page.

MLN   Modern Language Notes.

MLR   Modern Language Review.

Montrose   Louis Montrose, '"Shaping Fantasies": Figurations of Gender
and Power in Elizabethan Culture', *Representations*, 1.2 (1983), 61–94.

MP   Modern Philology.

MRDE   Medieval and Renaissance Drama in England.

MSR   Malone Society Reprints.

Mustard   W. P. Mustard, 'Notes on John Lyly's Plays', *SP*, XXII (1925),
267–71.

Nashe   *The Works of Thomas Nashe*, ed. R. B. McKerrow, rev. F. P. Wilson,
5 vols (Oxford University Press, 1958).

N&Q   Notes and Queries.

Neale   J. E. Neale, *Queen Elizabeth* (London: Jonathan Cape, 1934).

OED   The Oxford English Dictionary (second edition).

PBSA   Publications of the Bibliographical Society of America.

Peele   *The Life and Major Works of George Peele*, G. T. Prouty, gen. ed. (New
Haven: Yale University Press, 1952–70).

Perella   Nicolas James Perella, *The Kiss Sacred and Profane* (Berkeley: University of California Press, 1969).

PMLA   Publications of the Modern Language Association (PMLA).

PQ   Philological Quarterly.

Puttenham   George Puttenham, *The Arte of English Poesie*, ed. Gladys
Doidge Willcock and Alice Walker (Cambridge University Press, 1936).

Q   [John Lyly], *Endimion: The Man in the Moon. Played before the Queen's
Majesty at Greenwich on Candlemas Day at Night, by the Children of Paul's*
(London, printed by I. Charlewood for the widow Broome, 1591).

Read   Conyers Read, *Lord Burghley and Queen Elizabeth* (New York: Knopf,
1960).

RenD   Renaissance Drama.

RenP   Renaissance Papers.

RES   Review of English Studies.

*Revels   Documents Relating to the Office of the Revels in the Time of Queen
Elizabeth*, ed. Albert Feuillerat. Materielien zur Kunde der älteren
Englischen Dramas, XXI (Louvain: Uystpruyst, 1908).

Rose   Mary Beth Rose, *The Expense of Spirit: Love and Sexuality in English
Renaissance Drama* (Ithaca, N.Y.: Cornell University Press, 1988).

SAB   South Atlantic Bulletin.

Saccio, *Court Comedies*   Peter Saccio, *The Court Comedies of John Lyly: A
Study in Allegorical Dramaturgy* (Princeton University Press, 1969).

Saccio, 'Oddity'   Peter Saccio, 'The Oddity of Lyly's *Endimion*', *The Elizabethan Theatre V*, ed. G. R. Hibbard (Hamden, Conn.: Archon, Shoe
String Press, 1975), pp. 92–111.

Scot   Reginald Scot, *The Discovery of Witchcraft* (London: W. Brome, 1584).

Shakespeare   *The Complete Works of Shakespeare*, 4th edn, ed. David
Bevington (New York: HarperCollins, 1992).

Shapiro   Michael Shapiro, *Children of the Revels: The Boy Companies of
Shakespeare's Time and Their Plays* (New York: Columbia University
Press, 1977).

ShS   Shakespeare Survey.

SP   Studies in Philology.

S. R.   The Stationers' Register.

Spenser   Edmund Spenser, *The Faerie Queene*, ed. J. C. Smith, 2 vols (Oxford University Press, 1909).

Thomas   Susan D. Thomas, '*Endimion* and Its Sources', *CL*, xxx (1978), 35–52.

TN   Theatre Notebook.

Weltner   Peter Weltner, 'The Antinomic Vision of Lyly's *Endymion*', *ELR*, III (1973), 5–44.

Wilson   F. P. Wilson, *A Dictionary of English Proverbs.*

Giovanni Piero Valeriano Bolzani, *Hieroglyphica*, Lyons, 1586, p. 572

Introduction

THE TEXT

The Stationers' Register for 1591 contains the following entry:

4to Octobris [1591] mystres Broome Wydowe Late Wyfe of William Broome Entred for her copies vnder the hand of the Bishop of London: Three Comedies plaid before her maiestie by the Children of Paules th one Called. Endimion. Th other.Galathea and th other, Midas. . . . xviij^{d}.[1]

The acquisition of these plays by a publisher may have been occasioned by the closing down of the boys' acting companies in 1590.

Earlier in 1591, William Broome had issued reprints of *Campaspe* and *Sappho and Phao* in quarto, without any record of transfer in the Stationers' Register to Broome from their previous owner and publisher, Thomas Cadman. Cadman had issued several quartos of these two plays in 1584, when they were new, but had published nothing since 1589. Perhaps he transferred the rights to these plays to Broome by informal agreement, or the copyright may have seemed derelict. Broome died in 1591. Subsequently, in an S.R. entry of 12 April 1597,[2] his widow Joan confirmed her rights to these two plays. Broome's widow thus came into possession of all but one of Lyly's plays that were to be published as *Six Court Comedies* in 1632.

Endymion appeared in 1591 with the following title page:

[Q] ENDIMION, / The Man in the / *Moone.* / Playd before the Queenes Ma-/iestie at Greenewich on Candlemas day / at night, by the Chyldren of / Paules. / [ornament] / AT LONDON, / Printed by I. Charlewood, for / the widdowe Broome. / 1591.

'The Printer to the *Reader*' is on sig. A2; 'The Prologue' is on sig. A2v. The play occupies fifty-three leaves of sigs B–K. The Epilogue is on K3v. Copies of Q (*S.T.C.* 17050) are to be found in the British Library, the Huntington Library, and some others.

This was to be the only quarto of *Endymion*, in a clear sign of the dramatist's declining fortunes during the early 1590s. *Campaspe* had required three quarto editions in 1584 and another in 1591, while *Sappho and Phao* went through two editions in 1584 and a third in 1591. The Broome family of husband and widow made an attempt to resusciate Lyly's reputation in 1591 with *Campaspe, Sappho and Phao*, and then (after Broome's death) *Endymion*, followed by *Gallathea* the next year, but evidently without much success. *Midas*, to which the widow gained entitlement in 1591 along with *Endymion* and *Gallathea*, was printed in quarto in 1592 by Thomas Scarlet 'for I. B.', but seems to have needed no second printing. *Mother Bombie* alone among Lyly's six major plays went through two quarto printing in the 1590s, in 1594 and then in 1598.

The rights to *Endymion*, along with *Campaspe, Sappho and Phao, Gallathea*, and *Midas*, were tranferred from 'mystres Brome Lately deceased' to George Potter on 23 August 1601. Potter's evident decision not to capitalise on this acquisition may again point to a low ebb in Lyly's reputation as a dramatist. Eventually, these five plays and *Mother Bombie* (which had been registered to Cuthbert Burby on 18 June 1594) were registered on 9 January 1628 to Edward Blount,[3] and then published by him in the following collection of 1632:

> [Blount] SIXE / COVRT / Comedies. / Often Presented and Acted / *before Queene* ELIZABETH, / by the Children of her Ma-/iesties Chappell, and the / Children of Paules. / *Written* / By the onely Rare Poet of that / Time, The Wittie, Comicall, / *Facetiously-Quicke and* / vnparaleld / IOHN LILLY, Master / *of Arts*. / Decies repetita placeabunt. / [ornament] / *LONDON* / Printed by *William Stansby* for *Edward* / *Blount*. 1632.

Given pride of first place in this volume, *Endymion* follows the Preface without a separate title page. The Prologue appears on sig. A6v. The play occupies the sixty leaves of sigs B–F in duodecimo. The Epilogue is on sig. G; Gv is blank. The text is reprinted from Q with minor variations, all of which are attributable to compositorial work and not to authorial sources, except, importantly, for the songs and a dumb show. Whether the songs newly added at this point to Lyly's major plays were his own or were adapted by Blount from other song-writers of the period is a matter of debate, but prevailing opinion generally sides with G. K. Hunter in supposing that the songs, written by Lyly himself, were copied out separately for the boy choristers and were then held back from original publication as part of the boy actors' repertory. The songs in *Endymion* are well integrated into the text. The song to awaken Tophas at III.iii.119 mentions his name and that of Dipsas in a series of wry comments on his ridiculous sleeping; that at IV.ii.127 jests about the Man in the Moon and the watch; and that at IV.iii.33 differs textually from a

comparable version in Thomas Evans's *Old Ballads* (1810) by specifically mentioning Endymion and making fun of the spotted
Corsites. On the other hand, Blount fails to provide texts for songs
that seem to be needed on two occasions, at II.iii.52 and III.iv.0.2, so
that his numbering of 'The First Song' and 'The Second' and 'The
Third' is misleading.[4] The dumb show at II.iii.68.1–14 is also found
for the first time in Blount.

Some emendations in Blount are commonsensical and recom-
mend themselves to the modern editor, but are without authority.
Lyly seems not to have involved himself in correcting new editions
of his plays.[5] Copies of Blount (*S.T.C.* 17088) are to be found in the
British Library, the Huntington Library, the Boston Public Library,
and the Library of Congress, as well as in the libraries of Yale
University, Indiana University, the University of Chicago, and some
others.

Q is an excellent text, with very few printing errors (see below). It
reads like a text prepared by the author himself for publication, with
characters' names grouped at the beginning of each scene, in the
literary and classically sanctioned 'continental' style later adopted by
Ben Jonson in his highly literary Folio of 1616. The sparsity of
printing errors suggests that the manuscript was accurate and consistent. Lyly was, after all, involved in the production of his own
plays, so that no prompter need have been required to mark up his
copy for production. The speech headings are uniformly accurate
and consistent, probably not because a 'prompter' regularised them
but because Lyly's own manuscript was a highly finished product.

Stage directions are accordingly sparse yet practical and accurate.
Along with the grouped names at the head of each scene (where the
word *Enter* is omitted but clearly implied), the text generally indicates entrances in mid scene; the chief omission is the entrance of
Samias and Dares at v.ii.53.1. Sometimes, as at I.iii.4.1 and IV.ii.5.1,
the entrance of a character soon after the scene begins is simply
implied by the inclusion of the name in the scene's opening roster.
The text is occasionally vague about some entrances even at the start
of a scene; Act III, scene i, for example, indicates the entrance of *three
lords* without specifying who they are (Corsites, Zontes, and
Panelion), and neglects to mention Semele and Eumenides. The
stage direction *Enter the watch* at IV.ii.77.1 does not specify how
many are to enter and speak. A vague '*etc.*' at v.i.10.1 and at
v.iv.36.1–2 accounts for one or more of Cynthia's retinue.

The text is normally careful about exits. The few unnoted exits, usually near the end of a scene (i.i.87, ii.ii.164, iii.i.47, v.ii.118), may indicate an option for the actors in their departure at a scene's end, and are not likely in any case to puzzle the reader. At v.i.159.1, the bare indication of an *Exit* vaguely allows the reader to guess that most of Cynthia's entourage exits with her, leaving three speakers onstage.

Details about costume, such as the ridiculous armour that Sir Tophas wears (i.iii.4.1) or his sporting gear (ii.ii.58 ff.), are left to the acting company and its impresario, Lyly. Implied gestures of swaggering, embracing, kneeling, taking aim with a weapon, speaking aside or sotto voce to another actor, withdrawing to one side of the stage, and the like, are left to the rehearsal process. Several thematically and theatrically significant gestures are indicated: *He falls asleep* (ii.iii.27), *He sleeps* (iii.iii.72.1), *He lifts* (iv.iii.10), *The fairies dance, and with a song pinch him, and he falleth asleep . . . They kiss Endymion and depart* (iv.iii.32–45.1), *She kisseth him* (v.i.29). Other important pieces of stage business are implied in the dialogue, especially the apparent concealment of Endymion from view while he sleeps on his lunary bank (see ii.iii.67.12), the provision of a fountain (iii.iv.0.1), the application of spots to Corsites's flesh and their subsequent removal (iv.iii.43–142), the ageing of Endymion and the sudden restoration of his youthful appearance (v.iv.187), and the ageing of a tree that is ultimately metamorphosed back into Bagoa (v.iv.296.1). Stage locations, such as the lunary bank, the fountain, and the castle of Corsites, are not specified in stage directions.

The omission in Q of the dumb show at ii.iii.67.1–12 seems especially to underscore the literary nature of this text. Rather than upstage Endymion's own account of his dream in v.i with a purely theatrical description of stage action, Lyly omits the dumb show from his text. The dumb show is not necessary for sense in reading the play, and clearly Lyly does not intend his text as a record of theatrical performance.

An analysis of the printing of Q starts with a brief article by Donald Edge, demonstrating that at least some of Q of *Endymion* was printed from 'cast-off' copy, that is, printed not seriatim but in stints. Edge notes that the running titles alternate from gathering to gathering in the latter two-thirds of the play, starting in the middle of ii.ii: gatherings A, B, C, E, G, and I feature the italic word '*Endimion*' with a cursive capital *E*, whereas gatherings D, F, H, and K have the initial capital letter in roman. The roman capital is sufficiently battered to be visibly distinctive as a recurring typeface, indicating that the running titles were part of a skeleton used again and again in the printing process. 'Only one skeleton forme was used to impose the type pages of both formes of sheets D, F, H, and K', writes Edge. 'It seems that in at least four sheets the pages were set not in seriatim order but by formes from cast-off copy. There is other evidence of this method of composition in two "tight" pages (sigs D2v, K2r), the first of these being remarkably crowded.'[6]

Proceeding from this information, I have investigated to see if spelling characteristics can identify two compositors, one for each grouping of gatherings. A distinction is, I believe, demonstrable. Two compositors need not have divided their stints according to the skeleton formes, but they appear to have done so in this instance. I have labelled the first group of gatherings (A, B, C, E, G, I) the work of Compositor A and the other (D, F, H, K) of B. In the case of the word 'do', 7 uses of 'do' and 9 of 'doo' appear, all in the work of Compositor B, whereas 'doe' appears 24 times in A's work and 16 in B's. From this evidence we can theorise that B preferred 'do' and 'doo' but was influenced at times by his copy, which tended to read 'doe'. (Spellings in the printer's copy surely were not entirely consistent, as Renaissance documents generally were not, but the marked distribution of spellings noted here in the pages of the two compositors is too consistent to be accounted for by the vagaries of Elizabethan spelling.) Similarly, the word 'heart' is spelled 'hart' by Compositor A 24 times, by B only 7 times, whereas B has 'heart' 8 times, A only 3.[7]

In several samplings, we see a preference on A's part for 'y' spellings in place of 'i'. Compositor A uses 'theyr' 13 times to B's once, whereas B uses 'their' 15 times to A's once. The words 'fair' and 'fairies' also show strong differentiation: A prefers 'fayre' (11 uses to B's 5) and 'fayries' (3 uses to B's 1), whereas B prefers 'faire' and 'fairies' and 'fairenesse' (11 uses, to A's 6). Compositor A uses 'thys' 9 times, B never; B uses 'this' 31 times to A's 34, suggesting that the copy tended to read 'this' and that A sporadically but unmistakably imposed his preference for 'thys'. Compositor B uses 'neither' 5 times, 'neyther' never, whereas Compositor A uses 'neyther' 8 times; he also uses 'neither' (14 times), but 'neyther' is strictly an A spelling. In a similar word, Compositor A uses 'eyther' 4 times and 'either' not at all, whereas B uses 'either' and 'eyther' indifferently (5 times each). In the use of proper names in speech headings and in the text proper, Compositor A markedly prefers

'Gyptes' (A 6 times, B none) and 'Pythagoras' or 'Pyth.' (A 8, B 1), whereas B prefers 'Giptes' (B 3, A 0) and 'Pithagoras' (B 1, A 0). On the other hand, 'dye' seems to be a B spelling (8 times to A's once), 'die' an A spelling (7 times to B's twice).

Some other words do not offer clear differentiation, like 'sweet' and 'sweete', 'less' and 'lesse', 'me' and 'mee'. Compositor B may tend to prefer 'bloud' (2 uses) but also uses 'blood' (2 times); A uses 'blood' 5 times. B may prefer 'speaches' to 'speeches', though the sample is again small. Some words are generally spelled the same in both compositorial stints, such as 'little' (12 uses, as against only one 'lyttle'), 'like' (13 uses, no 'lyke'), 'sleepe' (35 uses, 'sleep' only thrice, in Compositor B's stint, though he plentifully uses 'sleepe'), 'passe' (7 times, 'pass' never), 'extreame' (5 uses, no 'extreme'), and 'immortall' (9 times, no 'immortal').

These tests tend to support the hypothesis that *Endymion* was set into type by two compositors, probably working concurrently. That idea suggests in turn that the whole of the play was set from cast-off copy. The quality of work is high, pointing in part to a scrupulously prepared printer's copy. Although speech headings vary between abbreviated and unabbreviated forms (*Top. Tophas*; *Cynth. Cynthia*; *End. Endimion*; *Zon. Zontes*; *Flos. Flosc. Floscula*; *Eu. Eum. Eumenides*, etc.), sometimes to meet the demands of available space, the variations are normal, and all speeches are correctly assigned—an unusual degree of accuracy in dramatic texts, for which the printer's copy again must deserve a major share of the credit. I count only nine substantive verbal errors in the entire text,[8] all but one of which (and an uncertain one at that, at v.iv.252) are in Compositor A's stint. There are perhaps twelve passages in which the compositors may have substantively mishandled the punctuation of their original,[9] more or less evenly distributed between the two compositors, and also about nine typographical errors,[10] for which Compositor A (who had a slightly larger stint overall) is responsible in about two-thirds of the cases. This is exemplary printing for a Renaissance play, and leaves little uncertainty as to how the text should be established in a modern edition.

Lyly may not have been involved in the actual publication of the 1591 Quarto, even though he may well have been in the publication of *Campaspe* and *Sappho and Phao* in 1584. The note provided by 'The Printer to the *Reader*' in the 1591 Quarto of *Endymion* speaks of 'certain comedies' that have come 'by chance' into the printer's hands 'since the plays in Paul's were dissolved', with *Endymion* as the first of these to be published and others to follow if this one can 'pass with good liking'. The printer, John Charlewood, did proceed to publish *Gallathea* in 1592. No mention is made in the *Endymion* 1591 Quarto of John Lyly, in the printer's note to the reader or on the title page. The lack of Lyly's name is not particularly significant; the 1584 quartos of *Campaspe* and *Sappho and Phao* similarly omit Lyly's name, as do those of *Midas* (1592) and *Mother Bombie* (First Quarto, 1594, Second Quarto, 1598). Only with *The Woman in the Moon* (1595 and 1597) and *Love's Metamorphosis* (1601) does the name of 'Iohn Lyllie' appear on a title page of one of his plays, well after Lyly's currency as a dramatist had disappeared. (Shakespeare's name first appeared on a quarto title page in 1598.) The printer's note to *Endymion*, on the other hand, is unlike anything found in the dramatist's earlier quartos, and bespeaks a distancing of Lyly from the process of publication. With the dissolving of the theatrical enterprise at Paul's, Lyly was no longer directly involved. He seems to have made no authorial contributions to the reprinting of *Campaspe* and *Sappho and Phao* in 1591.[11] The manuscript of *Endymion* that had come into the hands of 'the widow Broome' and Charlewood was manifestly a good one, and very close to what Lyly had written, as were the texts of *Campaspe* and *Sappho and Phao*, but they were under no obligation to consult him as they sought to capitalise on what was now their property.

Editorial choice for a modern edition of *Endymion* seems clear. Q is the authoritative text, except for the dumb show (II.iii.67.1–12) and the songs, which first appear in the Blount edition of 1632 and must be edited from that text. Otherwise, Blount shows no evidence of its publisher's having consulted anything other than the original quarto.

DATE AND AUTHORSHIP

Although Lyly's name does not appear on the title page of Q, and is not directly associated with *Endymion* until Blount's *Six Court Comedies* (1632) attributed all six plays to him on its title page, Lyly's authorship of this play (and of the others) has never been in doubt. His distinctive style, his connection with the Children of Paul's who, according to the title page of Q, played it 'before the Queen's Majesty at Greenwich on Candlemas day at night', and the play's numerous echoes of *Euphues* and Lyly's earlier plays all confirm Lyly as the dramatist.

Candlemas is the traditional name for the Feast of Purification of St Mary the Virgin, celebrating her ritual purification after Jesus's birth and the presentation of her holy child at the temple in Jerusalem. In Protestant England, as Carolyn Ruth Swift Lenz observes, this day was dedicated to the idea of purifying oneself and seeking the highest knowledge of God.[12] The feast was celebrated on 2 February with a great display of candles. *Endymion* appears to have been acted at court on this date in 1588, for Elizabeth's court was at Greenwich in February of that year, and in no other year between 1580 and 1591 is there a Candlemas payment to Paul's boys.[13] The *Acts of the Privy Council* records make clear that the payment to Thomas Giles (or Gyles) for Paul's boys on 2 February was indeed in 1588.[14] This evidence confirms the Revels account indicating that Paul's boys played before Elizabeth 'betwixte Christmas and Shrovetid' at Greenwich in that same year, that is, before Ash Wednesday and the beginning of Lent.[15]

Evidently, *Endymion* was acted before the Queen a bare month after a performance of some other play by Paul's boys; their master, Thomas Giles, also received payment for a performance on New Year's Day of 1588 in addition to that on 2 February. George Hunter and others plausibly suppose the New Year's play to have been *Gallathea*, which must have been written prior to its being entered in the Stationers' Register on 1 April 1585 but which may have been delayed by the break-up of the combined company of the Children of the Queen's Chapel and the Children of Paul's under the sponsorship of the Earl of Oxford that had performed *Campaspe* and *Sappho and Phao* in 1584. Some time in 1588, Hunter argues, after Lyly wrote *Endymion*, the connection with Oxford was dissolved. Lyly, encouraged in that same year by the Queen to aim his hopes at the Mastership of the Revels, was again active as a producer of his plays. The court performances of *Gallathea* on 1 January and *Endymion* on 2 February were soon followed by *Midas*, probably in November 1589 at Paul's and then on 6 January 1590 at court, capitalising on the recent defeat of the Spanish Armada.[16] Soon thereafter, in 1590, Paul's boys were forbidden to present plays to the public.

The favour that Queen Elizabeth showed towards Lyly in 1588 may well explain the tone of *Endymion*'s Epilogue. Speaking on behalf of the acting company and its playwright, the Epilogue begs their 'Dread sovereign' to bear in mind 'the malicious that seek to overthrow us with threats'. Even though such blusterings 'do but stiffen our thoughts and make them sturdier in storms', the speaker is acutely aware that all depends on the Queen: 'If Your Highness vouchsafe with your favourable beams to glance upon us, we shall not only stoop, but with all humility lay both our hands and hearts at Your Majesty's feet.' The kneeling gesture at the end of performance is a conventional acknowledgement of the Queen's greatness, to be sure; at the same time, as Hunter notes, the tone of relief and gratitude for deliverance from 'the malicious' is appropriate to the situation of a playwright who had evidently weathered nearly four years of non-performance of his plays at court and who now appeared to be enjoying a renewal of opportunity.[17] The hiatus in royal favour, the Epilogue suggests, was the work of Lyly's enemies at court.

Such a context makes better chronological sense, in any case, than the various hypotheses, once current among historical critics, that *Endymion* was part of a campaign for the Earl of Leicester or James VI of Scotland. Leicester, who headed a faction opposed to that of the Earl of Oxford with whom Lyly had been aligned, had fallen into disgrace with the discovery in 1579 of his third marriage the previous year to Essex's widow Lettice. Conceivably, a play about a courtier who suffers banishment from Cynthia and is eventually restored to her favour could be making a case for Leicester's reinstatement. Long before 1588, however, this scandal would have ceased to be the subject of court gossip; Leicester, nearing the end of his life, was a trusted adviser. The story of Leicester's prospects of marriage with Mary Queen of Scots (a possible candidate for Tellus in the play, according to Bond) goes still further back in time to 1563–65.[18] Josephine Waters Bennett presents a more substantial case for identifying Endymion with the Earl of Oxford and Tellus with Anne Vavasour, who bore Oxford's illegitimate child in 1581. Once again, however, this hypothesis suffers the chronological disadvantage that the affair was long since over and done with by 1588, so that the play would have to be viewed as a belated commemoration of such an event rather than as a campaign urging the Queen to forgive Oxford.[19]

Moreover, as Bond notes,[20] the echoes of *Euphues* in *Endymion* are far less insistent than in *Sappho and Phao* and *Campaspe*, plays written in 1584, and thus bespeak a later date; by this same measure, *Gallathea* (1584–85) is also an earlier play. Stylistically and topically, *Endymion* seems well suited to its apparent date of performance in early 1588.

SOURCES

As Ovid, Lucian, and Apollonius of Rhodes tell the tale, Endymion was a shepherd on Mount Latmos in Caria (in Asia Minor) who was beloved of the moon. Another Endymion, described by Pausanias, Ibycus, and others as King of Elis (in the western Peloponnese) and the father of three sons and a daughter, is the protagonist of a different legend usually unconnected with sleeping or the moon, though sometimes the two Endymions of Latmos and Elis are conflated. Apollodorus, for example, tells of Endymion that he was the son of Calyce and Aethlios, that he led some Aeolians from Thessaly to found Elis, and that he was beloved of the moon for his great beauty. Calyce, the daughter of Aeolus, was legendary ances-tor of the Aeolian Greeks in Thessaly and Boeotia; her husband, Aethlios, was a son of Zeus.[21]

In the most common legend about Endymion, Selene, the moon, falls so in love with him that she contrives to have him put into a perpetual sleep, so that she can descend every night to embrace him. In some accounts Endymion fathers a child, Aetolus, but not by Selene. According to Hesiod, Selene is the daughter of Hyperion and the Titaness Theia, and is sister of the sun (Helios) and the dawn (Eos), though other genealogical accounts are available.[22] The moon is often associated with Artemis or Diana, the virgin goddess of the hunt and, especially in the Renaisance, of chastity. The legend of Endymion as beloved by the moon recurs in English literature especially in Michael Drayton's 'Endimion and Phoebe' (1593) and in John Keats's 'Endymion' (1818).

Lyly's version is by all odds the most adventuresome of English accounts in its departures from this traditional legend. The legend as told by Ovid, Lucian, and others plays upon the irony that the gods are so vulnerable to human beauty that the goddess of chastity herself cannot resist falling in love. Hyginus indeed offers Endymion as one among many in a list of mortals beloved by the gods; Apollonius has the moon compare her infatuation for Endymion to that of Medea for Jason; and Lucian frames the story of Endymion as a debate between Aphrodite and Selene in which those goddesses agree to hold Cupid or Eros reponsible for Selene's lovesickness. Lyly, to the contrary, presents us with a Cynthia who is invulnerable to unchaste desire and even to wedded affection.

Yet Lyly's inversion is not without classical precedent. As Susan Thomas points out, Apollodorus tells of an Endymion of surpassing beauty who responds to the moon's adoration by requesting that Zeus allow him 'to sleep for ever, remaining deathless and ageless'. Plato, Aristotle, and Cicero follow in the tradition of seeing Endymion as one who 'cannot feel a thing' in his blissful state of being alive and yet spared the agony of sentient experience.[23] Although this Endymion does not age as does Lyly's, and is still the object of love rather than the initiator of it, he resembles Lyly's protagonist in that he is not the moon's active lover; she does not descend nightly to sleep with him. Cicero is, moreover, alone among ancient commentators in mentioning the kiss; he, or his mythographic followers like Conti and Cartari, may well have provided Lyly with a source for this climactic gesture in *Endymion*.[24]

Even more to the point, Pliny alludes to an Endymion who is said to be the moon's lover, not the object of her attentions. In this account Endymion is an astronomer, one whose fascination with the moon leads not only to scientific discoveries (including the moon's waxing and waning, eclipses, and erratic movement) but to envious rumours about his amorous entanglement. Susan Thomas is surely right that Lyly knew not only Pliny (whose presence is found everywhere in *Euphues* and the plays) but the mythographers such as Fulgentius who retold his stories and who were attracted to the astronomical Endymion as a type of Renaissance explorer.[25]

Aided then by the revisionist accounts of Apollodorus, Cicero, and especially Pliny, and by the mythographers who knew these Greek and Roman sources, Lyly consciously reverses the generally received Greek account of an Endymion who is the beloved of the moon. Lyly's doing so is much in accord with the strategy of George Peele in *The Arraignment of Paris* (c. 1581–84). In that courtly confection, staged by the Chapel Children before Queen Elizabeth, the fateful story of Paris's awarding an apple to Venus for her beauty and of his incurring the jealousy of Juno and Minerva is transformed with deliberate outrageousness into a fable of Elizabeth as the triumphant arbiter of all quarrels about beauty, wisdom, and regal authority. *Endymion* similarly belongs to a whole genre of encomiastic literature designed to show that England of the 1580s and 1590s, and its brilliant queen, could outshine the glory that was Greece and Rome.[26]

Important as that royal praise is to Lyly's design, it is not his only consideration in recasting an old story and adding complementary narrative. The plots of Eumenides and Semele, Geron and Dipsas, and Sir Tophas and the pages ring changes on familiar Renaissance debating topics such as love versus friendship, military honour versus courtship, Mars versus Venus, men versus women, age versus youth, reason versus emotion, the spiritual versus the earthly, strength versus beauty, and the like. For his conception of an ascending ladder of attitudes towards love, from the absurd venalities of Sir Tophas and the sensuous enslavement of Corsites to the self-denying friendship of Eumenides and the exalted worship of Cynthia by Endymion, Lyly was indebted to Neoplatonists like Giordano Bruno and to Cardinal Bembo's vivid depiction of the ascent of the soul from erotic desire to divine contemplation in Book IV of Castiglione's *The Book of the Courtier*.[27] Lyly may indeed have been familiar with a Renaissance Cabalistic interpretation of the Endymion myth, promulgated especially by Giordano Bruno, Giovanni Piero Valeriano Bolzani, and Giulio Camillo, in which Endymion's sleep signifies the ecstatic striving of the soul to seek union with God through contemplation, and in which Cynthia's chaste kiss signifies the receptivity of the Divine to that noble longing.[28] The conflict between spiritual and earthly passion in *Endymion* also owes much to the Courtly Love tradition and to the Petrarchan conceits and stereotypes that manifest themselves in Endymion's worshipping of a goddess-woman who is unattainably above him, in his cataloguing of her virtues, in his melancholic recital of his unhappiness, and the like.[29]

As Noemi Messora argues, Lyly's structural technique of centring his plays on debating themes like love and friendship or the nature of kingship, and his development of the debate not so much through plot as through soliloquies and disputations in a rhetorically balanced style, may owe something to the Italian *comoedia nova* and especially to the genre of the *trattati d'amore*, in which *dubbi* and *questioni d'amore* provided an elegant entertainment for well educated courtly circles in Italy and Europe. Carlo Turco's *Agnella*, for example, performed at Ascola in 1550, features debating themes that are dramatised in paired romantic stories offering a wealth of repeated types of characters seen from contrastive viewpoints, including that of parodic subplot.[30]

These sources show Lyly's acquaintance with learned and continental traditions. Yet he is no less at home in his native England. Some of the features Lyly could have learned from the Italian *comoedia nova*, as Noemi Messora acknowledges, were also available to him in plays like Henry Medwall's *Fulgens and Lucrece* (1497–1501) and John Heywood's *A Play of Love* (1533–34);[31] dramatised debate was a staple of courtly entertainment in England in the mummings and disguisings of John Lydgate, William Cornish, and a host of other purveyors of quasi-dramatic spectacle for the Yorkist, Lancastrian, and Tudor monarchies. Medwall's *Fulgens and Lucrece* had aptly demonstrated how an Italian humanistic source could be adapted to native traditions of indoor courtly interludes. Tournaments and other courtly spectacles made use of debate material. Similarly, medieval romance makes its presence felt in Eumenides's quest for a means of rescuing his friend, in the motif of the magical fountain that grants the true lover a single wish, in the story of a deserted husband living fifty years as a hermit, in the story of an enchanted sleep imposed on the hero by a baleful witch, in Tellus's imprisonment in a desert castle under the watchful eye of Corsites, and the like.[32] Folk legends about magic spells and fairies are essential to the story, and make use of improbability in a way that the more severely neoclassical critics like Sir Philip Sidney deplored.

Lyly's learning is thus broadly eclectic—no doubt deliberately so in a play that is at once 'classical' in its five-act structure and home-grown in its love of English lore. Lyly's familiarity with astronomical and geophysical commonplaces and theories about the motions of the heavenly spheres, volcanic eruptions, alchemical processes, and the like is evident everywhere in *Endymion* (see, for example, III.iv.113–14 and v.iv.87–98 and notes). He is plainly at home with ancient Greek and Roman myths besides the Endymion story: the chimera (Prologue, l. 6), Phaethon (I.i.86–7), Medea (I.ii.4–11), Io (I.ii.73–4), Janus (II.i.52), Vesta (II.i.92), Cassandra (IV.i.46–8), and many others. He cites Virgil (I.iii.55, Cicero (III.iii.29–30), Ovid everywhere, Aelian (II.i.35–7), Terence (III.iii.169), Plautus (V.ii.50), Aristotle (III.iv.142–3), and so on, with grace and ease. He knows many details of Pliny's *Natural History*, as at I.i.40–52 and III.iv.155–6. His characters' names reveal a knowledge of Greek, as in 'Eumenides' from the Greek '*eumenes*' or 'well-wisher' and 'Epiton' from '*epitemnein*', to cut short. His extensive Latin (inherited, as it were, from his grandfather William Lilly, co-author of the official Latin grammar) enables Lyly to lard his parodic scenes with Latin quotations and arch wordplay like that he must have heard and used in school. He knows the Bible well (see, for example, I.ii.20–6). At the same time, Lyly's knowledge of proverbial lore is extensive, as in *Euphues* and the early plays, even if Lyly is less likely in *Endymion* to concoct the outrageous pseudo-learned proverbs and analogies that marked his Euphuistic style in its earlier manifestations. He is indebted to Erasmus's *Adagia* for many sayings, especially one on eagles and beetles that provided him with important details of Endymion's enigmatic dream (see v.i.143–6 and n.).

Nowhere is Lyly's combining of classical and native traditions more entertainingly visible than in his creation of Sir Tophas. The name comes from Chaucer. In part, Sir Tophas is a *miles gloriosus*, recognisable as such by his military bluster, his elaborate equipment that turns out absurdly enough to be fishing gear, his habit of inflating his foes from harmless fish and sheep into monsters, and his comic cowardice. He kills by the dozen—or so he reports—like Pyrgopolinices in Plautus's *Miles Gloriosus*, for whom the stage type is named. Like Thraso in Terence's *Eunuchus*, he is vain of his knack at crushing repartee and yet is easily duped. At the same time, Sir Tophas bears a marked resemblance to characters on the English stage who had been modelled on the braggart soldier: the absurd hero of *Thersites* (1537, possibly by Udall), who, for all his grandiloquent boasting, lives in terror of a mere snail, and the Vice Ambidexter in Thomas Preston's *Cambyses* (*c.* 1558–69), fitted out in armour that travesties medieval knighthood.[33] Sarah Deats sees Sir Tophas as in part a kind of gluttonous parasite, like the title figure of Udall's *Ralph Roister Doister* (1545–52) and Pasiphilo in Gascoigne's *Supposes* (1566).[34]

Violet Jeffery cites many resemblances between Sir Tophas and the *capitano millantatore* and the *pedante* of Italian *commedia dell'arte*, but, as Boughner points out, the shared features can generally be accounted for by a common indebtedness to Plautus and Terence.[35] More certainly, Sir Thopas is a burlesque version of the Neoplatonists' heroic lover, striving to overcome fleshly desire in pursuit of divine contemplation; instead of purging that fleshly desire, Sir Tophas sinks into carnal lethargy. He is also a vehicle for a thoroughly English satire directed at social climbing, affected Petrarchan posing, infatuation with one's beard and fashion of dress, sonneteering, affectations of learning, and other mannerisms of the courtly hanger-on.

ALLEGORY AND SYMBOL IN *ENDYMION*

A characteristic of good allegory, as several recent critics remind us, is that it should lend itself to supple and complex interpretation. Eumenides says of the moon in *Endymion* that it is impossible to fit 'a coat to her form, which continueth not in one bigness while she is measuring' (i.i.26–7), and the same is surely true of any critical attempt to express what Cynthia signifies in Lyly's play.[36] Cynthia is all paradox: growing to completion only to decay, becoming old only to be born anew, always changing and yet eternal, neither a goddess in the fullest sense nor yet a mere mortal. The play that surrounds her is similarly undefined, in its uncertain sense of place (vaguely on earth or in the heavens), its dreamlike quality, its romantic and magical impossibilities.[37] Such a play especially must put us on our critical guard against taking allegory as a simple equation in which 'a poet's meaning is properly understood when it is translated into another group of statements, either more or less abstract or general'; we must be wary of allegory that 'does not provide us a way to think about things which we do not already know'.[38] Literary and Biblical exegetes of the medieval period and Renaissance may have been urging a similar plurality of approach when they insisted that inter-pretation could be at once literal, allegorical, anagogical (concerned with mystical and spiritual meanings), and moral; and that allegory itself could be simultaneously historical, religious, moral, social, personal, and satiric.[39] (To be sure, these multiple approaches could easily harden into their own forms of orthodoxy.) Another flexible method is to explore the uncertain boundary between allegory and symbolism, in which levels of possible meaning need not be as formally structured as in allegory.

Endymion seems to invite interpretation as allegory. The name 'Cynthia' suggests many identities: the moon, Selene; the classical goddess Artemis or Diana (from 'Cynthus', a mountain in Delos, supposed home of Artemis and Apollo); Queen Elizabeth; and the idea of unapproachable beauty worshipped by the Petrarchan son-neteers, who regularly named the objects of their adoration 'Phoebe', 'Stella', 'Diana', 'Caelia', and the like.[40] Similarly, the name 'Endymion' invites multiple interpretation. As we have seen in a study of the play's sources, the myth of Endymion was variously interpreted in the Renaissance as suggesting that the gods them-selves (and, *a fortiori*, human beings) are slaves to Eros, and con-versely that the human soul longs for contemplative union with the divine. The profound ambivalences contained in these traditions gave Lyly room to dramatise a shifting and delicate relationship in which love is at once guilty and selfless, enslaving and ethereal.[41]

Cosmic and neoplatonic allegory

Endymion gains a cosmic dimension from its constant expansion into astronomical and geophysical realms. Cynthia is a name for the moon, and Endymion, as the play's very title page assures us, is 'The Man in the Moon'. Whatever this witticism may suggest about Endymion's special place in the moon's affections, the image certainly directs our gaze towards the heavens and towards the anthropomorphic legend of a human face in the heavens. The moon is a unique heavenly body in Ptolemaic astronomy. It forms the boundary between that which is eternal and that which is 'sublunary' or transient. Physically the moon expresses this liminal status by its paradoxical ability to be constant in its incessant changing. To a civilisation that believed the stars and even the planets to circle immutably about the earth at the centre of the cosmos, the moon had to occupy a special place because it was the one heavenly body that did visibly change. The moon was thus the perfect emblem of a 'mutability' expressing the complex harmonies of the *concordia discors* that philosophers and writers saw also in the constant warring among the four elements, or between the sea and the land, dark and light.

The Cynthia in Lyly's play is certainly like the moon. Endymion worships her for keeping 'a settled course' ever 'since her first creation', not altering 'one minute in her moving', despite the fact that 'unkind men' have 'christened her with the name of wavering, waxing, and waning'. She is like the moon in giving to the sea its 'virtue' of 'ebbing and flowing'. 'Being in her fullness', she 'decayeth'. Uniquely among women, she 'waxeth young again' just when she has reached 'the pride of her beauty and latter minute of her age'. What man could fail to be happy in loving one who, having reached 'ripe years and infinite virtues, great honours and unspeakable beauty', is then able to 'grow tender again, getting youth by years and never-decaying beauty by time' (i.i.35–66)? Endymion's first long hymn of praise to Cynthia is an elaborate conceit comparing his mistress to the moon. The marked element of hyperbole in any such Petrarchan love song warns us to make allowance for exaggeration (especially since we know that the ageing Queen Elizabeth was lauded in just such extravagant terms) and to imagine Cynthia as a human woman, but we also see what marks her as apart from all other women. Even seemingly casual allusions to Cynthia speak of her as though she were a celestial body: 'Cynthia beginneth to rise', says Corsites to Tellus (IV.i.72–3).

Tellus, Cynthia's opposite and rival for Endymion's affections, is, as a woman, contrasted with Cynthia in every way: she is changeable, vengeful, spiteful, malicious. She is also, as her name plainly signals, like the earth in her mundane rage of possessiveness. Like Mundus in *The Castle of Perseverance*, she refuses to give Endymion up. Lyly plays up the cosmic dimensions of her rivalry with Cynthia in Tellus's first conversation with her servant Floscula ('little flower'). To Floscula's contention that there can be no comparison between the 'meanness' of Tellus's fortune and the greatness of Cynthia's state, Tellus replies as though she were an archetypal goddess of vegetation:

> No comparison, Floscula? And why so? Is not my beauty divine, whose body is decked with fair flowers, and veins are vines, yielding sweet liquor to the dullest spirits, whose ears are corn to bring strength, and whose hairs are grass to bring abundance? Doth not frankincense and myrrh breathe out of my nostrils, and all the sacrifice of the gods breed in my bowels? Infinite are my creatures. (I.ii.20–7)

What is more, Tellus as earth knows that her hold over Endymion must be limited to his fleshly being and that her reign over his sensual existence must come to an end. Endymion may dote, but not 'for ever in this delight', not unto death—the very thought of which renders Tellus's heart 'in sunder, in putting me in remembrance of the end' (ll. 69–71). She will succeed in tangling Endymion's affections in a 'sweet net' of desire and thereby dominate 'the prime of his youth and the pride of his time' (ll. 44, 65), but she knows that she will lose at the last.

This cosmic fable is not limited to the play's opening action. As late as the final scene, Tellus confesses a fury of resentment and possessive desire that has been virtually volcanic in its internal operation:

> Feeling a continual burning in all my bowels and a bursting almost in every vein, I could not smother the inward fire, but it must needs be perceived by the outward smoke; and, by the flying abroad of divers sparks, divers judged of my scalding flames. (V.iv.87–91)

Endymion has sworn that her affections, in respect to his, were 'fumes to Etna, valleys to Alps' (ll. 97–8). Elsewhere, Tellus describes her pent-up malice as 'scorching flames', kindled afresh by Endymion's indifference to her (IV.i.12). Cynthia expects that Tellus will some day 'melt herself in her own looseness' (IV.iii.131–2). Subplot characters like Scintilla and Favilla, with names connoting 'sparks' and 'cinders', can also express elemental strife; to see them weep is 'to see water come out of fire', since 'It is their property to carry in their eyes fire and water, tears and torches' (II.ii.54–6).[42]

Tellus's lover, Corsites, can pull forty-year-old trees out of the ground, roots and all, like a hurricane (IV.iii.15–17). The extended metaphor recaptures the ancient mythological conflict in which the Giants of the earth rose against the gods and were imprisoned in the earth as volcanic mountains for their presumption. Tellus is descended from these menacing earth deities.

Tellus's association with the earth and with chthonic powers is in evidence throughout the play. Even in her resemblance to the jealous Juno, her intent is to 'turn Jupiter's lovers to beasts on the earth' (I.ii.73–4). The image casts Tellus as a Circean enchantress. In her desire to win Endymion's unwilling affection, she relies upon the substances of the earth, especially those with alchemical properties: 'herbs, stones [minerals], spells, incantation, enchantment, exorcisms, fire, metals, planets' (I.iv.16–17). She commands the obedience of Dipsas who, like Medea, is able to 'darken the sun' by her skill and 'remove the moon out of her course', 'restore youth to the aged', and 'make hills without bottoms', though significantly she does differ from the gods in that she is 'not able to rule hearts' (ll. 22–7). Corsites laments that such a 'flower of beauty' should be doomed by Cynthia to 'wither in prison' in the desert castle (III.ii.4–5). Tellus is a Proserpina-like figure able to cast Endymion into a deathlike, ageing sleep. She is balefully associated with foison and abundance that turn into decay. Yet Endymion is laid to rest on a bed of lunary, a fern with magical properties plainly associated with the moon (Luna), and it is lunary that Gyptes uses to remove Corsites's shameful spots (IV.iii.137–42). Growing things thus occupy a pivotal role in the play's cosmic struggle between the heavens and the sublunary world.

So does Endymion. The world and its ways are not unbeautiful to him, especially at first. He reluctantly concedes that Tellus is not only 'fair' but wise, honourable, and fortunate (II.iii.12–18). His attitude towards her is not entirely consistent or even straightforward. He claims to have used her 'but as a cloak for mine affections, that others, seeing my mangled and disordered mind, might think it were for one that loveth me, not for Cynthia' (II.i.25–8), and insists in the play's final scene of reckoning before Cynthia that Tellus lied when 'she said I loved her and swore to honour her' (V.iv.152–3), but the evidence of the play refuses to support him in this. Earlier, he protests to Tellus that 'the sweet remembrance of your love is the only companion of my life, and thy presence my paradise, so that I am not alone when nobody is with me, and in heaven itself when thou art with me' (II.i.60–4). When Tellus responds by asking 'Then you love me, Endymion?' the hero replies with a prevarication: 'Or else I live not, Tellus' (ll. 65–6). This can mean, for her ears, 'I can't live without your love', but also suggests to our understanding that Endymion perceives the danger he is in once her vengeance is awakened. As an example of the 'cloaking' of his affections that Endymion professes to use to throw people off from any suspicion of his loving Cynthia, this courtier-like doublespeak is cannily enough motivated, and technically it may rescue Endymion from the charge of actually having sworn his affection to Tellus, but it hardly squares with his insistence to Cynthia in v.iv that he has never led Tellus to believe in his love for her.

Moreover, the play gives us reason to believe that Endymion has indeed been involved with Tellus. She calls him 'treacherous and most perjured' (I.ii.1), not to his face but in bitter private reflection on his behaviour towards her. 'Were thy oaths without number, thy kisses without measure, thy sighs without end, forged to deceive a poor credulous virgin?' (ll. 7–10), she apostrophises him. Even allowing for some self-pitying exaggeration in this outburst, we can only suppose that Endymion has deceived her. His misogynistic jeering at women for being dissemblers (II.i.68–76) is all the less admirable for his having just admitted in soliloquy that he is consciously dissembling with Tellus (ll. 25–7, 51–2). In the final scene, when Tellus recounts how violently she fell in love with Endymion, and describes how he swore that his affections were vastly greater than hers, and 'made me believe that (which all of our sex willingly acknowledge) I was beautiful', Endymion allows her testimony to stand unchallenged (v.iv.68–120).

Endymion, then, in his relationship with Tellus, is perjured, treacherous, forsworn, misogynistic, and sanctimonious. Tellus responds by being treacherous, vengeful, malicious, vain, and cynical. Both are capable of better things. She is beautiful, witty, loved by many men, and penitent at the last. Endymion, for his part, has long realised that his better self loves Cynthia.[43] The play hints strongly that Endymion has had a carnal relationship with Tellus; in allegorical terms, she represents the trammels of the flesh in a familiar contest of body and soul. The 'picture of Endymion' she is finally allowed by Cynthia to 'possess and play withal', a picture she has 'wrought' during her banishment to the desert castle (v.iv.262–5), signifies in part the flesh that the World can cling to as Mankind flourishes, ages, and dies. The 'picture' is also suggestive of a child, the product of sexual desire. Cynthia, conversely, comes to represent what the human psyche longs for as it learns to give up its dependency on the pleasures of this corrupted world.

Cynthia appears to be everything that Tellus is not. She is matronly, queenlike, imposing—an exemplary figure for a play acted at court before a virgin Queen on the Feast of the Purification of St Mary the Virgin. Cynthia represents a love that is 'unspotted'—a word that resonates through *Endymion*.[44] She also represents that which is heavenly, in the astronomical, moral, and spiritual senses of that term. Endymion's thoughts are 'stitched to the stars' in his adoration for Cynthia; he is resolved to 'possess the moon herself' (i.i.5–19). What he longs for most is a 'constancy not to be matched' in other women, a mistress who is not 'fickle' (ll. 37–45). She is of 'ripe years and infinite virtues', and her beauty is not subject to the decay of time (ll. 60–3). In personal and romantic terms, she is Endymion's idealised woman, one whom he can worship and prostrate himself before, like the lover of the Petrarchan sonnet but without the fleshly longing that normally attends that relationship. She is, in Endymion's self-censored fantasy of her, not a desired sexual object but indeed the very opposite of that, a woman who releases the guilt-ridden man from his obsession. She thus seems to be a welcome refutation of dark misogynistic fears and resentments—though in fact, as we shall see, her association with witchcraft and her power over men render her more problematic than at first appears. As such, she bears a striking relationship to Queen Elizabeth, who made use of her power as an unmarried virgin among men who were both eager to win her and anxiously resentful of being subordinated to a dominant and flirtatious woman.[45] Hence, in Lyly's play, the troubled male suitor longs to find constancy in himself at long last by loving honourably a woman who is, in a spatial metaphor, 'above' carnal desire.

Correspondingly, in the allegory of heaven and earth, Cynthia represents the Platonic Form or Idea as contrasted with unformed matter. Floscula aptly explains to Tellus the contrast between Cynthia and Tellus in terms of substance and shadow, real concept and illusory sense experience:

> But know you not, fair lady, that Cynthia governeth all things? Your grapes would be but dry husks, your corn but chaff, and all your virtues vain, were it not Cynthia that preserveth the one in the bud and nourisheth the other in the blade, and by her influence both comforteth all things and by her authority commandeth all creatures. (i.ii.29–34)

Cynthia is like the mind of God, the truly creative force that organ-
ises chaotic matter into patterned life, without which the seeming
vitality of existence lacks all direction and purpose. Like the gods
embodied in the planets and sun and moon, she sheds 'influence' (l.
33), that is, a stream of ethereal fluid acting upon the character and
destiny of sublunary men. She exercises 'virtue' (I.i.44 and elsewhere), another key word in this play signifying power, authority,
'influence', essential quality, and moral excellence.[46] Not only
Endymion but Eumenides and Geron know that Cynthia 'worketh
by her influence, never standing at one stay', and that her 'virtues,
being all divine, must needs bring things to pass that be miraculous'
(III.iv.181–92).[47] Her philosophers are so in awe of her that they are
prepared to 'fall from vain follies of philosophers' and turn instead
to the noble practicalities of 'virtues as are here practised' (V.iv.300–
1). In worshipful strains they proclaim their intent to 'live by the
sight of Cynthia' (l. 306), much as Endymion has done in his long
sleep of contemplation.

Small wonder, then, that Endymion longs for spiritual union with
Cynthia and for release from his own carnality. His quest is
Promethean, in both a positive and a negative sense. Bystanders like
Floscula admire the 'greatness of his mind' for 'being affected with
a thing more than mortal' (I.ii.18–19). Others, even those closest to
him like Eumenides, worry that he is committing 'idolatry' and that
he will 'blaspheme' if he is not prevented (I.i.77–8). Endymion
himself knows that his quest is hopeless, quixotic, even perverse. Yet
he cannot be content to be like Eumenides, 'whose thoughts never
grow higher than the crown of thy head' and whose fortunes 'creep
on the earth' (ll. 81–5). If Endymion's presumptuous wish to 'fly' to
his fortunes is 'desperate' and is bound to lead to a 'fall' like that of
Icarus or Phaethon, so be it: 'yet shall it come by daring' (ll. 85–7).
Endymion's dilemma provides a tension in this seemingly uneventful play because it is so resonantly human. It is the stuff out of which
Marlowe creates a tragic dilemma for Doctor Faustus, though in
Lyly's hands it is made essentially comic through Cynthia's 'virtue'—her power to encourage Endymion's best self.

Endymion's sleep

Endymion's sleep thus becomes an event of major signification, not
simply because it is what Endymion does through most of the play
but because it evidently expresses his tortured emotions and

motivations in questing after Cynthia and disentangling himself
from Tellus. In part, the sleep may be escape and intellectual sloth.
'Sleep would do thee more good than speech', Eumenides exhorts
his friend. 'The moon heareth thee not, or, if she do, regardeth thee
not' (I.i.79–80). Even though the long sleep is the result of a magical
spell, it may also reflect his own paralysis of will. Sleep seems to
express for him Cynthia's apparent indifference and great distance.
In such a sleep he can dreamingly contemplate her from afar without
offence and without commitment on his part. He claims that he has
already devoted nearly seven years of 'solitary' contemplation of
Cynthia without visible reward (II.i.16, 44–8), even if the solitariness
has evidently been relieved by his dissembling game with Tellus and
his involvement in some unspecified factionalism in Cynthia's court
(ll. 19–23). In his unhappiness he naturally wants to see 'if I can
beguile myself with sleep' (II.iii.4–5), and proceeds to do so, thinking
of both Cynthia and Tellus. He speaks of sleep as a kind of death
wish (l. 21). At the same time, he does notice that the longing for
sleep that comes upon him so heavily is unexplainable and sudden
(ll. 22–6). Is it weariness, he wonders, or melancholy, or what? Sleep
finely expresses the indeterminacy of his not knowing what to make
of his dilemma.

In part, certainly, the prolonged sleep becomes the consequence
of magical spells inflicted on the already sleeping Endymion by
Dipsas and Bagoa at the behest of Tellus. The sleep constitutes
Tellus's revenge and her enslavement of him, the entanglement in a
'sweet net' that he cannot escape. Tellus will thus force Endymion
to spend his youth in 'melancholy passions, careless behaviour,
untamed thoughts, and unbridled affections' (I.ii.66–7). The World
can hold hostage the body, the senses, the emotions, the corrupted
will. These 'traps' that are laid for Endymion (l. 90) are those that
wickedness practises against the unwary, and suggest that Endymion
is a victim of a malicious conspiracy even if his human weakness
contributes to the fall. The fact that Dipsas can induce a physical
state like sleep but is unable 'to rule hearts' (I.iv.27) corresponds to
Christian teaching that the devil can tempt humankind and prevail
upon the body and physical surroundings but must ultimately depend on human participation to complete the temptation. Only
grace can protect, as both Luther and Calvin insisted. Cynthia's role
as divine deliverer completes here the picture of a soul-struggle in
which fallen humankind is released from spiritual captivity through
a grace immeasurably exceeding desert. Cynthia's rebuke of Tellus

and Dipsas for practising black magic on Endymion is one they acknowledge to be richly deserved, for at the last they are not diabolical figures in an allegory of salvation but erring powers whom Cynthia can reclaim.

These interpretations of Endymion's sleep as an expression of spiritual enslavement in sin or as a melancholic seeking after oblivion are valid up to a point but are not complete. The sleep also appears to represent Cynthia's way of teaching Endymion how to purge his lusts that stand in the way of a more perfect union. Those lusts are not expressly erotic; indeed, we have seen how he turns to Cynthia as a release from his own carnality. His desires for her are none the less possessive and self-serving, politically as well as more personally. The play hints repeatedly at a court factionalism in which he has been at the mercy of powerful enemies. 'Whom have I not contemned for thee?' he beseeches in soliloquy the apparently unheeding Cynthia. 'Have I not crept to those on whom I might have trodden, only because thou didst shine upon them? Have not injuries been sweet to me if thou vouchsafest I should bear them? Have I not spent my golden years in hopes, waxing old with wishing?' (II.i.19–24). The pertinence of such complainings about unfulfilled hopes is poignant in the context of Lyly's own unsuccessful attempts to become Elizabeth's Master of the Revels. In the play, these frustrations and resentments point to attitudes in Endymion which must be cured before he can rise to the top as Cynthia's model courtier. The lesson is a painful one to learn because it is so paradoxical: only by renouncing personal ambition can a courtier like Endymion hope to become fully worthy of and accepted by the Queen. Such lessons take time and require the wisdom that comes with age.

Cynthia's own role in this curative process as guide and ruler seems at last perfectly plain. She has not been indifferent to Endymion or unaware of his fate; she has inquired often into his condition and has solicitously sent her wise men into various countries in search of a remedy. She bestows on him a kiss 'which yet never mortal man could boast of heretofore, nor shall ever hope for hereafter' (v.i.27–9). 'I favoured thee, Endymion, for thy honour, thy virtues, thy affections', she assures him. Still, a restraint on him was necessary to bring him around. 'But to bring thy thoughts within the compass of thy fortunes, I have seemed strange, that I might have thee stayed' (IV.iii.83–6). The word 'stayed' (also 'stay') is another term that reverberates through the play; as here, it can

mean 'hindered' but also 'staid, fixed'.[48] Staidness is constancy, and
it is this quality Cynthia desires to foster in Endymion just as he
quests for constancy through his adoration of her. He must learn
constancy through being 'stayed', hindered in his inappropriate
desire for more than 'the compass of his fortunes' can allow. The
soul can learn to love God only by striving for the perfect selflessness
that God represents; the ideal subject can learn how to be a perfect
courtier only through self-abnegating obedience that puts aside all
petty self-interest.

   In these terms that are at once romantic, moral, religious, and
political, sleep becomes at its best a secret life of contemplation.
Endymion has of course contemplated the moon for years in his
lonely vigil, but has been able to find 'no rest' in his uncertainty as
to how to settle his steps or his thoughts (II.iii.1–2). Sleep has been
'impossible' (l. 22), oddly enough in one who is mythically famous
for his long sleep. He is miserable until the rest he has longed for
descends upon him (ll. 22–7). Viewed in this light, the sleep is not a
wicked enslavement visited upon Endymion by Dipsas so much as a
relief from suffering and a chance to gain wisdom through decades
of pure contemplation. He goes to sleep with Cynthia's name on his
lips and pronounces the name of 'Fair Cynthia, divine Cynthia' as
he awakes (v.i.50–1). He can scarcely remember his own name, or
that of Eumenides. 'Only divine Cynthia, to whom time, fortune,
destiny, and death are subject, I see and remember' (ll. 61–3). He
professes gratefully that 'There hath none pleased mine eyes but
Cynthia, none delighted mine ears but Cynthia, none possessed my
heart but Cynthia' (v.iv.159–62). Cynthia at last pronounces him
worthy of acceptance. 'Endymion, this honourable respect of thine
shall be christened "love" in thee, and my reward for it "favour".
Persevere, Endymion, in loving me, and I account more strength in
a true heart than in a walled city' (ll. 177–80). The contemplative
man is finally subsumed into the complete courtier. Endymion is
one of the Elect.

Endymion's dream

If sleep in *Endymion* is thus multifaceted in meaning, dreaming is
bound to be no less so. Endymion's dream, portrayed first as a
dumb show (missing from the Quarto edition) at II.iii.67 and then in
Endymion's narrative recollection at v.i.88 ff., bristles with potentially topical suggestions of court rivalry, but also with insights into

the personal dilemma that has led to the long sleep. The lady 'passing fair' who seems about to cut Endymion's throat in his sleep until her looking glass reveals to her 'how ill anger became ladies' (v.i.88–92) must reflect to some extent the ambivalent feelings in Endymion's psyche concerning Cynthia; if his dream accuses her implicitly of violent behaviour and 'unmovable cruelty' (l. 111), it does so as a way of expressing Endymion's own guilty sense of deserving anything Cynthia chooses to do to him. In any event, this lady shows queenlike qualities in her ability to restrain herself from vengeance, however justly deserved.

As a representation of Cynthia, who teaches herself to overcome 'anger' with 'mercy' and in whose 'heavenly face' appears a 'divine majesty mingled with a sweet mildness' (ll. 105–7; compare Dante's *Vita Nuova*), the lady in the dream is appropriately accompanied by a pair of damsels serving as counsellors, one intent upon 'mischief' and the other sadly forgiving—much as any authority figure conventionally embodies the divergent impulses of menace and mercy. At the same time, this pairing draws once again upon Endymion's polarised attitude towards women and especially towards Tellus and Cynthia. The 'settled malice' he detects in the first damsel associates her with a word ('malice', 'malicious') that is a regular attribute of Tellus throughout the play and is also used by the Epilogue, speaking on behalf of Lyly and his company, to characterise those who have sought their 'overthrow'.[49] The two attendants are thus antithetical attributes of the Cynthia-like central figure, unreconciled to the last as 'an unmovable cruelty' and 'a constant pity' (ll. 94–5, 111).

The aged man with a book would appear to be Endymion's idea of a wise counsellor, ready to offer sage advice and to be disdainfully angry at a young man for failing to see the advantage of 'counsels' and 'policies' thus offered (l. 118). The aged man's role resembles that of the Sybil who offered to Tarquin the Sybilline verses that were at first refused but became in time the prophetic texts of Rome's cultural heritage (see note at II.iii.67.9). Endymion, in his dream, does accept 'pictures' on the third offering, perhaps because they are more graphically persuasive than more abstract counsels or policies, but also lest he offend and because 'some strange thing' moves him with a feeling that he should acquiesce (v.i.127–8). We as audience note that the old man is like Geron offering good advice to Eumenides; in both cases the young man struggles with inner conflict and ultimately accedes to the advice, presumably to his benefit.

In this present dream, the context is markedly political; 'policies' have to do chiefly with court affairs, and have the matter-of-fact connotation of political sagacity and cunning.

In the nightmare logic of a dream, Endymion discovers in the third segment that he is indeed at court, presumably that of the beautiful lady who incorporates into herself the dual identity of malice and mildness. The 'picture' Endymion has accepted from the old man (anticipatory perhaps of the 'picture' of Endymion Tellus is allowed to keep at v.iv.264–6) shows him a frightening catalogue of what 'policies' can lead to: emulous factionalism among wolf-like courtiers barking at Cynthia and biting one another to death, ingrateful hangers-on 'gazing for benefits' (i.e. interested only in what pensions and emoluments they can gain) and turning on their patrons in bitter dissatisfaction, treacherous villains who smile while they murder, the envious who aim at those above them only to suffer the consequences of their own malice, and bloodsucking parasites attacking the monarchy itself (v.i.131–46). Although these figures are personified as female abstractions, in the conventional misogyny of medieval allegory they bespeak a world of courtly intrigue, cynicism, treachery, and violence. Both Cynthia and Queen Elizabeth are implicitly figured in the princely eagle being attacked by the drones or beetles. This heroic royal figure is not only blameless of the factionalism at court but is its chief intended victim. Endymion's dream thus ends on a hysterical note of widespread conspiracy to which the anxious dreamer is of course not sympathetic; the enemies of whom he complained earlier may be Cynthia's enemies as well, though Endymion also concedes that he has put up with many injuries from persons whom Cynthia has vouchsafed to tolerate or even encourage (ii.i.19–23). Endymion's worry that Cynthia (and, implicitly, Elizabeth) is served by persons not worthy of her trust makes its way into his dream as a nightmare about drones or beetles.

In sum, the dream has the effect of placing Endymion's imperfect quest for heavenly contemplation in the context of political strife at court. The errant protagonist must learn to eschew not only fleshly desire (in the person of Tellus) but also base political ambition if he is to become worthy of Cynthia's love. Here again the long sleep serves the function of weaning Endymion from worldly longing for acquisition of power. Cynthia, aware of his virtues and of his weaknesses, wishes to 'bring [his] thoughts within the compass of [his] fortunes' (iv.iii.84–5). Medieval allegorical tradition lends a general perspective to this need for purification: the mankind hero must

purge his attachment to World, Flesh, and Devil, to worldly emi-
nence, to carnal desire, and to the sins of the spirit like Treachery,
Ingratitude, and Envy.

Political and religious allegory

A political reading of the allegory in *Endymion* raises inevitable
questions about the pertinence of such a reading to the Elizabethan
court in early 1588. A significant degree of correspondence between
Cynthia and Queen Elizabeth is undeniable, as we have seen;
Elizabeth encouraged mythological propaganda in which she was
the virgin queen, the Diana or Cynthia of her grateful nation. By the
same token, any sophisticated audience in 1588 would have detected
manifold resemblances between Endymion's dream of dangerous
political emulation and the kind of factionalism they all knew, or at
least knew about, in Elizabeth's court. Did such resemblances encourage more particular identifications?

The case for the Earl of Leicester, reviewed briefly above under
'Date and Authorship', seemed attractive to early historical critics
like Halpin and Bond because Leicester was a great favourite of
Elizabeth who had none the less suffered an eclipse in her favour
owing to a secret marriage in 1578; moreover, he had been proposed
as a husband for Mary Queen of Scots in the mid-1560s.[50] Neverthe-
less, the connection is improbable because Leicester's period of
disgrace in 1579 was such an old story in 1588 and because Leicester
was a rival of Lyly's patron, the Earl of Oxford. The case for Oxford
is more substantial because it does put forward Lyly's former patron
as the Endymion-like courtier who is ultimately anointed as the
Queen's special favourite. Oxford too had suffered a period of
enforced absence from the court.[51] Once again, however, the details
of the case seem woefully out of date in 1588 when one centres on
the story of Oxford's having fathered a child by Anne Vavasour in
1581. Oxford had been officially received back into Elizabeth's presence in 1583.[52] The unsatisfactoriness of such topical readings has
led a number of recent critics (myself among them) to doubt that
topical meaning in *Endymion* goes much further than to identify
Cynthia as Queen Elizabeth in her triumph over erotic love and as
a benign, wise ruler deserving the rhetoric of praise that is so lavishly
bestowed on her here and in *The Arraignment of Paris, Campaspe,
Sappho and Phao*, and the like.[53]

Without denying the centrality of this panegyric function in

Endymion, and its indebtedness to a venerable classical tradition of
rhetorical praise and advice to a monarch like that we see in
Erasmus's *The Education of a Christian Prince*, I now wish to argue
that Lyly's play also enfolds in itself a particular issue of great
moment in 1587–88. It is even possible that the episode of Oxford's
fathering a bastard may be delicately alluded to in the piquant detail
of the 'picture' of Endymion which Tellus has 'wrought' in the
desert castle (possibly suggesting the child Anne bore to Oxford, for
which they both suffered a time of disgrace; see v.iv.264–8). I wish
to argue, on the other hand, that the offence for which Oxford
needed to beg pardon in the 1580s was far more serious. Indeed, it
still hung over him like a dark cloud in 1588 as the day of the Great
Armada approached. I refer to his suspected Catholicism.[54] Oxford
may have been imprisoned briefly in December of 1580 on suspicion
of Catholic involvement, though this is uncertain; it is certain that he
was arrested in 1581 over the affair with Anne Vavasour, all of which
added to his disgrace. He confessed to having been a secret Catholic
since his return from Italy in 1576,[55] and the very fact of his having
been a Papist kept him under suspicion among some members of
Elizabeth's administration in the days of the Armada threat. To be
sure, he had been restored to the Queen's graces by early 1588, and
had voted to condemn Mary Queen of Scots, so that the restoration
of Endymion to the graces of Cynthia might seem, appropriately
enough, to celebrate a reconciliation that had already occurred when
the play was written (perhaps in early 1587) and performed (perhaps
in late 1587, in anticipation of court performance in February of
1588). Yet fears about English Catholics were mounting during
these same years. Oxford was not alone in needing to plead for
understanding of his having entertained Catholic loyalties. Whether
justly or not, many Catholic-inclined Englishmen like Oxford were
being counted on by Philip of Spain, Parma, Mendoza, and other
architects of 'the Enterprise' to join them against Elizabeth when
foreign troops landed on English soil.

   We need to consider what a courtly audience might have been
thinking about in early February of 1588 when they saw a play at
court by John Lyly centred on a Queen named Cynthia. Lyly had
something of a reputation for writing plays that could be subjected
to topical interpretation. His pious hope, in the Prologue to
Endymion, that 'none will apply pastimes, because they are fancies'
(ll. 7–8) neither confirms or denies that the play contains topical
material, but it certainly bespeaks an awareness of what his audience

might have expected. He was, of course, known to have been a protégé of Oxford, under whose sponsorship he had produced his first plays in 1584.

Some degree of identification between Cynthia and Queen Elizabeth goes without saying. What then would an audience in early 1588 make of Tellus, Cynthia's chief rival? Reaching back for Anne Vavasour in 1581 seems far less compelling than to suppose that Tellus may have some connection with Mary Queen of Scots. Elizabeth had consented—reluctantly, tearfully, angrily—to the execution of Mary at Fotheringay in the previous February. She imprisoned her principal Secretary of State, William Davison, who had transmitted the order for execution, in a classic move of scapegoating. She had it given out in various European centres of power that the execution had been against her will. In the play, of course, Cynthia pardons Tellus, but the difference between fact and fantasy may be little more than idealisation of what Elizabeth clung to emotionally after acceding to the hard realities of international politics. Quite possibly, too, Lyly had been working on *Endymion* while Mary was still alive in early 1587. Mary had long been Elizabeth's rival—politically, religiously, personally. As long as Mary lived, hopes of a Catholic succession lived with her, for she was a direct descendant of Henry VII's daughter Margaret and James IV of Scotland. Stories abound attesting to Elizabeth's longstanding personal jealousy of Mary, as for instance when (in 1564) she grilled Mary's ambassador, Sir James Melville, about the colour of Mary's hair, her dancing ability, and the like.[56]

And, of course, Mary was determinedly and dangerously Catholic.[57] Pope Pius V had issued the bull *Regnans in excelsis* in 1570 denouncing Elizabeth as a heretic and absolving her people of any ties of obedience to 'her pretended right to the throne'. Dr William Allen, founder and president of the English College at Douai in northern France and co-founder of the English College at Rome, was busy training priests for the clergy that were to serve England in a post-Elizabethan regime. English Catholics, urged by Rome to declare their faith openly, had done so in the Northern Rising of 1569. This attempt at violent overthrow of Elizabeth's Protestant government had been put down, but there were still huge numbers of Catholic sympathisers in England. The extent of their loyalty to the English crown was a burning issue of 1588 as the Armada force was being assembled on the Continent.[58]

Many great families of England were Catholic, especially in the north and west: the Nevilles of Westmorland, the Percy clan of Northumberland—names that are prominent in the Northern Rising of 1569 and that re-emerge, via Holinshed, in Shakespeare's *1 Henry IV.*[59] If that play in 1597 or so could capitalise on continued anxiety about the Northern Rising and all that is connoted in terms of Catholic plotting against the crown, what must the sensations have been in 1588 as England prepared for invasion? Other powerful names, like Lord Henry Howard and the Earls of Derby, Arundel, Cumberland, Southampton, and Oxford were potential supporters of the Catholic cause in the nervous guessing game that divided neighbour from neighbour. With whom would these lords side?[60]

Even before he wrote *Endymion*, John Lyly had celebrated Elizabeth's deliverance from her treacherous enemies on the Catholic right. Significantly for our purposes, he couched this celebratory tribute in terms of parables about wolves and an eagle whose nest is beset by beetles—the very metaphors that occupy the centre of Endymion's dream. In a long paean honouring England and her Queen entitled 'Euphues' Glass for Europe', Lyly praises Elizabeth as 'a glass for all princes to behold'; she is a prince 'endued with mercy, patience, and moderation', is 'adorned with singular beauty and chastity', etc. (*Euphues*, II.208–9). Yet she is surrounded with enemies. She is

> that mighty eagle that hath thrown dust into the eyes of the hart that went about to work destruction to her subjects, into whose wings although the blind beetle would have crept, and so being carried into her nest, destroyed her young ones, yet hath she with the virtue of her feathers consumed that fly in his own fraud.
>
> She hath exiled the swallow that sought to spoil the grasshopper, and given bitter almonds to the ravenous wolves that endeavoured to devour the silly lambs. (*Euphues*, II.215)[61]

Lyly can only be pointing, in 1580, to Elizabeth's defeat of the northern lords and to anxieties stirred up by the known arrival in England of the Jesuits Edmund Campion and Robert Parsons that year. This is also the year in which Oxford undertook to expose shortly before Christmas an alleged Catholic conspiracy featuring charges and counter-charges about a mysterious book containing painted pictures of treasonable prophecy.[62]

The chief person whom Oxford accused of disloyalty and of religious heresy was Oxford's own cousin, Lord Henry Howard, afterwards Earl of Northampton, second son of the poet Surrey and

brother of the Duke of Norfolk whom Queen Elizabeth had executed in 1572 in the wake of the Northern Rebellion. Oxford
dragged up the old charges against Howard, that he had exchanged
tokens with Mary Stuart in 1574 and had for years supplied her with
political information and advice. Howard, banished in 1579, had
made unsuccessful attempts to reinstate himself at court. When
Oxford attempted in 1581 to implicate Howard in the treasonous
exhibition of a 'book of painted pictures of prophecy' in the possession of Charles Arundel, Arundel and Howard countered the
charge so effectively that Oxford found himself embroiled in controversy. The Queen was distressed by this quarrel, for she was fond of
the young men involved in it, and was disposed to tolerate Catholicism at court so long as it did not spill over into treasonous plotting;
and Burghley continued to support his son-in-law, however dis-
approving of his conduct. Oxford himself had been accused of
helping the Duke of Norfolk to escape overseas in 1571 before
Norfolk's execution, and of joining with English Catholic refugees in
the Lowlands during a sojourn there in 1573, but Elizabeth seems to
have forgiven Oxford even these grave indiscretions.[63]

   John Lyly appears to have been affected by this quarrel of the
cousins in 1581; since Oxford was his patron, he suffered under
Oxford's disgrace. Oxford was accused by Arundel and Howard
of keeping the infamous book of prophecies in his writing desk in
his Greenwich apartment, where he was under house arrest after
Burghley had secured his release from the Tower in June 1581.[64]
Oxford was alleged to have had a taste for prophetic books. When
Lyly wrote to Burghley, Oxford's father-in-law, in July 1582, lamenting the disfavour into which he had fallen and to protest his innocence of any 'treachery' or indulgence in 'factions', he added in a
postscript, 'Loath I am to be a prophet, and to be a witch I loathe.'
The language may suggest a rueful wariness of being implicated in
Oxford's dabbling in the politically occult. Howard went on in 1583
to write his *Defensative against the poison of supposed prophecies*, attempting unsuccessfully to distance himself from this ominous and
controversial prophetic book to which he refers as 'Sybilline';
Howard was sent to the Fleet in late 1583 on a charge of carrying on
a secret correspondence with Mary. If in fact Lyly knew about the
incriminating book of prophecies—and we must stress the uncertainty of this matter—Lyly's dream in *Endymion* takes on substantial
significance. In that dream, an Old Man offers Endymion three
leaves in a patent reworking of the old story of the Sybilline verses

offered by the Sybil in three phases to Tarquin II (see note at
II.iii.67.9).[65]

By early 1588, Lyly had long been in the Earl of Oxford's employment. Even though the formal connection may have ended later that
year, in the summer, *Endymion* was almost certainly written and
produced well before Lyly left Oxford's service. The case to be made
on behalf of Oxford and of Catholic-inclined lords like him was by
this time urgent. Hysteria had been heightened in late 1583 by the
arrest of Francis Throckmorton, a Catholic nephew of Sir Nicholas
Throckmorton, on a charge of conspiring on behalf of Mary Queen
of Scots.[66] No evidence points to any direct involvement on Oxford's
part with Mary, but he was known to have connections with Spain
from 1580 onward. The execution of Mary in February of 1587
meant that war with Spain (and, in effect, with the Papacy and the
Holy League) was inevitable. An English army led by Leicester was
already fighting in the Lowlands against the dangerously able Duke
of Parma. Most significantly for *Endymion*, this all meant that
late 1587 and early 1588 had to be a time of decision for English
Catholics.

If this topical context has any validity, it suggests that the play is
concerned with Endymion's loyalty to the Queen and with the
widely held suspicion that he has been dallying with her chief rival
and enemy. Whether Oxford and other Catholic lords were involved
in conspiracy[67] is less to the point than is the obvious fact that their
loyalty was suspected. Audiences at Paul's and at court in 1588
would surely remember that Mary Stuart had been accused, in a
petition of Parliament to Elizabeth in 1572, of seeking 'by subtle and
crafty means to withdraw the late Duke of Norfolk . . . from his due
and natural obedience to your Highness, and against your Majesty's
express prohibition to couple herself in marriage with the said
Duke'.[68] Such alleged disloyalty in 1572 was still suspected in 1586,
when the so-called Babington Conspiracy brought to light an apparent plot of a Catholic 'invasion with the assistance of civil rebellion',[69] and in 1588, even after Mary's execution, in view of the
impending Armada.

The English Catholic lords had every reason to reassure the
Queen and her government that they were trustworthy. Hence,
perhaps, the play's insistence on constancy as a theme. Hence too its
concessive rhetoric of allowing that Endymion has indeed been
humanly imperfect in his attachment to a very beautiful and alluring
object of worship. The image of the Roman Catholic church as
outwardly beautiful and inwardly corrupt was of course a common-

place; it forms the centre of the political-religious allegory in Book I of Spenser's *The Fairie Queene*. Conceivably the 'Duessa' figure in this play may also be represented by Dipsas, as we shall see shortly. Tellus, leagued in evil with Dipsas, can then resonate with suggestions not simply of Mary herself but of Catholicism as popularly understood in Protestant propaganda as the Whore of Babylon. Tellus is appropriately malicious; as we have seen, the word follows her throughout the play. She is duplicitous, vengeful, beautiful but also terrifying.

She is of course also forgiven in this play. If a political-religious allegory is at work, it might suggest that, just as Elizabeth would have preferred to spare Mary's life and win her loyal submission (long a royal hope in the 1570s and 1580s), so also the play asks for royal tolerance of English Catholics provided they take the crucial step of proclaiming their loyalty and renouncing ultramontane notions of an international church to which they might owe a prior allegiance. This issue was again a burning one in 1588. Sentiment for a resolution of strife along the lines proposed, of loyal submission to the crown, was evidently strong in England. The crucial matter was whether English Catholics were ready to make that commitment. Dr Allen, the hated Jesuit Robert Parsons, and Edmund Campion were not. Lyly's play seems to argue that Oxford and many other lords are fully ready. The play seems also to flatter Elizabeth by implying that those Catholics who remain unloyal do so solely for venal reasons. Endymion's quest is spiritual, aiming at a higher order of truth and constancy by putting aside worldly concerns. Catholic meddling in the overthrow of Elizabeth is seen as a deplorably worldly endeavour, one that any idealistic and honourable Englishman will eschew.

Tellus's sinister alliance with the witch Dipsas may well suggest that Dipsas represents an aspect of Catholicism as well, and a particularly dire one. If Tellus is like Mary in a number of ways, Dipsas is more expressly a Protestant image of the ugly Whore of Rome. Dipsas and Cynthia are polar opposites in ways that recall Protestant stereotypes about the conflict between the Roman Church and the English Establishment: Dipsas is an enchantress, Cynthia is charismatic and transcendent. They are locked in a power struggle in which evil is destined to be circumscribed at last, because God is on Cynthia's side. As Cynthia proclaims to Dipsas in her scene of justice triumphant:

> Thou hast threatened to turn my course awry and alter by thy damnable art the government that I now possess by the eternal gods. But know thou,

Dipsas, and let all the enchanters know, that Cynthia, being placed for
light on earth, is also protected by the powers of heaven. (v.iv.6–11)[70]

Dipsas has been practising her witchcraft for 'almost these fifty
years' (v.iv.3; III.iv.5), a span of time that, as Joel Altman points out,
takes us back to the 1530s, when Henry VIII broke with Rome.[71]
'Fifty years' may be a round sum of no great significance, perhaps,
but in 1588 an audience may have thought more particularly about
their own recent history. Dipsas and Tellus together may thus
represent the hatred that many English people—including Elizabeth—felt for the Papacy, along with the more ambivalent feelings
they entertained for Mary.

Endymion's flirting with Tellus, indeed his deep involvement with
her, might also be interpreted in 1588 as a backward look at what
happened to English loyalties in 1553 to 1558, during the reign of
another Mary, Mary Tudor. Protestant morality plays of the 1560s
and 1570s, such as George Wapull's *The Tide Tarrieth No Man* and
William Wager's *The Longer Thou Livest the More Fool Thou Art*,
repeatedly characterised England's turning away from the true path
during those years as a fall from grace, the very sort of disobedience
and perversity that the human race is so prone to discover in itself.[72]
Calvinist theology, with which this early Elizabethan popular drama
is heavily infused, underscored the human depravity that alone
might explain how God's chosen people could worship false gods
with such blatant folly. And because this narrative of fall and salvation could rely so extensively on the archetypal Biblical story of
Adam and Eve, *Endymion* too perhaps takes on an inclusive dimension. Its comic resolution gently punishes and reclaims those who
have erred, no matter how grievously, and rewards the faithful
protagonist whose human weaknesses have led him too into folly but
whose inherent good nature deserves a second chance. The architect
of this comic benison is a goddess and a woman who understands
human frailty and can forgive in excess of human deserving. She is
Cynthia, also Elizabeth, who reclaimed England from her Catholic
sister in 1558, went on to discipline the northern lords in 1569, and
stood poised in 1588 at a moment in history when her wooing of
English Catholics would decide England's failure or success.

Although the main lines of the play's political allegory seem
reasonably clear, Lyly's own position remains uncertain. The situation was a delicate one for him. As one long indebted to Burghley
and no doubt hopeful of future favours, he could not afford to

alienate that powerful lord. Lyly was indebted to Burghley, who had
continued to support his son-in-law Oxford throughout the crisis of
impending invasion and at the same time championed a hard line
against Mary Stuart and her followers. One can well imagine that
Lyly's connection to Oxford, even if no longer formal, was still
important to the dramatist; indeed, we cannot be sure that he did
not hope to depend on the lord in the years to come.

The play does not ask leniency towards those who continued to
pursue the policies of the now-dead Mary Stuart; Tellus is a menac-
ingly troublesome presence in the play and is forgiven only when she
recants entirely her wicked aspirations. If, as is argued here, the play
appears to suggest a rapprochement through the offering of assurance by the Catholic lords that they harbour no treasonous intent
and are thus deserving of trust, Lyly's position might be seen as a
mediating one acceptable to Burghley and Oxford. Perhaps, in a
world of shifting allegiances, the vulnerable dramatist sought to
placate two men who, though forming no single faction to which
Lyly could align himself, were none the less obliged to each other by
ties of marriage. In the process, too, he hoped to suggest a stance not
unwelcome to Queen Elizabeth, who had bitterly resisted the machi-
nations of her courtiers forcing her hand in the execution of Mary.
Importantly, too, he presented his play in the form of an allegory
that enabled him to disclaim any overt political stance and to direct
his audience's attention to the myriad other ways in which allegory
can invite interpretation.

Allegories of gender and power

Endymion in fact invites another quite different sort of political
reading, one in which Cynthia's identification with Queen Elizabeth
is central but in which the focus is not specifically on the Catholic
threat. The political anxiety here at issue is what Louis Montrose
calls 'the interplay between representations of gender and power in
a stratified society in which authority is everywhere invested in
men—everywhere that is, except at the top'.[73] As Montrose argues,
anxieties about male subjection to a virgin queen found literary
expression in the 'shaping fantasies' of many Elizabethan authors,
including Lyly and Shakespeare. In a conscious attempt to appropriate to Elizabeth the worship formerly bestowed on the Virgin Mary,
and thus to foster a cult of Elizabeth, the Queen's propagandists
made bold use of erotic and maternal symbolism: she was the life-

rendering pelican mother, the bountiful wetnurse, the paradoxical
virgin and mother who was 'part Madonna, part Ephesian Diana'.
Her male courtiers, accustomed to a world in which public and
private forms of authority were invariably vested in fathers, husbands, and employers responded to the gendered inversion at the
top of that social structure with ambivalence. The ambivalence takes
the form, in *A Midsummer Night's Dream*, of a widely shared fantasy
in which a queen forms a liaison with a lowly subject and in which
she is at once nurturing and domineering, dependent and autocratic,
tender and threatening. In Montrose's view, we are given 'a fantasy
of male dependency upon women' that is 'expressed and contained
within a fantasy of male control over women'.[74] Elsewhere in the
play as well, Theseus's male need to tame an Amazonian queen
bespeaks an insistence on patriarchal control that was threatened at
the top of Elizabethan society by a queen who used the game of
courtship and flirtation as a weapon of political control.

Philippa Berry draws on Montrose and on Mary Beth Rose
(whose work we have cited earlier),[75] among others, to demonstrate
how aptly Elizabeth's use of her unmarried situation can apply to a
reading of *Endymion* and other of Lyly's plays. Berry's argument is
that Lyly gives us 'a mysticism of contemplation rather than of
action' in his attempt to define an ideal relationship between female
monarch and male courtier. Endymion withdraws into 'the private,
emotional and feminine sphere of experience symbolized by the
moon—the planet which was now becoming the privileged emblem
of her [Elizabeth's] courtly cult'. The move is not, however, without
its consequences of unease, as the baffled male courtier considers
what his role is to be in a court so gynocentrically defined.[76]

In part, the contemplative stance seems well suited to Lyly's
artistic, aesthetic, and political agendas, as Berry demonstrates.
Neoplatonism provided Lyly with the symbolic language and imagery of contemplative worship. Lyly's dependence on Burghley encouraged his espousal of a non-aggressive stance attuned to a foreign
policy of non-intervention and implicitly sceptical of the interven-
tionist policies of the Leicester–Walsingham faction. Lyly was also
close to an unstable alliance of crypto-Catholics that included Oxford, Lord Henry Howard, and Arundel, among others, who could
at least agree in opposing all that Leicester represented in the Netherlands. Lyly's uncle George had been a Roman Catholic divine
under Cardinal Pole, whom Queen Mary appointed as Archbishop
of Canterbury; George served as Pole's domestic chaplain and

canon of Canterbury.[77] Even when Lyly himself later displayed a loyal and no doubt prudent Anglicanism in his contributions to the Martin Marprelate controversy, he did so in the name of vilifying the Puritans, who generally supported Leicester.

Yet, as Berry shows, the portraiture of female power in Lyly's plays and notably in *Endymion* is not without an uneasy and satirical suggestiveness of which the dramatist may be not wholly conscious. Because she is associated with the moon and thus with Selene, Cynthia conjures up not only positive images but also disturbing suggestions of the crone or the witch[78] that some contemporaries may have dared privately to compare with the ageing Elizabeth. Male friendship in *Endymion*, as in earlier plays like *Campaspe*, takes on an aspect of misogynistic rejection of the kind of dependency that is so likely, in this view, to overwhelm the male in his hapless quest for heterosexual union, even if in *Endymion* the solution is finally idealised. The female ruler's pretensions to authority in the world of the intellectual and the artist similarly threaten the autonomy of the male humanist and writer of courtly entertainments. An 'underlying fear of female sexuality' produces an unresolved 'division or fragmentation of the feminine' like that found in much Petrarchan and Neoplatonic writing. Having chosen a myth of Endymion that was widely associated in that literature with sublimated desire, Lyly ends his portrayal of his protagonist's struggle with desire not by fulfilling it in erotic terms but by retreating into passivity—as a courtier had to do. To the extent that Mary Queen of Scots hovers in the political allegory, argues Berry, it is to contrast the erotic and conspiratorial Tellus with her Platonic opposite (Cynthia) and thereby to polarise the figure of womanly authority into radically divergent images of whore and saint. Even so, Cynthia does not emerge unscathed from this implicit political contrast, for she too is associated with feminine mutability, with a motherly voraciousness, and with a supernatural power that is tainted by suggestions of witchcraft. In the play's subplot, as well, the revulsive catalogue of Dipsas's sagging breasts and toothless smile may contaminate by its proximity the image of Elizabeth herself.[79]

Allegory and multiple plotting

Berry's political reading of contemplative passivity implicitly supporting a foreign policy of non-intervention on the Continent is surely compatible with the political reading proposed in this Introduction, one in which an accommodation of English Catholics like Oxford plays a significant role. Perhaps both readings have the added advantage of suggesting highly personal and topical resonances that none the less avoid overly detailed workings out of the allegory in terms of court personalities and marriages. These readings do not insist on topical identifications for Eumenides, Semele, Corsites, Sir Tophas, Bagoa, Geron, Pythagoras, and the other characters of the play whose purported historical identities have driven into the realm of utter implausibility those many inter-pretations that insist on seeing *Endymion* as an elaborate *roman à clef*.

Clearly these other characters are important to the play's Neoplatonic allegory and symbolism, and even to its political rami-fications in the broad sense of that term 'political'. Lyly has added these characters to his basic myth of Endymion apparently in order to enrich the allegorical idea of a quest for constancy and for higher spiritual, religious, and political understanding. Nowhere is the play's schematic tendency more evident than in the arrangement of the play's sets of lovers. Endymion and Cynthia are at the apex of the play's structure by virtue of Cynthia's regal stature and the spiritualised nature of Endymion's love. Below them, in descending order on the Neoplatonic ladder from contemplative union down towards base fleshliness (although the exact order is sometimes debated), are Eumenides and Semele, Corsites and Tellus, Geron and Dipsas, and Sir Tophas and Bagoa.[80]

Eumenides is a wandering knight out of medieval romance. He is also at the centre of a debate between love and friendship. He journeys to the magic fountain to find a remedy for his sleeping friend. Since only faithful lovers are permitted to see the bottom of this fountain, Eumenides is by definition a faithful lover. As such he is a rare person, personating honour; Geron has seen many 'lusters' at his fountain, men and women, who have wept tears of love sorrow but to no avail because they are insufficiently constant. Eumenides is at once a loyal friend and a faithful lover. Yet his reward for such virtue appears to be cruelly paradoxical: he is bidden to 'Ask one for all, and but one thing at all' (III.iv.40, 85–6). He must choose whether to rescue his friend or win possession of his mistress, Semele. The debate that rages in his soul pours forth in one of the most highly wrought and antithetical Euphuistic passages of the play. It characteristically ends in a draw until the wise old Geron demonstrates with more Euphuistic prose how friendship is superior to love because it is not subject to time and fortune. Reinforced by

these elegant commonplaces, Eumenides chooses friendship. Ultimately, to be sure, he wins the love of Semele as well, and thus ends
up with both love and friendship. This plot illustrates the truism that
only the lover who is prepared to put friendship above all other
considerations is worthy of true love also. In the hierarchies that
stand behind this play at every turn, friendship ranks above love.
Friendship is reasonable, generous, intellectually nourishing, constant; erotic love (as distinguished from Neoplatonic love) is a
tickling of desire too apt to ebb and fade as beauty diminishes. Lyly
thus plays with truisms about love and friendship reaching back
at least to Chaucer's *Knight's Tale*, Sir Thomas Elyot's account of
Titus and Gysippus in *The Governour* (1531), and Richard
Edwards's *Damon and Pythias* (c. 1565).[81]

Semele, the desired object of Eumenides's romantic longings, is
womanish in a way that polarises the sexes and thereby reinforces
the misogynistic truisms that emerge everywhere in this play. Semele
is spiteful; the words 'spiteful' and 'spitefully' are repeatedly used to
characterise her.[82] She is also 'froward' or perversely ill-humoured;
Eumenides is 'fond' or infatuated (III.iv.62–3). They fence with each
other in brittle fashion.[83] Semele's mythological name is that of a
king's daughter who proudly desires to see her lover Zeus in all his
glory and is consumed by his lightning. She is thus, in this play, the
proud beauty of the Petrarchan sonnet. Cynthia is determined to
rein her in, and does so by imprisoning that 'saucy' part of her that
so offends: her tongue (IV.iii.69–77). Eumenides perceives that his
passion for Semele is so ruinously strong that he can only pray for
restraint: 'Let her practise her accustomed coyness, that I may diet
myself upon my desires. Otherwise the fullness of my joys will
diminish the sweetness, and I shall perish by them before I possess
them' (III.iv.104–7).

The resolution of their love story in Act V is that of a lovers'
quarrel put finally to rest: Semele is jealous that Eumenides has
chosen Endymion over her, but is content at last to love him when
he offers to take her punishment upon him and begs the Queen to
forgive Semele. Seemingly she understands now that friendship
has provided the remedy to the intemperateness of passionate love
and all the misunderstandings it so readily generates. Though
Eumenides is passionate also in his love of Endymion, this friendship provides a counterbalance that enables Eumenides to give the
right priority to his affections. He is thus a quester after the wisdom
that Endymion attains, but he is less successful, in that friendship

and love remain polarised for him between men and women. Only in the partnership of Endymion and Cynthia are love and friendship platonically indistinguishable.

Corsites and Tellus would seem to be one step below Eumenides and Semele on the Neoplatonic ladder. His name, 'heart-thirst', sugggests the essentially carnal nature of his infatuation for Tellus. He is, to be sure, an honourable soldier in the service of Cynthia, but when he is commissioned to be Tellus's keeper in the desert castle he quickly loses his heart to her. Tellus's role towards him is patently that of the insincere flirt; she cannot love him, but confesses to us that she will 'dissemble' with him in order to gain advantage. With practised coyness, she strikes a delicate balance between being too 'flexible' or available and too 'froward' or denying; one extreme would 'give him more hope than I mean', the other 'less liberty than I would' (IV.i.26–31). She succeeds so well that he undertakes to do anything for her, as a good Petrarchan wooer should. The task she assigns is one that she knows he cannot perform: to move the spellbound Endymion from his lunary bank. He recognises the language of bartering, and understands that his reward is to be sexual: 'As I would have none partaker of my sweet love, so shall none be partners of my labours' (ll. 70–1). Tellus sends him about a fool's errand with the matter-of-fact lack of compunction of a lady accustomed to being pursued by importunate men. She is playing games with him, in order that she may 'laugh with the other ladies at Corsites' sweating' (ll. 87–8). Corsites is taken in; 'Without doubt Tellus doteth upon me' (IV.iii.1–2).

Only when he awakens to see himself covered with spots of shame does Corsites realise that Tellus has practised 'deceit' out of 'despite' (l. 135). Yet he forbearingly refuses to seek revenge; she is still beautiful, and holds his heart captive. His continuing affection lends some plausibility to the conventional romantic ending in which they are paired off, though Tellus appears to take him simply as a way out of her difficulties with Cynthia. The Queen, in fact, offers her this marriage as the price of forgiveness: 'How say you, will you have your Corsites and so receive pardon for all that is past?' (V.iv.253–4). Still, Corsites is truly happy to have her, 'more happy to enjoy Tellus than the monarchy of the world' (ll. 257–8). Even if Tellus's thoughts are entirely upon Endymion still, she will have an obliging husband, and, more importantly no doubt, she will have shown obedience to Cynthia. Corsites and Tellus occupy a place on the Neoplatonic ladder below Eumenides and Semele, perhaps, because their relationship is so unreciprocal: doting on his part, cynical on hers.[84]

The pairing of Geron and Dipsas is even more one-sided, so much so that we can only wonder at the patience and forgiveness of an old man who has been deserted by his wife for fifty years and condemned to live a life of such loneliness that he esteems 'sorrow my chiefest solace' (III.iv.4–7). He cannot countenance the 'lewd and detestable course' of her witchcraft, but is more than happy to take her back when she renounces that black art (v.iv.278–80). Like Tellus, her accomplice, Dipsas welcomes penance because it allows her at last to show 'to Your Highness obedience'; and once again the wedding is Cynthia's price for forgiveness (ll. 269–75). The relationship of Geron and Dipsas mirrors and magnifies that of Corsites and Tellus.

In all the play's romantic resolutions, then, two elements are especially noteworthy. First, they are the creation of Cynthia, who takes charge of people's lives without hesitation, and who offers herself as the model of womanly perfection in her self-control and presumably benign authority over others. Second, in most of the male–female pairings in Cynthia's court, it is the woman who is most seriously at fault and who must be forgiven by the man. Even Semele, less guilty than Tellus and Dipsas, must be cured of her waspishness and unreasonable jealousy. Lyly's tendency to bifurcate women into deceivers and saints adopts the strategy of compensating for the threatening nature of his women by contrasting them with the unassailably virtuous queen at the centre of the play.[85]

To the extent that the play's marriages all come under the control of Cynthia, they resemble those of the Elizabethan court. Elizabeth was of course known for her touchiness on the subject of marriages among her courtiers and on her insistence in overseeing whatever matches were made. The reconciliation of Dipsas to Cynthia and her marriage to one of Cynthia's oldest and most loyal courtiers may be meant to reflect a hope on Elizabeth's part that even her Catholic enemies might be accommodated if only they would forswear disloyalty. After all, Elizabeth had once contemplated allowing Mary Stuart to marry Leicester or the Duke of Norfolk, however quick she was in fact to reject such ideas.[86]

Clearly at the bottom of the Neoplatonic ladder leading from concupiscence to ethereal contemplation is Sir Tophas. He is by ancestry, as we have seen, a braggart soldier, a parasite, a satiric type of social climber, and a burlesque version of the Neoplatonists' heroic lover. He is everything that Endymion is not or should not be, and is hence a reminder in this play that men can be insufferable too. His bravery is all sham, directed at innocent targets like birds, fish, and sheep, and easily turned aside into cowardice. His learning is pedantic and shallow, his self-conceit immeasurable. He professes at first to scorn love as a good soldier ought, and fends off the mocking flirtations of Scintilla and Favilla, but is soon infatuated in a way that exaggerates all the unattractive qualities in better men like Corsites and Endymion. Eros prompts him to lay aside all martial rigour and to pay excessive attention instead to his coiffure and wardrobe (III.iii.31–43). He quotes Ovid's *Ars Amatoria* and catalogues the absurdly inappropriate qualities of his mistress with epithets that are singularly foolish even in this play (ll. 55–64). He composes fatuous verse (IV.ii.26–9).

His sleep is a parody of Endymion's and, to a degree, Corsites's. Sir Tophas's is not a contemplative sleep but a sluggish and ener-vated one in which the dreams are replete with prognosticatory signs (an owl on his shoulder in the image of Dipsas) that lack any meaning other than mere foolishness (III.iii.141–6). Even after he awakes from this dream, he 'pineth in his bed and cometh not abroad', and 'would fain take a nap for forty or fifty years' (IV.ii.3–4, 19–20). Like Endymion, he 'ventureth on her whom none durst undertake', as Epiton punningly observes at Sir Tophas's expense (III.iii.75): Endymion ventures after Cynthia, who is ever above men's heads, whereas Sir Tophas ventures for a witch whom no other man would touch. Dipsas is a married woman at that. His aspiration is parodied by his disproportionate size: Epiton, his longsuffering page, is always there to point up by his diminutive size and his ready wit the grossness and fatuity of his master. Sir Tophas parodies not only Endymion's asiration but his struggles to be constant in his affection. Sir Tophas changes from love-rejecting soldier to enervated lover of Dipsas to one who is willing to take any woman in Dipsas's stead: 'so she be a wench I care not' (v.iv.293–4). To the extent that Sir Tophas is a part of Endymion, the beastly part of him, his discomfiture makes him the perfect scapegoat. Yet Sir Tophas too is included in the final round of forgiveness and rec-onciling marriages.

The secondary characters in *Endymion*, then, offer variations on the themes love and friendship, aspiration, and constancy, all in relation to the central configuration of Endymion, Cynthia, and Tellus. The secondary characters don't seem to have much to do with a topical historical allegory; attempts to find places for them in Elizabeth's court all founder on particularities that are unconvincing. Sir Tophas offers the most tempting target, though once again the identifications proposed by earlier historical critics (Sir Gabriel Harvey, Stephen Gosson)[87] strike me as too parochial and less demonstrable than a major player in contemporary history whom no one has proposed: Philip II, King of Spain, Portugal, the Netherlands, and Naples.

Within a year of so of *Endymion*, in 1589, following upon England's defeat of the Armada, Lyly was to make open fun of Philip of Spain in the person of King Midas. The isles north of Phrygia in *Midas* are plainly the British Isles, Lesbos is England, and the foolish king of Phrygia who longs to see all that he touches turn to gold is very like the Spanish king coveting his South American mines. Sir Tophas is no less a covetous fool in *Endymion*. Philip had been much laughed at in England for his bumbling and inconstant role as a wooer: he married four times, one of these times to Mary Tudor, and had even set his cap for Elizabeth in the early days of her reign. English authors had free licence to cast Philip as a sham soldier and coward, as Lyly did in 1589. Most importantly, Sir Tophas is courting Dipsas, who, as we have seen, may reflect English attitudes about the ugly conspiracies of international Catholicism. An allegorical reading along these lines would distinguish sharply between Sir Tophas's incurable folly, presumably characteristic of the Spanish Papists, and the recoverable decency of well-meaning English Catholics. In seeing Philip as the witless dupe and worshipper of Catholicism (Dipsas), Lyly's play could then be inviting satirical laughter at an enemy the English had already subjected to scorn and humiliation through Drake's raids of 1587, opposition to Parma in the Netherlands, and support for Henry of Navarre as victor at Coutras in October of 1587. This interpretion of Sir Tophas seems to me less certain than that of Cynthia, Endymion, Tellus, and Dipsas, but inviting none the less. In a more general sense, Sir Tophas may represent anyone, English or otherwise, who is so foolish as to be infatuated by Catholicism.

The Neoplatonic reading of *Endymion* as a set of variations on the themes of love and constancy has much to commend it, so long as it does not transform the play into a kind of Christian homily. C. C. Gannon does well to point out Lyly's familiarity with Renaissance interpretations of the Endymion story by Giordano Bruno, among others, in which sleep figures forth a union of the soul with Christ in death, or, short of that, the ecstatic contemplation by the soul of the divine. The moon's kiss thereby becomes a mystical *mors osculi* bespeaking a reciprocal desire for union between God and human-kind.[88] Edgar Wind interprets the Endymion myth in a similar way.[89] The Song of Solomon, alluded to in Lyly's play (i.ii.20–6), becomes severely allegorised in this reading from an erotic love song into the rapture of purely religious ecstasy. Because Bruno identifies his Diana figure with Queen Elizabeth, and his heroic furor (*gli eroici furori*) with a questing and suffering hero like Endymion, the Neoplatonic reading of *Endymion* allies itself effortlessly with Lyly's avowed purpose of celebrating Elizabeth's greatness and perhaps of urging that monarch to reclaim her loyal Catholic subjects. The Cabalists' search for a way to triumph over concupiscence is close to Lyly's wary mistrust of Tellus's beauty; their fascination with images of ascending calls to mind the Icarian images of daring flight and of fall in Lyly's play.

Similarly, the play's narrative of absence from and eventual resto-ration to grace in the person of Cynthia lends itself to a fable of redemption that can be found everywhere in Christian allegory. The emblems of Alciati, Whitney, and others, as Robert Knapp shows, turn again and again to images of falling from dangerous heights. 'Let mortal men, that are but earth and dust, / Not look too high, with puff of worldly pride', writes Whitney, in a truism with patent application to Endymion, even if the lesson must be read in a complex way. An emblem by Reusner from 1581 shows Diana holding Endymion in her lap, to signify Diana's (Christ's) releasing of Endymion from the flesh by means of the *mors osculi*.[90] Carolyn Ruth Swift Lenz pursues a possible liturgical connection between *Endymion* and the Feast of Purification of St Mary the Virgin, the day (2 February) on which the play was performed before Queen Elizabeth. The idea identifies *Endymion* as an allegory of wisdom in which mortal worshippers are invited to cleanse their souls and strive to learn the essence of God, and seems well illustrated by Abraham Fraunce's description of Endymion as 'a figure of the soul of man, kissed of Diana in [i.e., on] the hill—that is, ravished by celestial contemplation'.[91]

Yet there are dangers in Lenz's contention that the main events of *Endymion* are based on the apocryphal Book of the Wisdom of Solomon, even if that book did provide the lessons to be read on Candlemas Day; the audiences at Paul's in the weeks leading up to the court performance on 2 February cannot be assumed to have been thinking of Candlemas Day, and on balance the play quickly moves out of any imagined liturgical orbit. So too, the contention that the three ladies in Endymion's dream function as the four Daughters of God (Mercy, Justice, Peace, and Truth) in medieval allegorical tradition, as seen for example in the conclusion of *The Castle of Perseverance*, is to privilege Christian sources and themes in a way that perhaps obscures other more tangible influences.[92] Christian Neoplatonic idealism was so widely distributed in Renaissance culture that its presence in *Endymion* is both undeniable and, to a degree, unremarkable. Lyly makes elegant and entertaining theatrical use of its truisms as he does of proverb lore, Pliny, Ovid, and other elements that are anything but Neoplatonic in tone.

It is instructive to see that Peter Weltner is able to read the idealistic themes of *Endymion* in persuasive Jungian terms that have nothing explicitly to do with Christianity. The Endymion of classical legend is, for Jung, a mortal hero transformed into a half-god as he seeks to expand his human consciousness from its dark and limiting origins (typified by Tellus as the 'devouring Mother' of the unconscious) towards spiritual enlightenment (embodied in Cynthia as the 'luminous body'). Only when humankind learns to come into vital contact with the anima within can the human being 'transform himself and realize his higher nature', writes Weltner in summarising Jung's ideas. 'Otherwise, he is condemned to the destructive force of nature which will, at last, embrace him and draw him back into its generative and putrescent earth. So, then, only when Cynthia has stooped and touched Endymion can Endymion release himself from the terrible and destructive hold of Tellus, the nature who loves him and longs to keep him hers.' The fact that Lyly's play lends itself so well to a post-Romantic interpretation provides support for Weltner's contention that Lyly's art is best described (like all fine art) as more symbolic than allegorical, 'neither abstract nor concrete, neither rational nor irrational, neither real nor unreal', but 'always both'. Cynthia, the central symbol of *Endymion*, unites in her dramatic person body and soul, flesh and spirit, the unconscious and consciousness.[93] In the dualism of Lyly's play, perhaps allegory and symbolism also merge as one.

STRUCTURE AND STYLE

In structure and language, *Endymion* is consciously antithetical. It pairs its characters and its various plots in such a way as to invite a contrastive juxtaposition. The several pairs of lovers resemble one another in order to reveal an ascending scale from carnal desire to contemplative union, from Sir Tophas and Dipsas (or, finally, Bagoa) to Geron and Dipsas, Corsites and Tellus, Eumenides and Semele, and Endymion and Cynthia. These parallel love situations explore antithetical issues of love and honour, love and friendship, carnality and chastity, perfidy and constancy, sovereignty and service, reason and passion, masters versus servants, men versus women, and the like. As Peter Saccio has shown of Lyly generally, the dramaturgy is 'situational': characters are revealed through an investigative mode in which a variety of discrete plots are juxtaposed, all aimed at defining propriety or decorum in the individual's social role as monarch, courtier, philosopher, page, friend, and so on.[94] Joel Altman argues that this mode of thinking about hypothesised questions through formal rhetorical debate is deeply ingrained in English education in the Renaissance and in courtly drama throughout the sixteenth century. The quintessential Lylyan plot, 'arising from a *quaestio*, is often really a pair of *theses* argued copiously, now through one order of the cosmos, now through another, until the whole universe seems caught up in the strife'. The questions in *Endymion*, says Altman, are traditional: 'What kind of relationship must the Courtier have with his sovereign? Should love or friendship bear the greater sway in determining men's actions? What constitutes royal justice?'.[95]

Lyly's famous Euphuistic style, with its elaborate rhetorical schemes and tropes of isocolon, parison, and paramoion (similarity of length, grammatical form, and sound in successive and corresponding phrases or clauses), alliteration, word repetition, *similiter cadentes* (similarity at the end of a phrase), metaphors from fanciful natural history, and the like, is elegantly suited to a drama of antithetical debate. The style, as Jonas Barish has shown, revels in parallels, logical structures, and syntactic oppositions, through which a thing may be defined by its opposite, or two things may be held in equilibrium, or one thing may be seen to possess contrary properties within it.[96] An example of the first in *Endymion* might be the contrast of Endymion and Sir Tophas, in which the cowardly knight is essentially all that Endymion is not; the second pattern appears in the debate of love and friendship, where much is to be said on behalf of each quality until they are finally reconciled in Endymion and Cynthia; and the third manifests itself in the debate within Endymion himself between worldly desire (Tellus) and spiritual contemplation (Cynthia).

All three patterns display themselves at the level of the individual phrase, sentence, and paragraph. Thus, to illustrate the first pattern of opposition, Floscula says of Tellus and Cynthia in speaking to Tellus:

> But know you not, fair lady, that Cynthia governeth all things? Your grapes would be but dry husks, your corn but chaff, and all your virtues vain, were it not Cynthia that preserveth the one in the bud and nourisheth the other in the blade. (I.ii.29–33)

Here the parison, isocolon, and paramoion, reinforced by alliteration and *similiter cadens* ('preserv*eth the* one *in the* b*ud* and nourish*eth the* other *in the* b*lade*'), underscore the parallel out of which symmetrical opposition arises. The holding of two ideas in equilibrium is illustrated with splendid virtuosity in Eumenides's *deliberatio* and *altercatio* on love and friendship as he debates whether to expend his one wish for Semele or Endymion: 'Tush, Semele doth possess my love.—Ay, but Endymion hath deserved it', and so on (III.iv.123–4), where the equal word lengths, grammatical repetitions, and sounds focus attention on the balance inhering in a difficult choice. Finally, the discovery of contrary qualities within a single entity can be seen in Cynthia as head of a court in which politics and idealism, justice and mercy, practical affairs and philosophy are at last reconciled. As she says to her wise men: 'if you cannot content yourselves in our court to fall from vain follies of philosophers to such virtues as are here practised, you shall be entertained according to your deserts' (V.iv.300–3). Cynthia's speech embodies rhetorical balance and antithesis just as her rule embraces all the healthful oppositions of a court in which faction has become meaningful debate.

Barish's fine perception that 'the more absolute of its kind a thing may appear to be, the more certain it is that somewhere within it lies its own antithesis, its anti-self'[97] aptly describes the seemingly total opposition between Endymion and Sir Tophas. They are opposites, to be sure, and yet, as we have seen, Endymion shares with his ludicrous *Doppelgänger* propensities towards intellectual sloth, sensual enslavement, and ambition that he must overcome in his quest for enlightenment. Lyly's style and characterisation work hand in hand to reveal the antipathies and contradictions in human nature, indeed the paradoxical inconsistency of the world itself. And because the contradictions of human existence manifest themselves with particularly comic vividness in mating rituals, love serves as the central theme in a play that is also about humankind's faltering search for the ethereal. Lyly's language is at once playful and serious, mannered and didactic, fanciful and in earnest, farcical (in the pages' scenes) and lyrical.[98]

Even the secondary personages in *Endymion* seem to exist as doubles of some other character or characters. Dares and Simias, pages to Endymion and Eumenides, exchange witticisms with each other and with the diminutive ladies-in-waiting, Scintilla and Favilla, whose similar-sounding names unite them as two of a kind. Epiton is seldom seen without his master, Sir Tophas, in a visual and verbal rhetoric of contrast: small and large, witty and obtuse, resourceful and enervated, self-aware and fatuous. Dipsas has her assistant, Bagoa, and is also paired with Tellus in a conspiracy of malice and witchcraft.[99] Thus the pairings overlap, much as Tellus is paired with Endymion and Corsites, Tellus also with her rival Cynthia, Endymion with Cynthia and Eumenides, Eumenides with Endymion and Semele. Philosophers come in pairs as Pythagoras and Gyptes; so do essentially supernumerary courtiers like Panelion and Zontes. The fair lady in Endymion's dream is accompanied by two ladies, one vengeful and one merciful. Lyly's view of human-kind, and of his theatre, is dialectical.

For all its studied mannerisms and its look-alike prose in which all the characters at first seem to be speaking in Euphuistic sentences, Lyly's style in *Endymion* is notably supple and varied. The play shifts appropriately from a measured and formal dialogue in I.i and I.ii to the more staccato rhythms of I.iii; throughout, the comic scenes involving Sir Tophas and the pages are more colloquial and punning than are the other parts of the play. Lyly has an operatic taste for long soliloquies, virtually sung at key points by his boy actors. They are not 'undramatic' simply because they are long any more than an aria is undramatic. Lyly's diction is richly varied, and his repertory of artful metaphors drawn from proverb lore, legendary natural history, and sheer invention is impressive in its self-conscious artifice.[100]

Dialogue of advice and exhortation is common in *Endymion* as in Lyly's other plays, as Eumenides cautions Endymion against blas-phemous ambition (I.i), Floscula warns Tellus to remember how much the state of Cynthia towers above her own (I.ii) and advises against the use of sorcery (I.iv), Tellus woos Dipsas to practise her witchcraft on Endymion (I.iv) and persuades Corsites to attempt to move the sleeping Endymion (IV.i), Geron talks Eumenides into choosing friendship over love (III.iv), and the like. Persuasion is at times ineffective or, worse still, pernicious; Lyly excels in a use of language that shows the very limitations of that language, and especially so in romantic encounters where language serves to dramatise the predicaments of lovers. Language isolates the lovers, as Robert Turner shows, and drives them into trapped corners where their speaking can express their frustrated desire to break out of an unsatisfactory situation.[101] Endymion laments his unresolvable dilemma in loving a queen who is not to be conquered; Eumenides reflects unhappily on Semele's unremitting scorn (III.iv.54–8); Tellus reveals a malicious envy that she must conceal from Endymion. Lyly makes of each situation a wry comedy showing how 'love cuts across our little plans and makes fools of us all'.[102] In these and still other ways, Lyly's dramatic prose demonstrates a virtuosity that is pyrotechnical in itself and yet integral to the play of comic absurdities and paradoxes in which his courtly drama excels.[103]

DRAMATURGY AND STAGING

Endymion was not staged at the Blackfriars theatre Lyly had used to present *Campaspe* and *Sappho and Phao* in 1584. By Easter term in that year, the Blackfriars lease had reverted to its erstwhile landlord, Sir William More, who evicted forthwith the children's troupes that had been playing there in 1583–84. Lyly sold off the lease he held on some rooms in Blackfriars. The two companies, the Children of the Royal Chapel and Paul's boys, that had been combined under the Earl of Oxford's patronage, with Lyly as playwright and impresario, went their separate ways; Thomas Giles, appointed on 22 May 1584 as Master of Choristers, assumed control as Master of the Childen of Paul's. By some time in 1588 Lyly as theatrical entrepreneur was no longer directly connected with Oxford. *Gallathea,* written in 1584–85, was evidently held up from production for some years, perhaps by 'the malicious' whom Lyly, in the Epilogue to *Endymion,* implicitly accuses of having sought 'to overthrow' him and Paul's boys. When circumstances allowed Lyly to return to his role as purveyor of plays in late 1587 and early 1588, culminating in court performances of *Gallathea* probably on New Year's Day 1588 and *Endymion* on Candlemas Day of 2 February, the acting company must have opened 'at Paul's', with Thomas Giles as the Master of Paul's boys and Lyly as playwright. We do not know with certainty the location of such a place; it may have been the boys' singing-school in the parish church of St Gregory's, or 'the Almonry House' leased by Sebastian Westcote as almoner from the cathedral, or some other hall on the cathedral grounds.[104]

Performances of Lyly's plays in so-called 'private' playhouses were, according to a useful fiction, 'rehearsals' to enable the players to perfect their shows before acting them in the Queen's presence. As purported rehearsals, such previews enjoyed the protection of the crown. More substantially, they were sources of revenue from paying spectators and means of showing off the dramatist's fare to a sophisticated clientele.[105]

We can only assume that the Paul's boys' theatre was more or less like that at Blackfriars, about which we have some information: a stage probably the full width of the hall, about 27 feet, and perhaps 14 feet deep, with stage 'houses' framed with painted canvas to provide fixed scenic locations. These 'houses' could be symmetrically located onstage, fitted on occasion with a curtain, or the doors themselves may have been sufficient in some cases to represent fixed locations like palaces and caves. The stage must also have provided means of exit and entrance 'offstage' on either wing or possibly through the audience. The theatre may have had no space for acting 'above'.[106] In all likelihood, Lyly designed his productions 'in Paul's', as at Blackfriars earlier, with a watchful eye to culminating court performances, so that his staging methods in the private theatres could be immediately transported to the great hall at Greenwich or at Whitehall.

These staging methods also owed much to traditions of courtly indoor entertainment throughout the years of Tudor rule down to 1584–88. A playing arena located in a great hall, fitted out as necessary with 'houses', provided a venue for a good deal of dramatic entertainment from Henry Medwall's *Fulgens and Lucres* (*c.* 1497) and Nicholas Udall's (?) *Thersites* (1537) down to John Pickering's *Horestes* (1567) and George Peele's *The Arraignment of Paris* (1581–84). Stage action was generally presentational, with no curtain to divide scene from scene; the stage 'mansions' or 'houses' were simultaneously visible and were constructed with little attempt at verisimilar illusion of a scene in perspective. Most action took place in a neutral acting space, from which symbolic journeys could be made to the stage 'houses' representing more fixed locations. Sets of this kind offered flexibility in matters of space and time. Dramatists generally did not worry about classical rules of decorum specifying an action in one place and within twenty-four hours.

Lyly's *Endymion* exploits just such a stage with assurance and familiarity. As in his earlier plays, Lyly sets up at least two anti-thetical fixed locations that are visible throughout the action. In *Campaspe* the opposition is between Apelles's studio and Dionysius's tub. Alexander's palace, probably indicated by a stage door, occupies a central location that gives the King access to these two worlds of emotion and reason, art and philosophy, against which to measure his own greatness and his own limitations as a monarch. *Sappho and Phao* sets off Sibylla's cave against Sappho's bedchamber, with Sappho's palace probably again centrally located at a stage door; Phao's station as a ferryman is somewhere in the neutral acting space that takes up most of the stage. Vulcan's forge, needed only in one late scene, may or may not be doubled with Sibylla's cave. In *Gallathea* we see the sacrificial tree on one side and perhaps a grove of trees opposite.[107]

Endymion calls similarly for an antithetical staging that visualises tensions and attractions between Cynthia and Endymion, Cynthia and Tellus, Endymion and Eumenides, Endymion and Corsites, Endymion and Sir Tophas, thus embodying in varying forms the tensions and attractions of love and friendship throughout the story. The play centres on Cynthia's court; her palace is indicated prob-ably by a stage door giving on to the main acting area. Peter Saccio's claim that 'no word in *Endimion* hints at a palace for Cynthia'[108] is incorrect; Gyptes refers to it at iv.iii.52. Elsewhere, as at iii.iv.201–8, characters announce their intent of going to her and seeking her aid, plainly at her court. Still, the lack of more overt gesturing towards an onstage 'palace' may suggest that a door in the playhouse façade is sufficient representation (as also probably in *Sappho and Phao* and perhaps in *Campaspe*), without necessitating a stage 'house'. Much of the action, in any event, takes place in an unmarked location that is understood to be at or near her court.

Flanking this central acting area, presumably, are fixed locations representing the castle in the desert and the lunary bank where Endymion sleeps. The lunary bank needs to be curtained off from view from time to time, much as Sappho is periodically concealed from the spectators in *Sappho and Phao* and Diogenes is hidden within his tub in *Campaspe*. (The lunary bank is referred to as a 'cabin', iv.iii.119, as is Diogenes's tub in *Campaspe*, v.iv.79 and 82.) The hermitage of Geron, where Eumenides reads the inscription at the bottom of a fountain, is, like the forge of Vulcan in *Sappho and Phao*, limited to a single scene (iii.iv); it may use the same location as the lunary bank, as Hunter suggests,[109] though, if this is indeed

the plan, the arrangement needs to allow for the continuing fiction
that Endymion remains asleep on his lunary bank whenever he is
concealed from view. I will argue shortly that the fountain is adjacent to the lunary bank but not physically identical with it, perhaps
(as Best proposes) onstage near the bank.

   Queen Cynthia does not enter to claim the stage as her courtly
space until the third act. Meantime, the play's initial strategy in
terms of stage location is to establish the central acting area as in the
vicinity of her court. Endymion confesses to Eumenides his love for
Cynthia; Tellus reveals to Floscula her plan of entangling Endymion
in a sweet net of desire, and commissions Dipsas to employ her
spells on the intended victim; the pages Dares and Samias, aided by
the pert maids Scintilla and Favilla, amuse themselves with Sir
Tophas's parodic behaviour as a would-be warrior and lover;
Endymion dissembles with Tellus and is put into a long sleep of
enchantment in which he sees a dumb show. None of this requires
any precise indications of location or any stage structure except at
the very end of Act II when, presumably, Endymion falls asleep on
the 'lunary bank'; it is not mentioned at this point, but will be
needed later when Corsites discovers him there. In the interim,
Endymion must be curtained off from view.

   Endymion's felt but invisible presence behind the curtain lasts a
long time; his ageing sleep is the chief plot of this largely uneventful
play. Not until Act IV, scene iii does Corsites find him on the lunary
bank, now considerably aged. Meantime, Cynthia banishes Tellus
for her presumptuous criticism of Endymion to 'the castle in the
desert' (III.i.42–3) and dispatches Eumenides and other courtiers in
search of remedy for Endymion. Where is the castle to be located?
Act III, scene ii begins with an indication of its specificity as a stage
location: 'Here is the castle, fair Tellus', Corsites tells her. 'Let us
in', he invites her at the scene's close, and they thus exit into the
'castle'. This exit may be into a stage 'house' flanking the central
acting area, but it could also be simply a stage door, opposite the
door used to signify Cynthia's palace.[110] The façade of the acting
space at Paul's or at court makes for a plausible castle exterior, be it
Cynthia's on most occasions or the desert castle when Tellus and
Corsites are onstage. Staging requirements are not extensive for this
desert castle; the two characters come onstage, exchange dialogue,
and exit. They use this location once again, in IV.i, when Tellus
vamps her infatuated captor into agreeing to move Endymion from
his place of enchanted sleep. Corsites refers to 'all the ladies of

the castle' (IV.i.53), but they are never seen and are simply to be imagined behind the scenes; Tellus exits at the end of this scene to 'in and laugh with the other ladies at Corsites' sweating'. Once again her exit through a stage door identifies the locus of this castle. Corsites, dispatched to move Endymion, presumably leaves the stage by some other exit a few lines earlier (l. 78.1). If central doors or 'houses' are used for Cynthia's palace and for the castle in the desert, there are also presumably offstage means of exit to either side or through the audience.

The other important stage location needed during the long hiatus of Endymion's sleep, from II.iii to v.i, is the hermitage of Geron and its magical fountain. Although it is used only once (III.iv), it is referred to at other times; Epiton, in the service of his lovesick master Tophas, resolves to 'see if I can find where Endymion lieth, and then go to a certain fountain hard by, where they say faithful lovers shall have all things they will ask' (IV.ii.71–4). This useful bit of information pairing Tophas as a parodic double of Endymion suggests that the fountain is to be located near the lunary bank but not precisely on the same spot. Some differentiation of the two, even if they are directly adjacent, has distinct advantages in the staging of this play. It allows both to exert their felt presences when they are not actively in use. Both would profit from the use of a curtain, to screen off Endymion from view during his long sleep and to conceal the fountain (if it was a practical stage structure) when it is no longer needed; alternatively, the fountain could be painted on such a curtain. Eumenides's scene (III.iv) with Geron begins in mid conversation, with a song; perhaps a curtain is used at this time to reveal the fountain. At the end of the scene, Geron and Eumenides exit in the direction of the court (ll. 199–208), presumably through a stage exit that does not signify the hermitage. The fountain is either curtained off from view or physically removed.

The lunary bank and its occupant are referred to often, implicitly and explicitly, during Endymion's sleep. Eumenides has visited the sleeper: 'I have seen him, to my grief' (III.i.25). Tophas's sleep onstage (III.iii.72.1–138) pairs this foolish knight iconically with the unseen sleeper out of view. Eumenides converses with Geron about his 'dearest friend, who hath been cast into a dead sleep almost these twenty years' (III.iv.18–19). Tellus sends Corsites to 'the lunary bank' on which 'sleepeth Endymion' (IV.i.59). Even Epiton knows where Endymion's bank is to be found (IV.ii.72). So do Dares and Samias. A watch appears, charged with keeping guard over the

sleeping Endymion; when Dares asks, 'But I pray, sirs, may we see
Endymion?' his request is denied (iv.ii.86–7). Cynthia, who has
ordered the watch, knows where her faithful servant lies asleep.
Throughout the central part of the play, then, Endymion's invisible
presence is strongly felt. Several mimetic journeys are made across
the stage to that location: by Corsites, by Dares and Samias, by the
watch, and, in iv.iii and v.i, by Cynthia and her entire entourage.
'Let us walk to Endymion', she commands (iv.iii.57); 'let us to
Endymion' (v.i.21). A few steps onstage signify a shift of location.

The place where Cynthia and her train find the sleeping
Endymion and Corsites, each under a kind of spell, is variously
called 'this grove' (iv.iii.171) and 'this green' (l. 141). The presence
'near by' of the sacred fountain is repeatedly evoked in the dialogue
(v.i.12). The fairy dance and song take place on this green
(iv.iii.32.1), presumably in the neutral acting space adjacent to the
lunary bank. When Cynthia and others first approach that lunary
bank, they do not see Endymion at first; 'I can do nothing till I see
him', opines Gyptes (l. 61), and accordingly the first business of the
assembled courtiers has to do with discovering and awakening
Corsites to his shameful condition of being spotted. Those spots,
like those of Wit in *Wit and Science* (1531–47), betoken the stains
on his spotted soul. Cynthia's bidding Corsites to 'rouse thyself and
be as thou hast been' effects a cure, aided by the lunary from
Endymion's place of rest. Corsites recovers his 'former state' (ll.
130–3), guided by Cynthia's wisdom, and the spots disappear. Presumably this action is quite literal onstage: the fairies anoint him
with spots, and the lunary enables him to rub them out.

Only when Corsites has been thus recovered do Cynthia and her
train appear to take notice of the sleeping Endymion. Because the
enchantment is too strong for Gyptes's skill, nothing is to be done at
present other than set careful watch over him, and so the fourth act
ends with a general exit and Endymion still asleep on the lunary
bank. His presence bridges the gap of an act division, carefully
marked in Lyly's text but not definably a scene break in the sense
that Endymion is still there. (Compare similar bridgings in *A
Midsummer Night's Dream*, where Titania, asleep onstage at what is
marked in the Folio but not in the First Quarto as the end of Act ii,
remains thus throughout the mechanicals' rehearsal of iii.i; similarly,
at the end of iii.ii, the four lovers remain asleep onstage throughout
the ensuing scene of Titania's being released from her infatuation
for Bottom until they are eventually awakened by Theseus and

Hippolyta.) A time lapse does occur between Acts IV and V, to be
sure, but no shift of location. Cynthia leads her entourage to the
sleeping Endymion and, in the play's climactic gesture, '*kisseth him*'
(v.i.29).

Much is made of Endymion's visible signs of age, including his
'grey beard', 'hollow eyes', 'withered body', and 'decayed limbs' (ll.
53–4); his 'curled locks' are turned to 'grey hairs' and his 'strong
body' to a 'dying weakness, having waxed old and not knowing it'.
Cynthia graciously allows him to sit down because his limbs are so
'stiff' and unable to 'stay' him (ll. 74–8). Yet, almost surely, the
other members of the court have not aged visibly along with him,
despite plentiful evidence of a long lapse of time ('forty years', by
Eumenides' account, l. 56, though contradicted elsewhere, as at
III.iv.19), and despite the conventional logic that would suggest that
they must have done so. True enough, if all were to age onstage
except Cynthia, the contrast between all other mortals and the
godlike queen would be striking,[111] but to strive for this effect in the
theatre would be to rob Endymion's ageing and renewal of its
centrality and would also necessitate an immense and potentially
ludicrous fuss of removing beards and such. Significantly,
Endymion alone is given back his youth by Cynthia: 'Your highness
hath blessed me', he says, 'and your words have again restored my
youth. Methinks I feel my joints strong, and these mouldy hairs to
moult' (v.iv.188–90). No other character is singled out in this fashion. The talk of moulting presumably suggests that the metamorphosis is to be effected onstage by the removal of a wig and beard.
The actor has his own gestures by which to indicate a renewed
vigour of limb—gestures that would be all the more amusing and
theatrically reflexive when undertaken by a boy actor.

The other climactic stage gesture of the play's finale is Cynthia's
enabling Bagoa to recover her human shape from that of the tree to
which she has been transformed by Dipsas for tattling about the
enchantment of Endymion. The gesture is manifestly a test of
Cynthia's virtuous power, and is explicitly paralleled to that of
restoring Endymion's youth. 'Endymion awaked, and at my words
he waxed young', the Queen tells Sir Tophas. 'I will try whether I
can turn this tree again to thy true love' (v.iv.290–2). The feat raises
several questions about stagecraft. How much of the tree's mythological history is shown in the theatre? We last see Bagoa in II.iii,
regretting her part in the enchantment of Endymion and being
threatened with dire punishment by Dipsas if she breathes a word of

what they have done (ll. 53–67). We are later told repeatedly that
Dipsas has 'turned her maid Bagoa to an aspen tree for bewraying
her secrets' (v.ii.85–6; see also v.iii.15–16 and v.iv.54).

This tree evidently becomes visually significant onstage. When
Endymion awakes, Eumenides bids him, 'behold, the twig to which
thou laidst thy head is now become a tree' (v.i.57–8). The tree is not
only present in this awakening scene but is remembered to have
been there as a 'twig' (though not necessarily visible) when
Endymion first fell asleep—when, in fact, Bagoa was last seen (ii.iii).
A tree would then be required at the beginning of Act V, for the
sleeping Endymion remains in view from this point until he is
awakened. The tree evidently remains onstage, with the lunary
bank, at the end of v.i; certainly it must be visible throughout v.iii,
since there is no break in the action between this scene and the play's
finale. The tree is thus visible while Zontes and Panelion lament
Bagoa's fate at having been turned into an aspen. The play provides
an opportunity for the tree to age in appearance, since the curtain
presumably conceals the lunary bank from the end of ii.ii to iv.iii.
Verbal images of twigs growing into trees occur throughout the play
(i.i.50, iii.i.37, iv.iii.15–17), offering a metaphorical idea of ageing for
which the stage action then provides a visible correlative.

How the final transformation of the tree back into Bagoa at
v.iv.297.1, in the last moments of the play, is to be carried off
theatrically is not indicated.[112] It seemingly cannot be done by
concealing the tree prior to this moment, since Cynthia pointedly
indicates her intention to try whether she can turn 'this' tree into
Bagoa some six lines before the transformation can take place (l.
292). A curtained 'discovery' of Bagoa may none the less offer a
practical solution, since the lunary bank and its tree appear to have
been located in a curtained space throughout the play.

Fundamental to Lyly's dramaturgy are simultaneity and juxtaposition. The theatrical signs of Cynthia's court are ever-present, even
as we journey to the desert castle or to the lunary bank or to the
magic fountain. Conversely, those symbolic locations exert a felt
presence even when not actually visible in the theatre. As in so much
medieval drama, where heaven and hell are structures located about
the acting space throughout the play, Lyly's secularised locations are
presentationally at work throughout *Endymion*. The protagonist's
stage location is his identity; unmovable on his lunary bank until the
very last, Endymion is finally released and incorporated into the
orbit of his heavenly queen. Ageing and sublunary frailty give way to

the timeless, the regal, the celestial. Endymion's seeming choice between Tellus and Cynthia expresses itself in the symmetrically opposite stage locations of desert castle and courtly palace. Eumenides, representing another alternative of loyal friendship, is identified with the magic fountain. Tophas's antics parody all these oppositions. The paradoxes of love and friendship, youth and age, mortality and immortality are at last resolved into a celebration of Cynthia's greatness, much as the staging locations of *Endymion* are all subsumed into a final scene at court in the presence of the Queen—Cynthia onstage, and Elizabeth as chief spectator. The stage now belongs entirely to Cynthia, and to Elizabeth. The barrier of illusion between theatrical fiction and the theatricality of Elizabethan court life hovers in uncertainty, all the more so because of Lyly's fanciful use of fairies, magic fountains, desert castles, and other deliberate impossibilities.

Lyly produced *Endymion* with the boys of Paul's, but also must have had at hand a number of adult male choristers. This resource raises the distinct possibility, amounting to a likelihood in my view, that Sir Tophas and the members of the watch were played by adults. Certainly the scenes involving Tophas and the pages and maids-in-waiting with whom he invariably appears offer plentiful opportunity for humour based on contrasts in size and age. Epiton, his hapless page, addresses Tophas as 'sir'; Tophas addresses his page as 'boy' and 'fool' (i.iii.6–17). The knight characterises Dares and Samias, when he first sees them, as 'two wrens' (l. 19). Epiton explains that they are 'two lads' and 'two little boys' (ll. 20–2). Tophas represents himself as twice their size; he will be 'half friends' with such 'unequal' companions. 'Reaching to my middle, so far as from the ground to the waist I will be your friend' (ll. 33–6). The joke could be at once a snobbism and a playful metatheatrical allusion to the visual contrast between adult choristers and juveniles. Tophas addresses the young people as 'my children' (l. 39), and grandly condescends to spare the boys' lives: 'You, Samias, because you are little; you, Dares, because you are no bigger' (ll. 66–7). When he proclaims that the pages' Latin has saved their lives from his terrible wrath (ll. 107–8), he speaks like a pedagogue. (The joke would be especially funny if Lyly himself played Tophas.) We learn later that Tophas is bearded, and vain about the style of beard he should wear as a lover (iii.iii.32–6).

On the female side, Scintilla and Favilla are petite 'sparks' and 'girls' (ii.ii.23, 29). When Dares jocosely addresses Favilla as 'good old gentlewoman' (l. 17), he is making comic capital out of her diminutiveness. Favilla similarly addresses Scintilla in jest as 'your matronship' (l. 32), and goes on to compare their sizes in the competitive terms we later find in the colloquies of Hermia and Helena (*MND*, III.ii.288–343) or Rosalind and Celia (*AYLI*, I.iii.113–14). 'You will be mine elder because you stand upon a stool and I on the floor', jeers Favilla, prompting Favilla to observe of Scintilla, 'it spited me to see how short she was' (ll. 34–45). Yet Tophas is far above them all. Upon his first encounter with them, Tophas greets them as 'children' and excuses his not having spoken to them earlier by his being too far above them in a literal sense: 'I seldom cast mine eyes so low as to the crowns of your heads' (ll. 107–8).

The members of the watch set to guard Endymion similarly make jokes about differences in age. A watchman addresses Samias as 'sir boy' (IV.ii.83). The boys in their turn address the watch as 'Masters' (l. 81). When told that 'no man' shall be allowed to see Endymion, Samias has his pert answer: 'Why, we are but boys' (l. 89). This witticism will not circumvent the downright literalism of the watch, however: 'so shall there no boys see Endymion' (l. 104). The Constable belabours a proverb, 'Children and fools speak true', playing on inversions of wisdom and folly that may depend on the visual contrast between a group of adult watchmen and diminutive boys. The watchmen speak to each others as 'neighbours' (ll. 90, 108, 114). Their homespun humour of drinking and domestic quarrels contrasts with the bantering tone of the play's wit combats in general, and seems suited to adult comic actors. Most significantly, perhaps, the watch seems to have been brought onstage mainly to join in a song, one in which the watchmen and the pages sing alternating exchanges until they join forces in a concluding refrain. The mix of adult and juvenile voices here is not demonstrable in the absence of the music, but it seems likely, and resembles a pattern found in other Lyly plays (e.g. *Sappho and Phao*, IV.iv.37–51).

To be sure, the presence in *Endymion* of this comedy of discrepant age and its relevance to the play's more serious concerns do not offer conclusive proof of the use of adult actors. Carter Daniel claims to the contrary that 'Tophas is clearly shorter than anyone else'. George Hunter opts more tentatively for a boy actor, though he sees a place for 'one or two older persons' in nearly all the subplots of the other plays, enabling the adult to sing bass in part singing.[113] I cannot agree that the case is at all as clear as Daniel asserts, and in

fact I believe the opposite, but it is true that a boy actor playing
Tophas could make comic capital out of his boasting if his claims to
superior size are visibly ridiculous. Tophas's manly beard appears to
be a sham, for his chin is but a 'quiller' yet; Epiton is able to locate
no more than 'three or four little hairs' where Tophas hopes he may
lay claim to 'my beard' (v.ii.19–23). Part of the joke about his falling
in love with Dipsas, 'that old crone', is that she is so much older than
he (ll. 24–5).

None the less, Tophas could well have been played by an adult
actor surrounded by juveniles. Historical precedents for such a
casting arrangement are not hard to find. Michael Shapiro offers the
analogy of 'Father' Grim the Collier in Richard Edwards's *Damon
and Pythias*, *c.* 1565, a play performed 'by the Children of Her
Grace's Chapel' when Edwards was master of the children, in which
Grim bids his fellows begin singing: 'Go to, then, lustily. I will sing
in my man's voice; / 'Ch'ave troubling bass buss' (ll. 1659–60).
Edwards himself was remembered as a 'great actor of plays' as well
as master of the Children of the Queen's Chapel.[114] Earlier, in 1538,
John Heywood received payment for 'playing an interlude with his
children before My Lady's Grace', the Princess Mary; the company
may have come from the Chapel.[115] Earlier still, in 1512, William
Cornish, Master of the Chapel Children, played a Chaucerian interlude of 'Troilus and Pandar' with 'the Children of the Chapel',
assisted by another adult actor, Harry Kite, 'Gentleman of the
Chapel'.[116] Medieval ceremonies of the Boy Bishop and the *Festa
Asinorum* involved adult and juvenile choristers and minor church
officials. Nor is all such evidence early; we know also that boys'
companies sometimes used adult actors as late as the 1580s. The
'Earl of Oxford's Company', playing at Bristol in 1581 shortly before
they joined forces with Paul's boys to produce Lyly's first plays,
consisted of 'i man and ix boyes'.[117]

In any event, *Endymion* is generally well suited to boy actors. The
predominance of female roles, especially of saucy young maids-in-
waiting, loyal waitingwomen, old crones, and vengeful neglected
beauties, yields many parts for which boys were invariably chosen, in
adult companies as well as in the juvenile troupes. Even the demanding role of Cynthia anticipates major and queenly parts written
by later dramatists, such as Webster's Duchess of Malfi. The daring
of presenting a stand-in for Queen Elizabeth onstage is perhaps
softened by the delicately parodic nature of juvenile acting; this
Cynthia is manifestly not Elizabeth, but a distant and fictive shadow

of a queen whom art cannot presume to represent in all her Jovial authority. Among the male parts, as in Lyly's plays generally, young men and pages predominate, or, conversely, the old men (Geron, Gyptes, Pythagoras, etc.) whom boy actors were adept at mimicking. The very business of transforming Endymion from a young man into a grey-bearded oldster plays directly into juvenile acting abilities, and invites reflexive laughter at the overt contrivances of a metatheatrical stage.

C. S. Lewis refers to a performance of *Endymion* at the Taylor Institution, Oxford, in 1944, noting that 'When I saw *Endmion* the courtly scenes (not the weak foolery of Sir Thopas) held me delighted for five acts'.[118] *The London Stage* refers to a masque of 'Endymion, the Man in a Moon' in September 1697,[119] but this is quite unlikely to have been Lyly's play. Otherwise, I have found no indications that the play has been performed since the original production of 1588.

NOTES

1 W. W. Greg, *A Bibliography of the English Printed Drama to the Restoration*, 4 vols (London, 1939–59), I.7.

2 *Ibid.*, I.13.

3 *Ibid.*, I.36.

4 George K. Hunter, *John Lyly: The Humanist as Courtier* (London: Routledge & Kegan Paul, 1962), pp. 367–72, and Michael Best, 'A Note on the Songs in Lyly's Plays', *N&Q*, CCX, n.s. XII (1965), 93–4. Compare W. W. Greg, 'The Authorship of the Songs in Lyly's Plays', *MLR*, I (1905), 43–52, and John Robert Moore, 'The Songs in Lyly's Plays', *PMLA*, XLII (1927), 623–40. Alfred Harbage, '*Love's Labor's Lost* and the Early Shakespeare', *PQ*, XLI (1962), 18–57, speculates that Shakespeare could possibly have joined the Paul's organisation in time to have written at least some of these songs (pp. 32–4).

5 George K. Hunter and David Bevington, eds, *John Lyly: 'Campaspe' and 'Sappho and Phao'* (Manchester University Press, 1991), pp. 147–50.

6 Donald Edge, 'Evidence of Cast-Off Copy in Lyly's *Endimion* and *Loves Metamorphosis*', *PBSA*, LXX (1976), 517–18. Edge's Ph.D. dissertation, 'Critical Editions of John Lyly's *Endimion* and *Love's Metamorphosis*', *DAI* 35:445A (1974, University of Rochester), gives further details.

7 Specific page assignments are as follows, with more uses than one on any single page indicated in parentheses: *doo*, B (2), B1v, B2 (2), B3 (2), B3v (2), B4v (2), C1v (3), C2 (2), C3v, D4 (2), E, F1v (2), F2v, F4 (3), G3 (2), H1v (2), H2, H3v (2), I (2), I1v (2), K1v, K2 (2); *doe*, D, D2, D2v, D3v, F1, F3 (2), H2 (2); *do*, D2v, D3v, H1v, H2 (2), K2, K3v. *hart*, B, B2, B3, B3v, C2 (2), C3, C4v, D2 (2), D3, E, E1v, E3, E3v (3), E4v, F3, G1 (2), G2, G4 (2), I3v (3), I4, K (2), K2v; *heart*, C4v, D2, D2v (2), D3 (2), D4, E2, I2v, K2, K3v.

Other word counts are available on application to the editor of this edition.

8 Substantive errors as follows (see collation notes): I.i.12, I.iii.45 and 46, I.iii.63, III.iii.47, IV.ii.40, V.ii.71, V.iv.77–8 and 252.

9 Mishandled punctuation: II.i.66, III.i.16, III.iii.33, III.iv.112, IV.i.39, IV.ii.4 and 6, IV.iii.22 and 31–2, V.iv.79–80, 128, and 253.

10 Typographical errors: I.iv.16, II.i.35, II.iii.60, III.i.53, III.iii.32–3, III.iv.154, IV.ii.108 and 11, V.i.9.

11 Hunter and Bevington, pp. 147–9.

12 Carolyn Ruth Swift Lenz, 'The Allegory of Wisdom in Lyly's *Endimion*', *CompD*, X (1976–77), 235–57.

13 To be sure, some records for 1585–87 are lost. See Josephine Waters Bennett, 'Oxford and *Endimion*', *PMLA*, LVII (1942), 354–69, pp. 363–4, n. 44; E. K. Chambers, 'Court Performances before Queen Elizabeth', *MLR*, II (1906), 1–13, p. 9; Chambers, *The Elizabethan Stage*, 4 vols (Oxford: Clarendon Press, 1923), IV.75–130, 'A Court Calendar', esp. pp. 100–3; Mary S. Steele, *Plays and Masques at Court During the Reigns of Elizabeth, James, and Charles* (New Haven: Yale University Press; London, Oxford University Press, 1926), pp. 91–7; Albert Feuillerat, *Documents Relating to the Office of the Revels in the Time of Queen Elizabeth* (Louvain: Uystpruyst, 1908), pp. 221, 319–97; Harold N. Hillebrand, *The Child Actors* (Urbana: University of Illinois Press, 1926), p. 141; and R. Warwick Bond, ed., *The Complete Works of John Lyly*, 3 vols (Oxford, Clarendon Press, 1902), III.11.

14 John Roche Dasent, ed., *Acts of the Privy Council of England* (1890–1906), XV (1587–8), 24; Chambers, *MLR* (1906), 9.

15 Peter Cunningham, *Extracts from the Accounts of the Revels at Court in the Reigns of Queen Elizabeth and King James I* (London: for the Shakespeare Society, 1842), pp. 198–9; Feuillerat, *Documents*, p. 378; and Frederick Gard Fleay, *A Biographical Chronicle of the English Drama, 1559–1642*, 3 vols (London: Reeves & Turner, 1891), II.41.

16 Hunter, *Lyly*, pp. 76–7, 187.

17 *Ibid.*, p. 77.

18 Those who champion Leicester as Endymion include Rev. N. J. Halpin, *Oberon's Vision* (London: for the Shakespeare Society, 1842); George Pierce Baker, ed., *Endymion*, by John Lyly (New York: Henry Holt, 1894); and Bond, III.81–103. For the theory that Endymion represents James VI of Scotland, attempting to distance himself from Mary Queen of Scots (i.e., Tellus) as his mother, see Albert Feuillerat, *John Lyly: Contribution à l'Histoire de la Renaissance en Angleterre* (Cambridge University Press, 1910, rpt. New York: Russell & Russell, 1968), pp. 141–90. For persuasive rebuttals, see Percy W. Long, 'Lyly's *Endimion*: An Addendum', *MP*, VIII (1911), 599–605, and C. F. Tucker Brooke, 'The Allegory in Lyly's *Endimion*', *MLN*, XXVI (1911), 12–15. The theory is briefly examined in David Bevington, *Tudor Drama and Politics: A Critical Approach to Topical Meaning* (Cambridge, Mass.: Harvard University Press, 1968), p. 179.

19 Bennett, 'Oxford and *Endimion*', pp. 354–69. The theory is criticised in Hunter, *Lyly*, pp. 187–8.

20 Bond, III.12.

21 The accounts that link Endymion with Mount Latmos in Caria include
   Ovid, *Heroides*, XVIII, ll. 61–5 (LCL, pp. 248–9); Ovid, *Ars Amatoria*, III.83
   (LCL, pp. 124–5); Lucian, *Deorum Dialogi* 19, discussion of Endymion by
   Aphrodite and Selene (LCL, VII, pp. 328–31); Apollonius Rhodius,
   Argonautica, IV, 54 ff. (esp. 58, LCL, pp. 298–9), with the Scholiast; and
   Cicero, *Tusculan Disputations*, I.xxxviii.92 (LCL, pp. 110–11). Those link-
   ing Endymion with Elis include Pausanias, *Description of Greece*, V.i.3–4
   (LCL, II.380–3); and Apollodorus, *The Library*, I.vii.5–6 (LCL, pp. 60–1).
   Hyginus, *Fabulae*, 271, identifies Endymion, 'whom Luna loved', as the
   son of Aethlios or Aetolus ('*Endymion Aethlii filius quem Luna amavit*';
   ed. Mary Grant, p. 172). Some of these are cited in Susan D. Thomas,
   '*Endimion* and Its Sources', *CL*, XXX (1978), 35–52. Pausanias describes
   Aethlios, first ruler of the Aetolians in Elis, as 'the son of Zeus and of
   Protogeneia, the daughter of Deucalion, and the father of Endymion'
   (V.i.3–4, LCL, II.380–3).
22 See Hesiod, *Theogony*, ll. 371–4 (LCL, pp. 106–7), on the genealogy of
   Hyperion, Helios, Selene, and Eos.
23 Thomas, '*Endimion* and Its Sources', citing Apollodorus, I.vii.5–6 (LCL,
   pp. 60–1); Plato, *Phaedo*, 17, 72C (LCL, pp. 250–1); Aristotle,
   Nicomachean Ethics, X.viii.7 (LCL, pp. 622–3); Cicero, *De Finibus
   Bonorum et Malorum*, V.xx.55 (LCL, pp. 454–7); and Cicero, *Tusculan
   Disputations*, I.xxxviii.92 (LCL, pp. 110–11). See *Herodas: The Mimes and
   Fragments*, ed. A. D. Knox, with notes by Walter Headlam (Cambridge
   University Press, 1922, reissued 1966), p. 380, for a list of references to
   Endymion in classical literature.
24 Cicero, *Tusculan Disputations*, I.xxxviii.92; Natali Conti, *Natalis Comitis
   Mythologiae* (originally published 1551; Venice, 1581), Bk IV, p. 222; and
   Vincenzo Cartari, *Le Imagini, con la Spositione de i Dei degli Antichi*, trans.
   into Latin as *Imagines Deorum* (originally published Venice, 1556; Lyons,
   1581), pp. 84–6. Cited in Thomas, '*Endimion* and Its Sources', p. 48. On
   Conti and Cartari as providers of subjects for Renaissance art and
   literature, see Jean Seznec, *The Survival of the Pagan Gods: The Mytho-
   logical Tradition and Its Place in Renaissance Humanism and Art* (New
   York: Pantheon, 1953), pp. 231–56.
25 Pliny, II.vi.41–3 (LCL, I.194–5); discussed in Thomas, '*Endimion* and Its
   Sources', pp. 37–9. Edward S. Le Comte, *Endymion in England* (New
   York: King's Crown Press, 1944), p. 25, quotes Artemidorus,
   Onirocriticon, IV.47, *Artemidori Daldiani*, . . . *de Somniorum Interpretatione
   Libri Quinque* (Lyons, 1546), p. 252, who argues that Endymion's re-
   searches amount to soothsaying and divination. Fulgentius reports that
   the moon is said have fallen in love with Endymion for one of two
   reasons, the first of which is that 'Endymion was the first man to
   discover the tracks of the moon, whereby having studied nothing in his
   life but this discovery he is said to have slept for thirty years'
   (*Mythologiae*, Book II, fabula 16, ed. Helm, pp. 57–8; trans. Leslie
   George Whitehead, p. 81).
26 Bevington, *Tudor Drama and Politics*, pp. 168–86.
27 Baldassare Castiglione, *The Book of The Courtier*, trans. Sir Thomas
   Hoby (London, 1561); Percy W. Long, 'The Purport of Lyly's
   Endimion', *PMLA*, XXIV (1909), 164–84; G. Wilson Knight, 'John

Lyly', *RES*, xv (1939), 146–63; and Philip Dust, 'The Kiss in Lyly's *Endymion*', *EM*, xxv (1975–76), 87–95. Nicolas James Perella, *The Kiss Sacred and Profane* (Berkeley: University of California Press, 1969), pp. 158–88, discusses also the contributions of Marsilio Ficino and Pico della Mirandola to the concept of Platonic love in the Renaissance.

28 C. C. Gannon, 'Lyly's *Endimion*: From Myth to Allegory', *ELR*, vi (1976), 220–43, citing Giordano Bruno, *Dialoghi Italiani*, ed. Giovanni Aquilecchia, 3rd edn (Florence, 1958), pp. 927–1178; Giovanni Piero Valeriano Bolzani, *Hieroglyphica* (Lyons, 1586), p. 572; and Giulio Camillo, *L'Idea del theatro* (Venice, 1550), p. 39.

29 Bernard F. Huppé, 'Allegory of Love in Lyly's Court Comedies', *ELH*, xiv (1947), 93–113.

30 Noemi Messora, 'Parallels between Italian and English Courtly Plays in the Sixteenth Century: Carlo Turco and John Lyly', *Theatre of the English and Italian Renaissance*, ed. J. R. Mulryne and Margaret Shewring (New York: St Martin's, 1991), pp. 141–60.

31 *Ibid.*, p. 142. On William Cornish and other devisers of English pageantry, see, among others, Gordon Kipling, *The Triumph of Honour: Burgundian Origins of the Elizabethan Renaissance* (Leiden University Press, 1977), and ed., *The Receyt of the Ladie Kateryne* (Oxford University Press, 1990).

32 Hunter, *Lyly*, p. 192.

33 Daniel C. Boughner, 'The Background of Lyly's Tophas', *PMLA*, liv (1939), 967–73.

34 Sarah Deats, 'The Disarming of the Knight: Comic Parody in Lyly's *Endymion*', *SAB*, xl (1975), 67–75.

35 Violet M. Jeffery, *John Lyly and the Italian Renaissance* (Paris: Librairie Ancienne Honoré Champion, 1928), pp. 98–102; see Boughner, 'The Background of Lyly's Tophas', pp. 967–73. Thomas, '*Endimion* and Its Sources', pp. 40ff., argues that Marc Antonio Epicuro's pastoral play *Mirzia* (published in Parma in 1582) is an important source, but again the resemblances point more surely to an analogue than to a direct source. David Orr, *Italian Renaissance Drama in England before 1625: The Influence of 'Erudita' Tragedy, Comedy, and Pastoral on Elizabethan and Jacobean Drama* (Chapel Hill: University of North Carolina Press, 1970), p. 84, sides with Boughner in believing that 'Lyly is just as likely to have gone to Latin as to Italian sources'; Italian influence is certainly possible, but Latin is 'actually a better contender'.

36 Robert S. Knapp, 'The Monarchy of Love in Lyly's *Endimion*', *MP*, lxxiii (1975–76), 353–67.

37 Peter Saccio, 'The Oddity of Lyly's *Endimion*', *The Elizabethan Theatre V*, ed. G. R. Hibbard (Hamden, Conn.: Archon, Shoe String Press, 1975), 92–111.

38 Peter Weltner, 'The Antinomic Vision of Lyly's *Endymion*', *ELR*, iii (1973), 5–44, p. 6.

39 Michael Murrin, *The Veil of Allegory* (University of Chicago Press, 1969).

40 *Endimion and Phoebe* by Michael Drayton (1595, ed. Hebel, 1.125 ff.), *Astrophel and Stella* by Philip Sidney (1581–83), *Diana* by Henry Constable (1592), and *Caelia* by William Percy (1594).

41 Huppé, 'Allegory of Love', reads the allegory as 'a statement of a conflict between two kinds of love within the lover's own heart' (p. 103). See also Long, 'Purport', pp. 164–84, and Henry Morley, *English Writers*, 11 vols (London: Cassell, 1892), IX.204–8.

42 Peter Saccio, *The Court Comedies of John Lyly: A Study in Allegorical Dramaturgy* (Princeton University Press, 1969), p. 172.

43 See Sigmund Freud on the kind of ambiguous attitude towards women that Endymion seems to represent: 'The Most Prevalent Form of Degradation in Erotic Life', *Sammlung*, Vierte Folge, first published in *Jahrbuch*, Bd IV, 1912; reprinted in *Freud: Sexuality and the Psychology of Love* (New York: Macmillan, 1963), pp. 58–70.

44 See I.iv.46, III.i.21, III.iv.125 and 160, IV.i.63, IV.iii.165, V.iv.167 and 213.

45 Mary Beth Rose, *The Expense of Spirit: Love and Sexuality in English Renaissance Drama* (Ithaca, N.Y.: Cornell University Press, 1988), pp. 12–42; Philippa Berry, *Of Chastity and Power: Elizabethan Literature and the Unmarried Queen* (London: Routledge, 1989), pp. 111–33; and Louis Montrose, '"Shaping Fantasies": Figurations of Gender and Power in Elizabethan Culture', *Representations*, 1.2 (1983), 61–94. Theodora A. Jankowski, 'The Subversion of Flattery: The Queen's Body in John Lyly's *Sapho and Phao*', *MRDE*, V (1991), 69–86, makes a similar point about Lyly's implied (even if partly unconscious) criticism of Elizabeth in *Sappho and Phao* of 1584. Marie Axton finds 'a legacy of resistance and criticism of the virgin ideal' in *Endymion*; see 'The Tudor Mask and Elizabethan Court Drama', *English Drama: Forms and Development*, ed. Marie Axton and Raymond Williams (Cambridge University Press, 1977), pp. 24–47. Susan Frye sees *Endymion* and dramatic entertainments like it as competing among themselves to represent Elizabeth as a self-sufficient and chaste queen who should none the less be subjected to 'masculinist control'; in the welter of competing voices, 'even the loudest praise encodes messages concerning the needs and claims of its author', and 'allegory became the trope of instability' (*Elizabeth I: The Competition for Representation* (Oxford University Press, 1993), p. 17).

46 See also at I.ii.31–3, III.iv.25 and 190, V.i.47, and V.iv.191.

47 Saccio, *Court Comedies*, pp. 173–4, noting the seeming oddity of Lyly's associating fruitfulness with the moon rather than with the sun, as in more conventional mythology, quotes Henry Cornelius Agrippa, who describes the moon as 'the wife of all the stars' and 'the most fruitful', receiving as it does 'the beams and influences of all the other planets and stars as a conception, bringing them forth to the inferior world as being next to itself' (*Three Books of Occult Philosophy*, tr. J. F. (London, 1651), II.xxxii, p. 284). Agrippa thus stresses the moon's 'influence' in the technical sense of an ethereal fluid, and its mediating function between the moon and the sublunary world.

48 See also I.i.3 and 52, III.iv.182, and V.i.78.

49 See I.i.55, I.ii.4 and 57, II.iii.41, III.ii.9, IV.i.9 and 64, IV.iii.155, V.i.94, V.iii.4, V.iv.49, and Epilogue 10.

50 Halpin, *Oberon's Vision*; Bond, III.81–103; Evelyn May Albright, *Dramatic Publication in England, 1580–1640* (New York: Heath, 1927), p. 110; C. F. Tucker Brooke, 'The Allegory in Lyly's *Endimion*', *MLN*, XXVI.1 (1911), 12–15; Fleay, *Biographical Chronicle*, p. 41. The theories

are reviewed and criticised in Long, 'Purport', 164–84, and 'An Addendum', 599–605, and in Bevington, *Tudor Drama and Politics*, pp. 178–9.

51 Bennett, 'Oxford and *Endimion*', pp. 354–69.

52 G. B. Harrison, *A Jacobean Journal . . . 1603–1606* (London: Routledge, 1941), p. 147, records the unreliable story (as told by John Aubrey in his *Brief Lives*, ed. Oliver Lawson Dick (London, 1949), p. 305) about Oxford's having had the misfortune to break wind in the Queen's presence, whereupon he absented himself from court for seven years, travelling abroad. When he finally returned, according to this account, Elizabeth graciously said to him, 'My lord, I had forgot the fart.'

53 Long, 'Purport', pp. 164–84 and 'An Addendum', pp. 599–605; Bevington, *Tudor Drama and Politics*, pp. 178–84; and R. Headlam Wells, 'Elizabethan Epideictic Drama: Praise and Blame in the Plays of Peele and Lyly', *Cahiers Élisabéthains*, XXIII (1983), 15–33.

54 Bennett, 'Oxford and *Endimion*', p. 357, and Le Comte, *Endymion in England*, p. 82, mention the Catholicism as a problem, but do not identify it as the underlying factor in Endymion's long sleep. My argument in this Introduction takes a more concretely topical line than in my *Tudor Drama and Politics*, pp. 179–84, but I still wish to stress that the portrait of Endymion is one of a generically ideal Elizabethan courtier. Oxford may be implicitly put forth as representative of that ideal.

55 Hunter, *Lyly*, p. 73. On Oxford's being still under suspicion in the days of the Armada threat and afterwards, see n. 58 below. I am indebted to Alan Nelson for several matters of fact in this account of Oxford's Catholicism.

56 Helen Morris, 'Queen Elizabeth I "shadowed" in Cleopatra', *HLQ*, XXXII (1969), 271–9.

57 As early as the 1550s, Cecil clearly perceived that Mary Stuart aimed at the English throne, and that the proposed Darnley match would, by linking two Roman Catholic claimants to the succession, galvanise support for Mary throughout the English Catholic community. See W. T. MacCaffrey, 'Elizabethan Politics: The First Decade, 1558–1568', *Past and Present*, XXIV (1963), 25–42, esp. p. 39. On the strategic hazards that Elizabeth incurred by her alignment with Continental Protestantism, see MacCaffrey, *Elizabeth I: War and Politics, 1588–1603* (Princeton University Press, 1992), esp. pp. 20–3.

58 This account is indebted to Garrett Mattingly, *The Armada*, Sentry Edition (Boston: Houghton Mifflin, 1962). Fears of this sort continued on until at least 1592, when, on 14 September, the priest George Dingley was 'again examined before the Lord Keeper, Lord Buckhurst and Mr John Fortescue about the things he had heard in Spain'. He declared 'that many of our nobility were believed to be discontented at not being advanced and would easily be moved to follow the Spaniard, who would promise to put them in places of authority if he should possess England'. Dingley continued: 'The Earls of Oxford and Cumberland, and the Lords Strange and Percy are much talked of as alienated by discontent. Their chief hope is the Queen's death; wherefore the Spaniard lingers in his attempt at again assaulting England because time will call her away, when they have certain hope of a debate between the two houses of Hertford and Derby, who will seek the throne, each for himself; during

which contention the Spaniard thinketh entry into England would be without danger' (G. B. Harrison, *An Elizabethan Journal . . . 1591–1594* (London: Constable, 1928), p. 167). A Scottish Jesuit named Creichton was found with incriminating papers in 1586 arguing various 'Reasons to show the easiness of the enterprise', i.e. the Armada, among which reasons was the claim that 'the faction of the Catholics in England is great, and able, if the kingdom were divided in three parts, to make two of them' (John Strype, *Annals of the Reformation*, 3 vols (Oxford: Clarendon Press, 1824), III.i.602–4). For statistics showing that 'a large majority of the English people' were opposed to the Elizabethan settlement, 1559–1587, see Brian Magee, *The English Recusants* (London: Burns Oates & Washbourne, 1938), pp. 23–36.

Yet these English Catholics were 'a flock without a shepherd' in the early part of Elizabeth's reign, and were largely untouched by Counter-Reformation fervour. Allowed to avoid the supremacy oath and left free to conduct religious affairs in their own households as they chose, the majority of English Catholic peers preferred not to be actively involved in support of the old religion. See Adrian Morey, *The Catholic Subjects of Elizabeth I* (Totowa, N.J.: Rowman & Littlefield, 1978), pp. 40–58, and Philip Hughes, *Rome and the Counter-Reformation in England* (London: Burns Oates, 1942), pp. 226–39. The Catholic clergy, lacking clear direction from Rome, were divided on such issues as conforming by attendance at Anglican services. Most English Catholics seem to have been shocked by the Papal bull *Regnans in excelsis* by which Elizabeth was excommunicated after the Northern Rising. See Philip Hughes, *The Reformation in England*, 3 vols (London: Hollis & Carter, 1950–54), III.272–80, and M. D. R. Leys, *Catholics in England, 1559–1829: A Social History* (London: Longmans, 1961), pp. 15–26. An attempted revival of Catholicism in England from about 1574 to the early 1580s was visibly beginning to fail in the latter half of that decade, under relentless pressure from Cecil, Walsingham, and others; at the height of the Armada crisis in 1588, those Catholics who spoke at all could be heard proclaiming loyalty to the throne. See William Raleigh Trimble, *The Catholic Laity in Elizabethan England, 1558–1603* (Cambridge, Mass.: Harvard University Press, 1964), pp. 9–176. A selection of useful documents is available in Alan Dures, *English Catholicism 1558–1642* (London: Longman, 1983), pp. 88–108.

The best account of Oxford's 'refusal' to cooperate in the fight against the Armada is by Irvin Leigh Matus, *Shakespeare, in Fact* (New York: Continuum, 1994), pp. 243–7.

59 The revolt of the northern earls in 1569 and its troublesome aftermath, prompted by Mary Stuart's residence in England and the attempt to marry her to the Duke of Norfolk, are succinctly reviewed in Wallace MacCaffrey, *The Shaping of the Elizabethan Regime* (Princeton University Press, 1968), pp. 293–398, in MacCaffrey, *Elizabeth I* (London: Edward Arnold, 1993), pp. 114–34, and in John Hungerford Pollen, S. J., *The English Catholics in the Reign of Queen Elizabeth* (London: Longmans, Green, 1920), pp. 111–84.

60 On Elizabeth's policy towards Catholic recalcitrance, see W. T. MacCaffrey, 'Catholic Dissent', *Queen Elizabeth and the Making of Policy, 1572–1588* (Princeton University Press, 1981), pp. 119–53.

61 Lyly is here relying on Pliny (x.5, LCL, III.302–3), on Aesop, *Fables*, no. 56, 'Of the Eagle and the Beetle' (1665 ed., pp. 139–41), and on Erasmus, *Adagia, Omnia Opera*, II.869 ff., for his images of eagles that attack stags and beetles that invade eagles' nests to attack their eggs. See v.i.143–6 and n.

62 As Le Comte reports (*Endymion in England*, p. 82), both sides in the contention about the Catholic conspiracy of 1580 were eager to deny having seen the dangerous book of prophetic pictures. Lord Henry Howard, brother of the Duke of Norfolk, sent to prison in 1583, published in that same year *A Defensative against the poison of supposed prophecies . . .which being grounded either upon the warrant and authority of old painted books, expositions of dreams, oracles, revelations, invocations of damned spirits, judicials of astrology, or any other kind of pretended knowledge whatsoever, De futuris contingentibus, have been causes of great disorder in the commonwealth, especially among the simple and unlearned people* (reprinted by W. Jaggard in 1629). Though admitting that he was examined on the painted treatise, he insisted that he was never 'admitted to this Sibylla's oracle' (pp. 120–120v). Bond (III.516) speculates that the Old Man of Endymion's dream is possibly intended for Burghley; see also Bennett, 'Oxford and *Endymion*', pp. 354–69. Certainly Burghley was the most unshakeable of Elizabeth's advisers in his wariness of the supposed Catholic menace (see Conyers Read, *Lord Burghley and Queen Elizabeth* (New York: Knopf, 1960), p. 421), and so Lyly had reason for tact in writing a play that might seem to defend the loyalty of English Catholics like Burghley's own son-in-law. Lyly's dependency on the favour of Burghley dates back to 1574, and he probably owed his position in Oxford's household to Burghley (Hunter, *Lyly*, pp. 45, 69).

63 In the *Calendar of State Papers, Spanish*, for 1581, the new French ambassador, Mauvissière de Castelnau, reports as follows: 'The Queen said to me, I knew quite well her favourable attitude towards Catholics who did not place their conscience in antagonism to the state.' Cited in Elizabeth Jenkins, *Elizabeth the Great* (London: Victor Gollancz, 1958), p. 233. See also B. M. Ward, *The Seventeenth Earl of Oxford* (London, 1928), p. 207, and E. K. Chambers, *Sir Henry Lee* (Oxford: Clarendon Press, 1936), pp. 154–5, on Oxford's appeal as a dancer and tilter. Oxford's attempt to free Norfolk from prison in 1571 was reported by an unidentified woman to the Privy Council in 1574, and may be confirmed by the French ambassador La Mothe Fénélon's report to the French court that Oxford was up to something in December of 1571. See Read, *Burghley and Elizabeth*, pp. 128–30.

64 *Calendar of State Papers, Domestic, Elizabeth, 1581–1590*, CXLIX.69 and CLI.42–57, pp. 23 and 38–40. Charles Arundel is not to be confused with Philip Howard, Earl of Arundel, son of the executed Duke of Norfolk; the Earl's troubles with the authorities are described in Arnold Pritchard, *Catholic Loyalism in Elizabethan England* (Chapel Hill: University of North Carolina Press, 1979), pp. 41–4, and David Mathew, *Catholicism in England, 1535–1935* (London: Longmans, Green, 1936), pp. 49–50.

65 Henry David Gray, 'A Possible Interpretation of Lyly's *Endimion*', *Anglia*, XXXIX (1916), 181–200; Feuillerat, *Lyly*, pp. 123–90. Lyly's letter

is reprinted in Bond, 1.28–9. Bond supposes that Lyly's disgrace is the result of 'falsification of accounts or appropriation of moneys', but there is no evidence for this or for Bond's contention that Lyly and Oxford may have fallen out over such matters. A likelier reason for the disgrace is the trouble over the prophetic book of pictures. On Burghley's immense importance in the system of patronage under Elizabeth, see Wallace T. MacCaffrey, 'Place and Patronage in Elizabethan Politics', *Elizabethan Government and Society: Essays Presented to Sir John Neale*, ed. S. T. Bindoff *et al.* (London: Athlone, 1961), pp. 95–126.

66 J. E. Neale, *Queen Elizabeth* (London: Jonathan Cape, 1934), pp. 263–5, and Christopher Hibbert, *The Virgin Queen: Elizabeth I, Genius of the Golden Age* (Reading, Mass.: Addison Wesley, 1991), pp. 203–4, are among those who give a lively account of the Throckmorton plot.

67 W. T. MacCaffrey, 'England: The Crown, and the New Aristocracy, 1540–1600', *Past and Present*, xxx (1965), 52–64, points out that English Catholic leadership was 'drastically enfeebled': with their clerical leaders imprisoned or forced into exile, the Catholic aristocracy adopted a timorous stance of waiting hopefully for a Catholic marriage to relieve them of their discomfiture. Such a vacillating position did not, however, prevent them from drifting 'through shallows of vacuous intrigue on to the shoals and shipwreck of fecklessly conceived rebellion' (p. 57).

68 *The Bardon Papers: Documents Relating to the Imprisonment and Trial of Mary Queen of Scots*, Camden Society Publications, 3rd series, vol. xvii (London: Camden Society, 1909), Appendix I, p. 114 (Caligula B.viii, ff. 240–6); quoted in Gray, 'Possible Interpretation', p. 193.

69 *Bardon Papers*, 'Sir Christopher Hatton's Notes on the Babington Plot', September 1586 (Egerton mss. 2124, ff. 43–4), p. 52. See also the Mary Stuart–Babington correspondence on pp. 26–41, Neale, *Queen Elizabeth*, pp. 271–8, and Read, *Burghley and Elizabeth*, pp. 343–6.

70 See Kurt Tetzeli von Rosador, 'The Power of Magic: From *Endimion* to *The Tempest*', *ShS*, xliii (1990), 1–13, on royal power vanquishing black magic.

71 Joel Altman, *The Tudor Play of Mind* (Berkeley: University of California Press, 1978), p. 225. Pope Leo X excommunicated Henry soon after the marriage to Anne Boleyn in 1527, but the Act of Supremacy was not promulgated until 1534 and the Statute of the Six Articles defining heresy in 1539. Feuillerat, *Lyly*, pp. 141–90, identifies Dipsas with the Papists but then takes the allegory into hazardous particularities by identifying Endymion as James VI of Scotland seeking to escape the influence of his mother Mary Queen of Scots—i.e. Tellus. See Long, 'An Addendum', pp. 599–605, for an effective rebuttal. Gray, 'A Possible Interpretation', pp. 181–200, identifies Tellus with Mary and Endymion with Lord Henry Howard, in a topical allegorical reading that implausibly relies on too early a date for the play (prior to 1583) and on a *fait accompli*. Gray also implausibly identifies Eumenides with Lyly himself. See Le Comte, *Endymion in England*, p. 78.

72 Bevington, *Tudor Drama and Politics*, pp. 131–9.

73 Montrose, ' "Shaping Fantasies" ', p. 61.

74 *Ibid.*, p. 65.

75 See note 45 above.

76 Berry, *Of Chastity and Power*, pp. 111–33. See also David Bevington, '"Jack Hath Not Jill": Failed Courtship in Lyly and Shakespeare', *ShS*, XLII (1990), 1–13.

77 Hunter, *John Lyly*, p. 26, cited in Berry, p. 115. See also *DNB* entry *s.v.* Lily, George.

78 Barbara G. Walker, *The Crone: Woman of Age, Wisdom, and Power* (San Francisco: Harper & Row, 1985). See also Lillian Faderman, *Surpassing the Love of Men: Romantic Friendship and Love Between Women from the Renaissance to the Present* (New York: William Morrow, 1981).

79 Berry, *Of Chastity and Power*, pp. 111–33. The *Endymion* passage is at III.iii.55–64.

80 Knapp, 'The Monarchy of Love', p. 356, puts Corsites and Tellus above Eumenides and Semele.

81 Catherine Belsey, 'Love in Venice', *ShS*, XLIV (1991), pp. 41–53, esp. pp. 49–50; and William Rossky, '*The Two Gentlemen of Verona* as Burlesque', *ELR*, XII (1982), 210–19.

82 See especially IV.iii.69 and 143.

83 David Lloyd Stevenson, *The Love-Game Comedy* (New York: AMS, 1966), p. 167.

84 Whether Corsites's role as the doting keeper of Tellus in the desert castle hints at the Earl of Shrewsbury's function as Mary Stuart's keeper, as argued by Bond and Gray, is a complex matter, all the more so since Shrewsbury was replaced in Mary's last months by the puritanical Sir Amyas Paulet. Quite conceivably, Lyly's audience might have wondered if an allusion to Shrewsbury's fourteen-year indulgent custodianship was intended.

85 In this polarisation, there is no real room, even at the last, for what Jean H. Hagstrum calls 'esteem enlivened by desire'; see *Esteem Enlivened by Desire: The Couple from Homer to Shakespeare* (University of Chicago Press, 1992).

86 Hibbert, *The Virgin Queen*, pp. 153–7, 174.

87 Halpin, *Oberon's Vision*, proposes Gosson; Bond, III.101, proposes Harvey.

88 Gannon, 'Lyly's *Endimion*', p. 225. See note 28 above. Perella, *The Kiss*, pp. 180–1, credits Pico with having introduced the *mors osculi* to Christian writers in the Renaissance. On Bruno in this context, see John Bossy, *Giordano Bruno and the Embassy Affair* (New Haven and London: Yale University Press, 1991). Bruno is here seen as anti-Spanish and an unreserved admirer of Queen Elizabeth.

89 Edgar Wind, *Pagan Mysteries in the Renaissance*, new and enlarged edn (New York: Barnes & Noble, 1968), pp. 154–9.

90 Knapp, 'The Monarchy of Love', pp. 354–6.

91 Abraham Fraunce, *The Third Part of the Countess of Pembroke's Ivychurch* (London: Thomas Woodcock, 1592), p. 43. Lenz, 'The Allegory of Wisdom', pp. 236–7 and n. 5, also cites Natale Conti, *Mythologiae* (Lyons, 1605), IV.viii.

92 See Huppé, 'Allegory of Love', p. 105, n. 33; J. A. Bryant, Jr, 'The Nature of the Allegory in Lyly's *Endymion*', *RenP* (1956), 4–11; and Saccio, *Court Comedies*, pp. 175–86.

93 Weltner, 'The Antinomic Vision', pp. 5–44, esp. pp. 8–9.

94 Saccio, *Court Comedies*, pp. 2 ff.; see also Michael R. Best, 'Lyly's Static Drama', *RenD*, n.s. 1 (1968), 75–86.

95 Altman, *Tudor Play of Mind*, pp. 206, 216.

96 Jonas Barish, 'The Prose Style of John Lyly', *ELH*, XXIII (1956), 14–35. See also Morris W. Croll, 'Introduction: The Sources of the Euphuistic Rhetoric', in Morris William Croll and Harry Clemons, eds, *Euphues* (London: G. Routledge, 1916), pp. xv–lxiv, rpt and edited by R. J. Schoeck and J. Max Patrick in *Style, Rhetoric, and Rhythm* (Princeton, 1966), pp. 241–95.

97 Barish, 'Prose Style', p. 22.

98 Jocelyn Powell, 'John Lyly and the Language of Play', *Elizabethan Theatre*, ed. John Russell Brown and Bernard Harris, Stratford-upon-Avon Studies 9 (London: Arnold, 1966), pp. 147–67.

99 Doris Brenan Braendel, 'The Limits of Clarity: Lyly's *Endymion*, Bronzino's *Allegory of Venus and Cupid*, Webster's *White Devil*, and Botticelli's *Primavera*', *HSL*, IV (1972), 197–215, elaborates on the play's balanced structure by positing that Eumenides's visit to the fountain (III.iv) is at the centre of the play, with scenes before and after it mirroring each other in order outward from the centre: III.ii–iii and Act IV, III.i and v.i, etc. This symmetry, though not 'mannerist' in any strict sense, is Florentine in character, as we see in the paintings of Botticelli.

100 Geoffrey Tillotson, 'The Prose of Lyly's Comedies', *Essays in Criticism and Research* (Cambridge University Press, 1942, rpt Hamden, Conn.: Archon, 1967), pp. 17–30. Walter N. King, 'John Lyly and Elizabethan Rhetoric', *SP*, LII (1955), 149–61, discusses Lyly's rhetoric in terms of *elocutio*, *inventio*, and *dispositio*.

101 Some of these examples are cited by Robert Y. Turner, 'Some Dialogues of Love in Lyly's Comedies', *ELH*, XXIX (1962), 276–88.

102 Marco Mincoff, 'Shakespeare and Lyly', *ShS*, XIV (1961), 15–24, aptly describes Lyly's theatrical world as a 'comedy of love's foolishness' in which the lovers 'pursue what is mostly a very unsuitable affair. They are at bottom only playing a game, though compelled to it by Cupid, and they are as miserable over it as any tragic hero' (p. 19). The description fits *Sappho and Phao* and *Gallathea* more perfectly than *Endymion*, but it is still apropos here.

103 See Knight, 'John Lyly', pp. 146–63, who argues cogently that the style of *Euphues* similarly reflects dramatic conflict and an antithetical balancing of contradictions.

104 W. Reavley Gair, *The Children of Paul's: The Story of a Theatre Company, 1553–1608* (Cambridge University Press, 1982), p. 99; Hillebrand, *The Child Actors*, pp. 112–24; Hunter, *Lyly*, pp. 74–5, 97, 358 (n. 35); Trevor Lennam, *Sebastian Westcott, the Children of Paul's, and 'The Marriage of Wit and Science'* (University of Toronto Press, 1975), pp. 44–8; Michael Shapiro, *Children of the Revels: The Boy Companies of Shakespeare's Time and Their Plays* (New York: Columbia University Press, 1977), p. 34; and Shapiro, 'The Children of Paul's and Their Playhouse', *TN*, XXX (1982), 3–13.

105 Chambers, *Elizabethan Stage*, II.496–7.

106 Michael R. Best, 'The Staging and Production of the Plays of John Lyly', *Theatre Research*, IX (1968), 104–17; Chambers, *Elizabethan Stage*,

I.213–34 ('The Court Play') and III.1–46 ('Staging at Court'); Irwin Smith, *Shakespeare's Blackfriars Playhouse* (New York University Press, 1964), pp. 130–63, esp. pp. 137–44; and Shapiro, *Children of the Revels*, p. 35.

107 Hunter and Bevington, pp. 181–91; Best, 'Staging and Production', pp. 104–17. On staging in great halls and similar venues, see Alan H. Nelson, *Early Cambridge Theatres: College, University, and Town Stages, 1464–1720* (Cambridge University Press, 1994), esp. p. 124. Nelson's demonstration that Cambridge stages often had permanent structures, erected year after year for performance at the upper end of the hall rather than in front of the hall screen, has implications for indoor courtly entertainments in Tudor England, including Lyly's Blackfriars.

108 Saccio, 'The Oddity of *Endimion*', p. 97.

109 Hunter, *Lyly*, p. 109.

110 Compare Saccio, 'The Oddity of *Endimion*', p. 97: 'On the public stage such a line ['Here is the castle'] would merely accompany a gesture at the tiring-house facade; on the court stage of the 1580s it probably indicates a genuine set-piece.'

111 Sallie Bond, 'John Lyly's *Endimion*', *SEL*, XIV (1974), 189–99, argues unpersuasively that the other courtiers should age visibly along with Endymion.

112 Saccio, 'The Oddity of *Endymion*', pp. 96–7. Werner Habicht, 'Tree Properties and Tree Scenes in Elizabethan Theater', *RenD*, n.s. IV (1971), 69–92, argues forcefully with many examples that emblematically significant trees were often physically present onstage, though he does not discuss *Endymion* in particular. George Hunter has pointed out to me an added instance of a tree property not discussed by Habicht: in William Percy's *The Faery Pastoral, or Forest of Elves*, 1603, a list of properties calls for 'A hollow oak with vice of wood to shut to'.

113 Carter A. Daniel, ed., *The Plays of John Lyly* (Lewisburg, Pa.: Bucknell University Press, 1988), p. 369; Hunter, *Lyly*, pp. 237–8.

114 Shapiro, *Children of the Revels*, pp. 105–6, and Richard Edwards, *Damon and Pythias*, c. 1565 (Malone Society Reprints, 1957), ll. 1659–60. See also Chambers, *Elizabethan Stage*, II.316 (about Nathan Field, born in 1587, who remained a member of the Chapel and the Queen's Revels until 1613) and 332 (about Edward Pearce, styled a 'Gentleman of Chapel' in 1589 and Master of Paul's in 1600); Hillebrand, *The Child Actors*, pp. 62 and n. 77 and 324; Hollybrand, *The French Schoolmaster* (1573), quoted in M. St Clare Byrne, ed., *The Elizabethan Home*, rev. ed. (London: Methuen, 1949), p. 33; and T. W. Craik, *The Tudor Interlude* (Leicester University Press, 1958), pp. 28–9 and 43.

115 Hillebrand, *The Child Actors*, p. 62 and n. 77, quoting *Privy Purse Expenses of Princess Mary*, p. 62 (March 1538).

116 Hillebrand, *The Child Actors*, pp. 54–5 and 324, quoting the *Records of the Exchequer, Miscellaneous Books, Treasury of Receipt*, vol. CCIX, p. 139.

117 John Tucker Murray, *English Dramatic Companies, 1558–1642*, 2 vols (London: Constable, 1910), I.344–5. The 'Erle of Oxenfordes lades' (i.e. 'lads') were also at Norwich in 1580–1; see *Norwich 1540–1642*, ed. David Galloway, Records of Early English Drama (University of Toronto Press, 1984), p. 61.

118 C. S. Lewis, *English Literature in the Sixteenth Century, Excluding Drama*, Oxford History of English Literature (Oxford: Clarendon, 1954), p. 316, cited in Hunter, *Lyly*, p. 363, n. 8. G. K. Hunter has kindly supplied me with the information about the Taylor Institution, noting further that the *Oxford Magazine* for 2 March 1944 (vol. LXII, 1943–44) provides on p. 142 an advance notice dated 24–6 February, stating that the performance was by the Eglesfield players (unidentified, but appearing in several other notices about this time). A review on p. 149 by 'J. R. P.' (unidentified) names Paul Haeffner as producer, Ian Smith as Eumenides, Christine Gibbs as Cynthia, Kenneth Miles as Endymion, Dorothy Thompson as Dipsas, Mary King as Tellus, Raymond Herod as Sir Tophas, and John Jepson as Epiton. Though some of the actors were inexperienced and some long speeches dull, in J. R. P.'s estimation, with not enough use being made of the apron stage, the groupings were generally well arranged, the scene changes smooth, and the nobility of several episodes authentically conveyed. This reviewer, unlike Lewis, found Sir Tophas 'the success of the evening'.

119 *The London Stage, 1660–1800, Part I: 1660–1700*, ed. William Van Lennep (Carbondale: Southern Illinois University Press, 1965), p. 486.

ENDYMION,
THE MAN IN THE MOON

Played before the Queen's Majesty at
Greenwich, at Candlemas Day at Night,
by the Children of Paul's

THE PRINTER TO THE READER

Since the plays in Paul's were dissolved, there are certain
comedies come to my hands by chance which were presented
before Her Majesty at several times by the Children of Paul's.
This is the first, and, if in any place it shall misplease, I will
take more pains to perfect the next. I refer it to thy indifferent   5
judgement to peruse, whom I would willingly please. And if
this may pass with thy good liking, I will then go forward to
publish the rest. In the meantime, let this have thy good word
for my better encouragement. Farewell.

---

1. *Since . . . dissolved*] The boys' acting companies, performing in the so-
called 'private' theatres like Blackfriars and Paul's, were closed during most
of the 1590s in a governmental reaction against their tendency to be satirical;
they were allowed to reopen in 1599. The publisher of *Endymion*, William
Broome's widow, may have benefited by the theatre closings in 1590 and the
resulting lack of need for the boys' companies to hold on to their play texts:
Endymion, *Gallathea*, and *Midas* were registered by her for publication in
1591, and her husband had published reprints of *Campaspe* and *Sappho and
Phao* in early 1591. See Introduction, pp. 1–2.
   5. *indifferent*] impartial.

[CHARACTERS IN ORDER OF APPEARANCE

ENDYMION, *a young man.*
EUMENIDES, *his friend.*
TELLUS, *a lady-in-waiting at Cynthia's court.*
FLOSCULA, *her servant.*
DARES, *Endymion's page.*   5
SAMIAS, *Eumenides's page.*
SIR TOPHAS, *a braggart.*

Characters in order of appearance] *Such a list was first supplied by Dilke (in hierarchical order).*

---

1. *ENDYMION*] in Greek mythology, a shepherd, who, in some accounts, required of Jupiter that he be perpetually young and allowed to sleep as much as he wished. Selene was so struck by the beauty of this youth as he slept on Mount Latmos that she descended from the skies each night to sleep with him. On variant narratives and on Lyly's transformation of the myth, see Introduction, pp. 10–11.

2. *EUMENIDES*] from the Greek *eumenes*, well-disposed, gracious. Aristotle, in his *Nicomachean Ethics*, VIII.ii.4 (LCL, pp. 456–7), describes a friend as 'one who wishes well for another' (Edge, 'A Crux', pp. 439–40); see note on Aristotle at III.iv.142–3. The well-known use of 'Eumenides' as a euphemism for the Furies, as in Aeschylus's *The Oresteia*, employs the same meaning; one speaks of the Furies as well-wishing in the hopes that they will prove so.

3. *TELLUS*] a divinity, the earth, the most ancient of the gods after Chaos; mother, by Coelus, of Oceanus, Hyperion, Ceus, Rhea, Iapetus, Themis, Saturn, Phoebe, Tethys, etc. The same divinity is honoured under the name of Rhea, Vesta, Ceres, Proserpine, etc. as a many-breasted goddess of fecundity. For a connection of Tellus with Medea, see under *Scintilla* below.

4. *FLOSCULA*] from the Latin *flosculus*, little flower—an appropriate name for one who is a confidante and lady-in-waiting of Tellus.

5. *DARES*] Dares the Phrygian, the priest of Hephaestus in Troy (*Iliad*, V.9), was reported to have written his own poem in Greek on the siege of Troy. A Latin work of the fifth century A.D., spuriously representing itself as a translation of this lost poem, was much used by medieval writers, despite its manifest absurdities. Another Dares, a boxer, is named in Virgil, *Aeneid*, V.369, 375 (LCL, I.470–1).

6. *SAMIAS*] perhaps from S*amios*, pertaining to the island of Samos; Ovid uses such an epithet for Pythagoras, born on Samos. Or possibly from *Samia*, the daughter of the river-god Maeander (Edge, 'Prosody', pp. 178–9).

7. *SIR TOPHAS*] On Lyly's indebtedness to Chaucer's Sir Thopas as well as to Plautus and to the *miles gloriosus* in English Renaissance plays like *Thersites* (1537) and *Roister Doister* (*c.* 1552), see Introduction, p. 14.

EPITON, *his page.*

DIPSAS, *an aged sorceress.*

SCINTILLA ⎫   10
FAVILLA ⎭ *maids -in-waiting at the court.*

BAGOA, *a sorceress, assistant to Dipsas.*

Three Ladies *and an ancient* Man, *in a dumb show.*

CYNTHIA, *the Queen.*

SEMELE, *a lady-in-waiting at Cynthia's court.*   15

CORSITES, *a captain.*

---

8. *EPITON*] a follower or companion (Greek); perhaps also suggesting *epitome*, an abridgement, from *epitemnein*, cut short, epitomised (Edge, 'Prosody', pp. 178–9)—a term suitable to a diminutive page attached to Tophas.

9. *DIPSAS*] the name given to an old, profligate bawd in Ovid, *Amores*, I.viii.2 (LCL, pp. 346–7). The word in Latin also connotes a kind of serpent whose bite causes violent thirst; from the Greek *dipsao*, to thirst. As a fire-drake, the serpent turns up also in Aelian, VI.51 (LCL, II.70–3; Dilke, II.19, quoting Stevens's note on *The Malcontent*). The further association of 'Dipsas' with herbs and witchcraft suggests Tellus's or earth's malevolent side as contrasted with the benign Floscula or 'flower'; both serve Tellus (Edge, '*Endimion*', p. 3).

10. *SCINTILLA*] a spark (Latin). The words *scintilla* and *favilla*, used to name Cynthia's two maids-in-waiting, are found linked in Ovid's account of Medea's rekindled love for Jason: '*quaeque / parva sub inducta latuit scintilla favilla / crescere*', 'as a tiny spark, which has lain hidden beneath hot embers, increases anew' (*Metamorphoses*, VII.79–81, LCL, I.348–9; see Edge, '*Endimion*', p. 3).

11. *FAVILLA*] hot cinders, embers (Latin). The name is similarly used in *Sappho and Phao* for a lady-in-waiting who dreams about fire. See the previous note on *Scintilla*.

12. *BAGOA*] perhaps suggested by the name Bagous or Bagoas, who is addressed in the vocative (Bagoa) as the guard of his mistress in Ovid's *Amores*, II.ii.1 (LCL, pp. 382–3; Mustard); or possibly a feminine form of *Bagoas* or *Bagosas*, a eunuch at the Persian court of Artaxerxes Ochus, *c.* 335 B.C.; hence, any guard of women.

14. *CYNTHIA*] a surname of Diana, in recognition of her having been born on Mount Cynthus, a high mountain of Delos.

15. *SEMELE*] in Greek mythology, the daughter of Cadmus by Harmonia, who was tricked by the jealous Juno into asking that her lover Jupiter should appear to her in his full majesty. Because he had sworn to honour her request, he reluctantly did so and consumed her in a flash of lighting and a bolt of thunder. In Renaissance art and literature she is a type of ruinous passion. See III.iv.101–4, V.iv.248, and notes.

16. *CORSITES*] perhaps suggesting 'thirsty of heart' or 'a wasting away of the heart'. The name also suggests 'a stone used as a remedy for venomous bites and for drugged or enchanted persons', since Corsites does attempt to undo Dipsas's magic charm; see Long, 'Purport', p. 176, and Fernand de Mely, *Les Lapidaires de l'Antiquité et du Moyen Age* (Paris: Ernest Leroux, 1898), Index.

PANELION ⎱
ZONTES ⎰ *lords at Cynthia's court.*

GERON, *a wise old man, estranged husband of Dipsas.*

A Constable. 20

Two Watchmen.

Four Fairies.

PYTHAGORAS, *a Greek philosopher at Cynthia's court.*

GYPTES, *an Egyptian soothsayer at Cynthia's court.*

SCENE: *at and near the court of Cynthia.*] 25

---

17. *PANELION*] perhaps from *panellenes*, all the Hellenes or Greeks. At III.i.52 the name reads 'Pantlion' in Q and 'Pantalion' in Blount, possibly suggesting Pantaleon, a king of Pisa who presided over the Olympic games in 664 B.C. Another Pantaleon was an Aetolian chief. The relevance of either figure is obscure here, but the name was at least known in ancient Greece.

18. *ZONTES*] Perhaps from Greek *zöon*, a living being, an animal, a figure, an image.

19. *GERON*] old man (Greek).

23. *PYTHAGORAS*] a Greek philosopher of pagan naturalism and a mathematician who died *c.* 497 B.C.

24. *GYPTES*] an aphetic form of 'Egyptian'. Egypt was renowned as the supposed home of the gypsies, who were noted for fortune-telling, divination, sooth-saying, and the like.

THE PROLOGUE

Most high and happy princess, we must tell you a tale of the
Man in the Moon, which, if it seem ridiculous for the method,
or superfluous for the matter, or for the means incredible, for
three faults we can make but one excuse: it is a tale of the Man
in the Moon.   5
    It was forbidden in old time to dispute of chimera, because
it was a fiction. We hope in our times none will apply pastimes, because they are fancies; for there liveth none under the
sun that knows what to make of the Man in the Moon. We
present neither comedy, nor tragedy, nor story, nor anything,   10
but that whosoever heareth may say this: 'Why, here is a tale
of the Man in the Moon.'

---

    1. *Most . . . princess*] Both Prologue and Epilogue in this play are for per-
formance at court before Queen Elizabeth. Compare *Campaspe*, which provides alternative prologues and epilogues to be spoken at Blackfriars and the
court, and *Sappho and Phao*, which provides prologues to be spoken at
Blackfriars and the court and an epilogue addressed to any viewer or reader.
    1–2. *a tale . . . Moon*] This proverbial expression (Dent T45.11) suggests a
tale that is far out, improbable, a mere 'fiction' or 'pastime' or 'fancy', as in
ll. 7–8, not to be read literally.
    6. *chimera*] a monster with three heads—lion, goat, and dragon—with
fore-, middle-, and hinder-parts to match. Chimera's union with its sibling,
Orthos, produced the Sphinx and the Nemean lion. To 'dispute' about such
monsters, or to call them by their true names, was forbidden as dangerous;
compare the term 'Eumenides', 'the kindly ones', as a propitiatory way of
referring to the Furies in Aeschylus's *Oresteia*.
    7–8. *apply pastimes*] read actual events into this entertaining play.
    8. *fancies*] imaginary constructions.
    10. *story*] history. Compare III.i.44 and note.

Act I

Actus Primus, Scaena Prima

[*Enter*] ENDYMION [*and*] EUMENIDES.

Endymion. I find, Eumenides, in all things both variety to
content and satiety to glut, saving only in my affections,
which are so stayed, and withal so stately, that I can
neither satisfy my heart with love nor mine eyes with
wonder. My thoughts, Eumenides, are stitched to the   5
stars, which, being as high as I can see, thou mayst
imagine how much higher they are than I can reach.

Eumenides. If you be enamoured of anything above the moon,
your thoughts are ridiculous, for that things immortal are

0.1 [*Enter*] ENDYMION [*and*] EUMENIDES] *Throughout, brackets in stage directions
signify editorial amplification. The following collation notes record substantive
changes only, as when new stage directions or portions of stage directions have been
added. The collation notes do not record routine amplifications such as the supply-
ing of an* [Enter] *where the entry is clearly implied in the Quarto original by the
listing of characters' names, or an* [and] *in a series of names. In Q, stage directions
are generally grouped at the beginning of scenes; where names are moved in this
present edition to what appears to be the correct location for entrance in mid-scene,
the relocation is noted.*

Actus Prima, Scaena Prima] Act and scene divisions are in Latin throughout. Characters' names are grouped at the head of each scene.

3. *stayed*] (*a*) staid, fixed (*b*) hindered (*c*) plagued with scruples. Compare
IV.iii.86. The word also is linked to *stately:* (*a*) deliberate and imposingly
dignified (*b*) having to do with matters of state. Compare also *stay*, verb, at
v.i.78, and noun, at I.i.52 and III.iv.182.

5–6. *stitched to the stars*] The proverbial idea of pointing or looking at an
unattainable star (Dent s825) is used by Apelles to describe his seemingly
hopeless love for Campaspe in *Campaspe*, III.v.41–2, 'stars are to be looked at,
not reached at', and in Sibylla's advice to Phao against ambitious love in
Sappho and Phao, II.i.154–5: 'keep . . . thine eyes upward and thy fingers
down'; compare also I.i.10. Similar sentiments occur in *Euphues*, II.46, 28–9:
'one may point at a star, but not pull at it', and II.204, 7–9.

8. *above the moon*] beyond the realm of the sublunary, hence immortal and
perfect.

9. *for that*] in that, since, because; as also at ll. 48 and 52, I.iv.14, II.ii.114,
III.i.27, III.ii.23, v.i.77, and v.iv.46.

79

not subject to affections; if allured or enchanted with   10
these transitory things under the moon, you show yourself senseless to attribute such lofty titles to such low
trifles.

Endymion. My love is placed neither under the moon nor
above.   15

Eumenides. I hope you be not sotted upon the man in the
moon.

Endymion. No, but settled either to die or possess the moon
herself.

Eumenides. Is Endymion mad, or do I mistake? Do you love   20
the moon, Endymion?

Endymion. Eumenides, the moon.

Eumenides. There was never any so peevish to imagine the
moon either capable of affection or shape of a mistress;
for as impossible it is to make love fit to her humour,   25
which no man knoweth, as a coat to her form, which
continueth not in one bigness whilst she is measuring.
Cease off, Endymion, to feed so much upon fancies. That
melancholy blood must be purged which draweth you to
a dotage no less miserable than monstrous.   30

---

12. low] *Bond;* loue *Q.*   28. Cease off, Endymion] *Baker;* Cease of
Endimion Q; Cease, Endymion *Dilke.*

---

12. *low*] Q's *loue* is not indefensible, since Endymion confesses to be in
love; possibly the word is picked up deliberately in line 14, playing on the
notion that *love* is *low*. Still, *low* is elegantly antithetical to *lofty* in l. 12, and
the compositor could easily have made such an error.

16. *sotted*] besotted, infatuated.

23. *peevish*] foolish, silly; mad; spiteful; perverse; petty.

25. *humour*] disposition, as also at 1.ii.54 and elsewhere.

27. *is measuring*] is being measured, as though for a new coat. The notable
fact about the moon is that its apparent size continually changes. *Measuring*
also suggests the moon's power to regulate and to traverse (*OED*, v. 1, 4, 11).

28. *Cease off*] cease, leave off. 'Cease of', the Q reading, is sometimes used
transitively, as in 'Sees of thy sawes', York *Temptation of Christ*, l. 157, but
here the construction appears to be the intransitive 'Cease off'.

29. *melancholy blood*] blood afflicted with too much black bile, a condition
thought to produce sadness and depression. Such blood was often *purged* or
bled off (l. 29) in a common medical therapy.

30. *dotage*] infatuation, folly.

Endymion. My thoughts have no veins, and yet, unless they be
   let blood, I shall perish.

Eumenides. But they have vanities, which being reformed, you
   may be restored.

Endymion. O fair Cynthia, why do others term thee un-   35
   constant whom I have ever found unmovable? Injurious
   time, corrupt manners, unkind men, who, finding a constancy not to be matched in my sweet mistress, have
   christened her with the name of wavering, waxing, and
   waning! Is she inconstant that keepeth a settled course,   40
   which since her first creation altereth not one minute in
   her moving? There is nothing thought more admirable or
   commendable in the sea than the ebbing and flowing; and
   shall the moon, from whom the sea taketh this virtue, be
   accounted fickle for increasing and decreasing? Flowers   45
   in their buds are nothing worth till they be blown, nor
   blossoms accounted till they be ripe fruit; and shall we
   then say they be changeable for that they grow from seeds
   to leaves, from leaves to buds, from buds to their perfection? Then why be not twigs that become trees, children   50

31–2. *be let blood*] be cured by blood-letting.

33. *vanities*] unprofitable and conceited thoughts (with wordplay on *veins*
at l. 31, suggesting *vainness*—close in pronunciation to *veins* and *vanities*).

35–6. *unconstant*] (*a*) changing in her monthly cycle (*b*) fickle. A similar
play continues in *unmovable* (*a*) constant (*b*) hardhearted. On the proverbial
nature of the moon's constant mutability, see Dent M 1111, and compare
Lyly's *The Woman in the Moon*.

37. *unkind*] (*a*) ungenerous (*b*) unnatural, disloyal.

40–52. *Is she ... stay?*] See Introduction, p. 16. The paradoxes in this
speech about the moon's waxing and waning, growing full only to decay and
then ageing only to become young again, being constant in her varying
course, derive ultimately from Pliny's *Natural History*, II.vi.41–3 (LCL, I.194–
5), and from Aristotle's ideas on organic form (*Physics*, Books II–IV), and were
also available to Lyly in the work of Renaissance mythographers, including
Erasmus (Thomas). Lyly may also have sensed in this idea a painful commentary on his own career, which was in danger of withering when he should
have been most honoured.

44. *virtue*] (*a*) influence and power inherent in a divine being (*b*) essential
quality (*c*) excellence. See also at III.iv.25 and 190, v.i.47, and v.iv.191.

46. *blown*] having blossomed and about to be past perfection; the 'blown
rose' is a decayed rose.

47. *accounted*] esteemed, taken account of.

48. *for that*] because; also at l. 52 and elsewhere.

49–50. *perfection*] completion of their organic destiny.

that become men, and mornings that grow to evenings
termed wavering, for that they continue not at one stay?
Ay, but Cynthia, being in her fullness, decayeth, as not
delighting in her greatest beauty, or withering when she
should be most honoured. When malice cannot object   55
anything, folly will, making that a vice which is the greatest virtue. What thing, my mistress excepted, being in the
pride of her beauty and latter minute of her age, that
waxeth young again? Tell me, Eumenides, what is he
that, having a mistress of ripe years and infinite virtues,   60
great honours and unspeakable beauty, but would wish
that she might grow tender again, getting youth by years
and never-decaying beauty by time, whose fair face
neither the summer's blaze can scorch nor winter's blast
chap, nor the numbering of years breed altering of   65
colours? Such is my sweet Cynthia, whom time cannot
touch because she is divine, nor will offend because she is
delicate. O Cynthia, if thou shouldst always continue at
thy fullness, both gods and men would conspire to ravish
thee. But thou, to abate the pride of our affections, dost   70
detract from thy perfections, thinking it sufficient if once
in a month we enjoy a glimpse of thy majesty; and then,
to increase our griefs, thou dost decrease thy gleams,
coming out of thy royal robes wherewith thou dazzlest
our eyes, down into thy swath clouts, beguiling our eyes.   75
And then—
Eumenides. Stay there, Endymion. Thou that committest

---

52. *stay*] fixed abode, continuance in a state (*OED*, sb.³ 6b–c), as also at
III.iv.182. Compare *stayed* at l. 3.

55. *object*] urge as an objection (*OED*, v. 4).

57–9. *What . . . again?*] What thing other than Cynthia, the moon, is able
to grow young again after having reached the perfection of beauty and grown
old?

61. *but would*] would not.

62. *getting youth by years*] (*a*) getting younger by many years (*b*) growing
younger as time advances.

63–5. *whose . . . chap*] Compare *Euphues*, I.202, 14–16: 'the fine face, the
beauty whereof is parched with summer's blaze and chipped with winter's
blast' (Bond).

75. *swath clouts*] swaddling clothes, betokening infancy.

idolatry wilt straight blaspheme if thou be suffered. Sleep
would do thee more good than speech. The moon
heareth thee not, or, if she do, regardeth thee not.   80
Endymion. Vain Eumenides, whose thoughts never grow
    higher than the crown of thy head! Why troublest thou
    me, having neither head to conceive the cause of my love
    or a heart to receive the impressions? Follow thou thine
    own fortunes, which creep on the earth, and suffer me to   85
    fly to mine, whose fall, though it be desperate, yet shall it
    come by daring. Farewell.   [*Exit.*]
Eumenides. Without doubt Endymion is bewitched; otherwise
    in a man of such rare virtues there could not harbour a
    mind of such extreme madness. I will follow him, lest in   90
    this fancy of the moon he deprive himself of the sight of
    the sun.   *Exit.*

Actus Primus, Scaena Secunda

[*Enter*] TELLUS [*and*] FLOSCULA.

Tellus. Treacherous and most perjured Endymion, is Cynthia
    the sweetness of thy life and the bitterness of my death?

---

87. s.d. *Exit*] Dilke.

78. *straight*] straightway, as also at v.ii.100.
suffered] allowed, as also at iv.i.4; see note at i.i.85.
Sleep] A prolepsis or anticipation of the main 'event' of this intentionally
static drama.
81. *Vain*] foolish, unavailing.
84. *the impressions*] the effect of Cynthia's beauty on my heart.
85. *suffer*] allow, as also at i.ii.35 and 73, ii.i.110, iii.i.62, v.i.165, and v.iv.21
and 195.
86–7. *whose fall . . . daring*] The apparent source passage in Ovid, *Metamorphoses*, ii.328—'*quem si non tenuit magnis tamen excidit ausis*', 'and though
he greatly failed, more greatly dared' (LCL, i.82–3)—is part of an epitaph for
Phaethon (Mustard). Endymion implicitly compares his desperate aspiration
with that of Phoebus's rash son. The image also recalls Icarus, and the fall of
man as told in Genesis. See Introduction, p. 13.
89. *rare*] (*a*) excellent (*b*) uncommon, as also at ii.i.3 and 42, iii.iv.120 and
145–6, iv.ii.61, and v.iv.213.
91–2. *deprive . . . sun*] i.e. commit suicide.

2. *of my death*] leading to my death.

What revenge may be devised so full of shame as my
thoughts are replenished with malice? Tell me, Floscula,
if falseness in love can possibly be punished with ex-   5
tremity of hate. As long as sword, fire, or poison may be
hired, no traitor to my love shall live unrevenged. Were
thy oaths without number, thy kisses without measure,
thy sighs without end, forged to deceive a poor credulous
virgin, whose simplicity had been worth thy favour and   10
better fortune? If the gods sit unequal beholders of injuries, or laughers at lovers' deceits, then let mischief be as
well forgiven in women as perjury winked at in men.

Floscula. Madam, if you would compare the state of Cynthia
with your own, and the height of Endymion his thoughts   15
with the meanness of your fortune, you would rather
yield than contend, being between you and her no comparison, and rather wonder than rage at the greatness of
his mind, being affected with a thing more than mortal.

4–11. *Tell me . . . fortune?*] Compare Medea in Ovid's *Heroides*, XII.181–2
and 89–92 (LCL, pp. 154–5, 148–9): '*dum ferrum flammaeque aderunt sucusque
veneni, / hostis Medeae nullus inultis erit*', 'while sword and fire and the juice of
poison are at hand, no foe of Medea shall go unpunished', and '*Haec
animum—et quota pars haec sunt!—movere puellae / simplicis, et dextrae dextera
iuncta meae. / vidi etiam lacrimas—an pars est fraudis in illis? / sic cito sum verbis
capta puella tuis*', 'Words like these—and how slight a part of them is here!—
and your right hand clasped with mine, moved the heart of the simple maid.
I saw even tears—or was there in the tears, too, part of your deceit? Thus
quickly was I ensnared, girl that I was, by your words' (Edge, 'Sources', pp.
179–80).
  8. *thy*] Addressed as an apostrophe to Endymion, as at l. 2.
  without measure] (*a*) innumerable (*b*) immoderate, unrestrained.
  10. *had been worth*] might have been thought worth (Bond).
  11–12. *If the gods . . . deceits*] On proverbial use of this idea, dating back to
Ovid, *Ars Amatoria*, I.633 (LCL, pp. 56–7), '*Iuppiter ex alto periuria ridet
amantum*', and Tibullus, III.vi.49–50, '*periuria ridet amantum / Iuppiter*' (*Elegies*, ed. Kirby F. Smith, p. 158), see Mustard, and Dent J82. Shakespeare's
phrasing in *Rom.*, II.ii.92–3, is close to that of Ovid and Tibullus: 'At lovers'
perjuries, / They say, Jove laughs' (Bond). By *unequal* (l. 11), Tellus asks if
the gods are prejudiced, capricious, and too far above human vicissitude to
be sympathetic and fair.
  12. *mischief*] revengeful malice.
  15. *Endymion his*] Endymion's.
  16. *meanness*] lowliness, scantness.
  19. *affected*] (*a*) afflicted (*b*) in love.

Tellus. No comparison, Floscula? And why so? Is not my   20
    beauty divine, whose body is decked with fair flowers,
    and veins are vines, yielding sweet liquor to the dullest
    spirits, whose ears are corn to bring strength, and whose
    hairs are grass to bring abundance? Doth not frankin-
    cense and myrrh breathe out of my nostrils, and all the   25
    sacrifice of the gods breed in my bowels? Infinite are my
    creatures, without which neither thou nor Endymion nor
    any could love or live.
Floscula. But know you not, fair lady, that Cynthia governeth
    all things? Your grapes would be but dry husks, your corn   30
    but chaff, and all your virtues vain, were it not Cynthia
    that preserveth the one in the bud and nourisheth the
    other in the blade, and by her influence both comforteth
    all things and by her authority commandeth all creatures.
    Suffer then Endymion to follow his affections, though to   35
    obtain her be impossible, and let him flatter himself in his
    own imaginations, because they are immortal.
Tellus. Loath I am, Endymion, thou shouldst die, because I
    love thee well, and that thou shouldst live it grieveth me,
    because thou lovest Cynthia too well. In these extremities   40
    what shall I do? Floscula, no more words. I am resolved:
    he shall neither live nor die.

---

23. spirits] *Q (sprits).*   24. hairs] *Q (heares).*   25. breathe] *Q (breath).*

20–6. *Is not . . . bowels?*] The imagery comparing the earth, with its vine-
yards, wheat fields, etc., to a woman's body and its fragrance of frankincense
and myrrh repeatedly echoes the Song of Songs; see Song of Solomon, i.13,
iii.6, iv.6, vii.1–13, etc.
  22. *and veins*] and whose veins.
  23. *corn*] grain, wheat. Compare Song of Solomon, vii.2.
  24. *hairs*] The play of assonance on *ears* in l. 23 is even more apparent in
the Q spellings, *eares* and *heares.*
  26. *of the gods*] to the gods. The phrase captures the Homeric imagery of
the fragrant smell of animal sacrifice.
  31. *virtues*] powers, as at I.i.44.
  32–3. *bud . . . blade*] means of survival in winter and summer. Alliteration,
parison, isocolon, and paramoion are prominent in this speech. See Introduction, pp. 46–7.
  33. *influence*] with suggestion of astrological influence (see note at
III.iv.182), as at I.i.44 and in note at l. 31 above.
  37. *immortal*] concerned with something immortal (Cynthia).

Floscula. A strange practice, if it be possible.

Tellus. Yes, I will entangle him in such a sweet net that he
shall neither find the means to come out, nor desire it. All   45
allurements of pleasure will I cast before his eyes, insomuch that he shall slake that love which he now voweth
to Cynthia, and burn in mine, of which he seemeth
careless. In this languishing between my amorous devices
and his own loose desires, there shall such dissolute   50
thoughts take root in his head, and over his heart grow so
thick a skin, that neither hope of preferment, nor fear of
punishment, nor counsel of the wisest, nor company of
the worthiest shall alter his humour nor make him once to
think of his honour.   55

Floscula. A revenge incredible, and if it may be, unnatural.

Tellus. He shall know the malice of a woman to have neither
mean nor end, and of a woman deluded in love to have
neither rule nor reason. I can do it, I must, I will. All his
virtues will I shadow with vices; his person—ah, sweet   60
person!—shall he deck with such rich robes as he shall
forget it is his own person; his sharp wit—ah, wit too
sharp, that hath cut off all my joys!—shall he use in
flattering of my face and devising sonnets in my favour.
The prime of his youth and pride of his time shall be   65
spent in melancholy passions, careless behaviour, untamed thoughts, and unbridled affections.

Floscula. When this is done, what then? Shall it continue till
his death, or shall he dote for ever in this delight?

Tellus. Ah, Floscula, thou rendest my heart in sunder, in   70
putting me in remembrance of the end.

---

43. *practice*] stratagem. See also at I.iv.17–18, v.i.158, v.iii.15, and v.iv.47–8.

47. *slake*] diminish the force or fury of (*OED*, v. 9).

54. *humour*] disposition.

56. *unnatural*] (*a*) supernatural; only to be procured by magic (*b*) cruel, inhuman.

58. *mean*] moderation; middle.

59. *I must, I will*] Tellus uses a commonplace pairing (Dent M1330.1) to emphasise her wilfulness.

60. *person*] body.

62–3. *sharp wit . . . joys*] The wit is *sharp* in that it has cut off Tellus; it also displays sharpness of judgement in determining to do so.

65. *pride of his time*] flower of his youth.

71. *the end*] death and divine judgement.

Floscula. Why, if this be not the end, all the rest is to no end.

Tellus. Yet suffer me to imitate Juno, who would turn
    Jupiter's lovers to beasts on the earth, though she knew
    afterwards they should be stars in heaven.   75

Floscula. Affection that is bred by enchantment is like a flower
    that is wrought in silk: in colour and form most like, but
    nothing at all in substance or savour.

Tellus. It shall suffice me, if the world talk, that I am favoured
    of Endymion.   80

Floscula. Well, use your own will, but you shall find that love
    gotten with witchcraft is as unpleasant as fish taken with
    medicines unwholesome.

Tellus. Floscula, they that be so poor that they have neither
    net nor hook will rather poison dough than pine with   85
    hunger; and she that is so oppressed with love that she is
    neither able with beauty nor wit to obtain her friend will

---

85. dough] *Q (dowe)*.

72. *end . . . end*] finale . . . purpose. Floscula's point is that, if Tellus cannot keep eschatological truths in mind, her minor triumphs in her present life
will avail her nothing. Tellus's answer indicates that she wilfully persists in
thinking of herself as a god.

73–4. *Juno . . . earth*] Tellus may be thinking of Io, whom the amorous
Jupiter changed into a heifer in an attempt to conceal her from the jealous
Juno. Juno, in the mythological account, did not turn Io into a beast, as
Tellus's analogy might suggest, but she did torment Io as heifer with a
malicious gadfly. Jupiter also changed himself into a bull in his affair with
Europa, though not in an attempt to fool Juno. Ovid (*Metamorphoses*, 1.738
ff., LCL, 1.54–5) does not place Io among the stars, though she is worshipped
as a goddess. Lyly alters legends of metamorphosis to suit his need.

76–8. *Affection . . . savour*] Floscula's insistence that love potions cannot
govern true affection is reiterated by Dipsas at I.iv.26–7 and recalls the
physician Psellus's advice to Philautus in *Euphues*, II.114, 7–9 and II.118, 20–
5 (Bond).

79. *if . . . talk*] if there is gossip about it.

82–3. *fish . . . unwholesome*] Lyly repeatedly uses this proverbial comparison (Dent F305.11) between fish caught by means of poisoned bait and the
procuring of love through witchcraft; see *Euphues*, II.108, 23–4 and *The
Entertainment at Cowdray*, 1591 (1.427, 20–2), as well as l. 85 in the present
scene (Bond). Lyly's source, according to Croll and Clemons, p. 322, is
either Erasmus's *Similia*, 1.574A (*Opera Omnia*; p. 165 in the Toronto translation), or Plutarch's *Conjugalia Praecepta*, §5, in the *Moralia* (LCL, II.302–3),
which Erasmus is translating.

85. *poison dough*] catch fish by means of poisoned dough-balls, i.e. use evil
means such as black magic.

87. *friend*] lover (*OED*, sb. and a. 4).

rather use unlawful means than try untolerable pains. I
will do it.   *Exit.*

Floscula. Then about it. Poor Endymion, what traps are laid   90
for thee because thou honourest one that all the world
wondereth at! And what plots are cast to make thee
unfortunate that studiest of all men to be the faithfullest!
                                                        Exit.

Actus Primus, Scaena Tertia

[*Enter*] DARES [*and*] SAMIAS.

Dares. Now our masters are in love up to the ears, what have
we to do but to be in knavery up to the crowns?

Samias. O, that we had Sir Tophas, that brave squire, in the
midst of our mirth—and *ecce autem,* will you see the devil?

Enter SIR TOPHAS, [*ridiculously armed and accoutred,
and*] EPITON.

Tophas. Epi!   5
Epiton. Here, sir.
Tophas. I brook not this idle humour of love. It tickleth not

---

4.1. S.D. *ridiculously armed and accoutred*] *This ed.*   4.2. S.D. [*and*] EPITON]
*Placement of Epiton's entrance as in Dilke; it is implied in Q by the indication of
Sir Tophas's entrance at this point.*

---

88. *try*] experience, undergo; *OED*, v. 14, listing *Euphues*, I.228, 6–7, as the
first instance of this now-obsolete meaning: 'the quiet life which I have tried,
being a maiden'.

90. *Then about it*] Floscula could say this to Tellus as she is about to
depart, but it can also said after her departure, in an ironic commentary,
as indicated in the Q placement of the stage direction. Compare the similar
note at II.iii.52.

1. *up to the ears*] To be over head and ears, or up to the ears, in love is a
proverbial idea (Dent H268).

2. *up to the crowns*] even higher than 'up to the ears' (l. 1).

3. *brave squire*] (*a*) intrepid gentleman (*b*) fine fellow (said ironically).

4. ecce autem] lo and behold.

will you see the devil] Compare the proverbial idea, 'Speak of the devil and
he will appear' (Dent D294).

7. *brook*] tolerate.

humour] mood, state of feeling.

my liver, from whence the love-mongers in former age
seemed to infer they should proceed.

Epiton. Love, sir, may lie in your lungs, and I think it doth,   10
and that is the cause you blow and are so pursy.

Tophas. Tush, boy, I think it but some device of the poet to
get money.

Epiton. A poet? What's that?

Tophas. Dost thou not know what a poet is?   15

Epiton. No.

Tophas. Why, fool, a poet is as much as one should say, a
poet. [*Discovering Dares and Samias*] But soft, yonder be
two wrens. Shall I shoot at them?

Epiton. They are two lads.   20

Tophas. Larks or wrens, I will kill them.

Epiton. Larks? Are you blind? They are two little boys.

Tophas. Birds or boys, they are both but a pittance for my
breakfast. Therefore have at them, for their brains must,
as it were, embroider my bolts.   25
           [*He takes aim at Samias and Dares.*]

---

18. S.D.] *Baker.*   25.1. S.D.] *This ed.;* SAMIAS *and* DARES *come forward* /
Baker.

---

8. *liver*] Regarded in ancient times as the seat of love and of the violent
passions generally, as in Theocritus, XIII.72 (LCL, pp. 162–3; Bond). *OED* sb.¹
2 cites Gower, *Confessio Amantis*, Book VII, l. 470 (ed. Macaulay, III.246),
Shakespeare's *Rape of Lucrece*, 47, *MV*, III.ii.86, *Wiv.*, II.i.112, *Ado*, IV.i.231,
and *TN*, I.i.36; Dilke cites *Wiv.*, II.i.112. See also II.ii.12–13 below.

9. *they should proceed*] that the violent passions (including love) should
emanate.

11. *blow*] pant, puff.

pursy] shortwinded, flabby, as in *Ham.*, III.iv.160: 'the fatness of these
pursy times'.

12. *the poet*] Tophas grandly invokes some vague idea of an ancient poet
who, for his own gain, devised myths about the seats of the emotions in the
body; but when challenged by the sceptical Epiton to explain himself,
Tophas offers only the most inane of definitions (ll. 17–18).

18. *soft*] wait a minute, as also at II.i.51, v.i.31, v.ii.53, and v.iv.287.

19. *wrens*] the smallest of common songbirds.

25. *embroider*] besmear with dirt or blood (*OED* 1b). Compare *Locrine*,
III.v.44–5 (ll. 1263–4 in the MSR edition of 1908): 'this great unwieldy club /
Which hath been painted with my foemen's brains'.

bolts] here, bird-bolts, blunt-headed arrows used for shooting small birds.
Tophas refers to them again at III.iii.40. Compare the proverb, 'A fool's bolt
is soon shot' (Dent F515).

Samias. [*To Sir Tophas*] Stay your courage, valiant knight, for
 your wisdom is so weary that it stayeth itself.

Dares. Why, Sir Tophas, have you forgotten your old friends?

Tophas. Friends? *Nego argumentum.*

Samias. And why not friends?   30

Tophas. Because *amicitia*, as in old annuals we find, is *inter
 pares*. Now, my pretty companions, you shall see how
 unequal you be to me. But I will not cut you quite off;
 you shall be my half friends, for, reaching to my middle,
 so far as from the ground to the waist I will be your   35
 friend.

Dares. Learnedly. But what shall become of the rest of your
 body, from the waist to the crown?

Tophas. My children, *quod supra vos nihil ad vos*, you must
 think the rest immortal because you cannot reach it.   40

---

26. s.d.] *This ed.*   31. annuals] *Q* (Annuals); annals *Blount.*

26–7. *Stay . . . stayeth*] calm . . . stops short.

27. *your wisdom . . . itself*] i.e. your wits fail you.

29. Nego argumentum] Compare *Sappho and Phao*, I.iii.44: 'I deny your
argument.' Lyly often supplies his pert boy-servants with such logical quips;
in Tophas's mouth they are doubly satirical.

31–2. amicitia . . . inter pares] friendship is strongest among equals. A
familiar proverb at least as old as Quintus Curtius Rufus, VII.viii.27 (LCL,
II.204–5): '*firmissima est inter pares amicitia*' (Mustard, Dent F761). Tophas's
snobbery is undercut by his ludicrous basing of social distinctions on physical
size (ll. 33–6). See notes at I.iii.48 and V.ii.122.

31. *annuals*] Many editors emend to *annals*, and the *OED* is reluctant to
recognise *annual* as a substantive referring to annual publication prior to
1689 (definition 4), but Lyly is certainly capable of word choice or coinage
pointing, as Bond suggests, to an almanac rather than a chronicle as a natural
source of proverbial lore. At the same time, Tophas could also mean *annals*
as establishing a pompous claim to ancient authority.

34–5. *reaching . . . waist*] Tophas is played either by an adult male chorister who towers over the boys or, as Daniel urges, by an especially diminutive
boy actor whose references to his height are satirically suited to his bombast.
See Introduction, pp. 57–9.

35. *so far . . . waist*] i.e. the grosser part of the human animal, as in many
composite images of centaurs, sphinxes, mermaids, etc. Compare *Lear*,
IV.vi.126–7: 'But to the girdle do the gods inherit; / Beneath is all the fiends'.'

39. quod . . . ad vos] that which is above you is nothing to you. A proverb
(Dent T206) found in Erasmus's *Adagia*, II.250A ('*Quae supra nos, nihil ad
nos*') and cited in *Euphues*, I.195, 26 in the Erasmian form. Here the interpretation parodies the play's serious interest in reaching for the unattainable, as
at I.i.5–6 and note.

Epiton. [*To Samias and Dares*] Nay, I tell ye, my master is
    more than a man.
Dares. [*To Epiton*] And thou less than a mouse.
Tophas. But what be you two?
Samias. I am Samias, page to Eumenides.   45
Dares. And I Dares, page to Endymion.
Tophas. Of what occupation are your masters?
Dares. Occupation, you clown? Why, they are honourable,
    and warriors.
Tophas. Then are they my prentices.   50
Dares. Thine? And why so?
Tophas. I was the first that ever devised war, and therefore by
    Mars himself given me for my arms a whole armoury, and
    thus I go as you see, clothed with artillery. It is not silks
    (milksops), nor tissues, nor the fine wool of Seres, but   55
    iron, steel, swords, flame, shot, terror, clamour, blood,

---

41, 43. S.D.] *This ed.*   45–6. Eumenides . . . Endymion] *Bond; Endimion
. . . Eumenides* / *Q.*   55. Seres] *Bond; Ceres* / *Q.*

42–3. *man . . . mouse*] The pages play with the proverbial contrast between
a man and a mouse (Dent M297) in such a way as to parody Tophas's self-
glorifying reflections on humanity as amphibiously half immortal (himself)
and half mortal (the pages).

45–6. *page to Eumenides . . . page to Endymion*] Q transposes 'Eumenides'
and 'Endymion' in these lines, seemingly in error, for the assignment of
Samias to Eumenides and Dares to Endymion seems unmistakable at
III.iii.77–82, IV.ii.1–2 and 78–86, and implicit at II.ii.1–5 and v.i.1–2 (Bond).
An easy compositorial error.

48. *Occupation*] Dares comically objects to Tophas's use of a term that
commonly has a bawdy meaning in Elizabethan English (compare Doll
Tearsheet's wry observation in *2H4*, II.iv.146–8) and that can connote menial
employment in a trade (*OED*, 4c), as in *JC*, I.ii.266 and *Cor.*, IV.i.14, though
it can also mean 'calling' (*OED*, 4b). Compare v.ii.122 and note, where
Tophas appears to be a *freeholder* or yeoman.

55. *milksops*] spiritless youths. (Addressed to the pages, with assonant
word play on *silks* in l. 54.)

    tissues] rich cloth, often interwoven with gold or silver (*OED*, sb. 1).

    fine wool of Seres] a silk celebrated in Virgil's *Georgics*, II.121 (LCL, I.124–5),
'*velleraque ut foliis depectant tenuia Seres*', 'and how the Seres comb their fine
fleeces from leaves' (Bond). The Seres lived in eastern Asia, probably China,
where they presumably made this soft cloth (a very soft wool) from the
filament cocoons left behind by silkworms feeding on mulberry leaves. Lyly
uses the image in *Euphues*, II.152, 22–3, and in *Sappho and Phao*, III.i.40. The
Q spelling, '*Ceres*', is presumably only a variant spelling; Ceres was goddess
of vegetation, not of flocks.

and ruin, that rocks asleep my thoughts, which never had
any other cradle but cruelty. Let me see, do you not
bleed?

Dares. Why so?   60

Tophas. Commonly my words wound.

Samias. What then do your blows?

Tophas. Not only wound, but also confound.

Samias. [*To Epiton*] How dar'st thou come so near thy master, Epi?—Sir Tophas, spare us.   65

Tophas. You shall live. You, Samias, because you are little;
you Dares, because you are no bigger; and both of you,
because you are but two; for commonly I kill by the
dozen, and have for every particular adversary a peculiar
weapon.   [*He displays his armoury.*]   70

Samias. May we know the use, for our better skill in war?

Tophas. You shall. Here is a birdbolt for the ugly beast, the
blackbird.

Dares. A cruel sight.

---

63. wound] *Fairholt;* confound *Q;* contund *Dilke.*   64. S.D.] *This ed.*
70. S.D.] *This ed.*   72. birdbolt] *Q (*burbolt*).*

---

57. *rocks*] The use of a singular verb after a plural noun is common
in Elizabethan English; see for example III.iv.147 below, *Ant.* I.iv.21 and 50,
and Abbott 333. The objects cited—iron, steel, etc.—make up a collectively
singular subject.

63. *wound... confound*] Dilke speculates that Q's *confound... confound*
may be a deliberate indication of Tophas's poverty of diction, as in 'a poet is
as much as one should say, a poet' (ll. 17–18), though he agrees with most
modern editors that the repetition here is more likely to be a compositor's
anticipation. Dilke's own emendation, *confound... contund,* seems unconvincing in that it uses a word seen nowhere else in English. Tophas and
Samias play with the proverb, 'Words hurt (cut) more than swords' (Dent
w839). Tophas ineptly reverses the connections, since *blows* normally *wound*
and *words confound.*

64–5. *How... Epi*] i.e. how brave of you, Epi, to be continually near such
a violent and dangerous warrior! (Said ironically.) To 'come near' a person
is also to score a point in verbal exchange, as in *Rom.*, I.v.21: 'Am I come near
ye now?'

69. *peculiar*] (*a*) particular (*b*) ill-suited. Tophas means the first; we may
hear the second.

72. *birdbolt*] a blunt-headed arrow for shooting birds, identical in meaning
with *bolt* in l. 25. Q's *burbolt* is an obsolete form.

Tophas. Here is the musket for the untamed, or, as the vulgar   75
    sort term it, the wild mallard.
                    [*He demonstrates, not heeding their talk.*]
Samias. O desperate attempt!
Epiton. Nay, my master will match them.
Dares. Ay, if he catch them.
Tophas. Here is spear and shield, and both necessary, the one   80
    to conquer, the other to subdue or overcome the terrible
    trout, which, although he be under the water, yet, tying a
    string to the top of my spear and an engine of iron to the
    end of my line, I overthrow him, and then herein I put
    him.   85
        [*He shows his gear and struts about, oblivious to their talk.*]
Samias. O wonderful war! Dares, didst thou ever hear such a
    dolt?
Dares. All the better. We shall have good sport hereafter if we
    can get leisure.
Samias. Leisure? I will rather lose my master's service than his 90
    company. Look how he struts. [*To Tophas*] But what is
    this? Call you it your sword?

76.1. s.d.] *This ed.*   85.1. s.d.] *This ed. Baker instead provides asides at ll. 86,
88, and 90.*   90. lose] *Q (*loose*).*   91. struts] *Q (*stroutes*).*   91. s.d.]
Baker.

75–6. *the untamed . . . mallard*] Touchstone parodies this sort of preten-
tious translation of vernacular (vulgar) English into aureate diction in his
pyrotechnic attack on William: 'Therefore, you clown, abandon—which is in
the vulgar, "leave"—the society—which in the boorish is "company"—of this
female—which in the common is "woman"' etc. (*AYLI*, v.i.46 ff.). Compare
also the inflated rhetoric of Don Armado, another *miles gloriosus*, at I.i.227 ff.
etc. in *LLL*. The comic exaggeration in the *miles gloriosus* is seen in Tophas's
extensive and ridiculous armoury used to shoot birds.
    78. *match*] be a match for. The intrepid Tophas will not flinch at confront-
ing a blackbird or mallard.
    80. *spear and shield*] either Tophas's grandiloquent terms for his fishing
rod and hamper, or actual weapons that he proposes to use in this comically
unheroic manner. A shield turned upside down might be used to carry fish.
    82. *although . . . water*] Tophas speaks as though the trout were an under-
water monster like Grendel, with whom he will have to grapple in an
unfamiliar element.
    83. *engine of iron*] i.e. fishhook.

Tophas. No, it is my scimitar, which I, by construction often
    studying to be compendious, call my smiter.
Dares. What, are you also learned, sir?   95
Tophas. Learned? I am all Mars and Ars.
Samias. Nay, you are all mass and ass.
Tophas. Mock you me? You shall both suffer, yet with such
    weapons as you shall make choice of the weapon where-
    with you shall perish. Am I all a mass or lump? Is there no   100
    proportion in me? Am I all ass? Is there no wit in me?—
    Epi, prepare them to the slaughter.
Samias. I pray, sir, hear us speak. We call you 'mass', which
    your learning doth well understand is all 'man', for *mas*,
    maris is a man. Then 'as', as you know, is a weight, and   105
    we for your virtues account you a weight.
Tophas. The Latin hath saved your lives, the which a world of
    silver could not have ransomed. I understand you and
    pardon you.

---

93. *scimitar*] an Asiatic curved sword first mentioned, according to the
OED, in 1548, having been introduced into England in the time of Henry VI
(Fairholt). The choice of an exotic foreign term denoting a weapon of fairly
recent note, in place of the hearty English 'sword', is characteristic of the
fashionmongering would-be swaggerer. For the laborious wordplay on *scimitar* and *smiter* in l. 94, compare III.iii.41 and note.

   construction] the mental building up of materials; construing (*OED* 2b, 5).

   94. *compendious*] succinct. Tophas laboriously suggests that by abbreviat-
ing 'scimitar' to 'smiter' he will save a letter or two while at the same time
making short work of his enemies.

   96. *Mars and Ars*] the personification of war and master of the skills
appropriate to peacetime—literature, art, music, etc.—that an accomplished
courtier should aim to be.

   97. *ass*] Samias's witticism is that Tophas is making an ass of himself.
Then, too, although the *OED* (sb.²) refuses to acknowledge *ass* as a colloquial variant of *arse* prior to 1860, the play in these lines on *Ars / ass*, and
Tophas's insistent questioning as to whether he is 'a mass or lump', 'all ass'
(ll. 100–1), surely register a vulgar witticism here. Compare *ass* at III.iii.120
and v.ii.89.

   104–5. mas, maris] The Latin root of 'masculine'; a male.

   105. *as*] a Latin unit of weight, coinage, measure, etc.

   106. *a weight*] (*a*) strong, courageous, valiant (*OED*, *wight*. a. 1) (*b*) a
wight, a person (*OED*, *wight*, sb.) (c) a *weight*, a heavy mass (*OED*, *weight*,
sb.¹ 11).

   107. *hath saved your lives*] i.e. serves as your neck-verse—usually the fifty-
first psalm, read by an accused person claiming benefit of clergy to save him
from the gallows.

Dares. Well, Sir Tophas, we bid you farewell, and at our next   110
  meeting we will be ready to do you service.
Tophas. Samias, I thank you. Dares, I thank you. But
  especially I thank you both.
Samias. [*Aside to Dares*] Wisely! Come, next time we'll have
  some pretty gentlewomen with us to walk, for without   115
  doubt with them he will be very dainty.
Dares. [*To Samias*] Come, let us see what our masters do. It
  is high time.   *Exeunt* [DARES *and* SAMIAS].
Tophas. Now will I march into the field, where, if I cannot
  encounter with my foul enemies, I will withdraw myself   120
  to the river and there fortify for fish; for there resteth no
  minute free from fight.   *Exit* [SIR TOPHAS *with* EPITON].

Actus Primus, Scaena Quarta

[*Enter*] TELLUS [*and*] FLOSCULA [*at one door, and*]
DIPSAS [*at another*].

Tellus. Behold, Floscula, we have met with the woman by
  chance that we sought for by travail. I will break my mind
  to her without ceremony or circumstance, lest we lose
  that time in advice that should be spent in execution.
Floscula. Use your discretion. I will in this case neither give   5
  counsel nor consent, for there cannot be a thing more
  monstrous than to force affection by sorcery, neither do I
  imagine anything more impossible.

---

114. S.D.] *Bond, subst. Baker instead supplies an aside after* Wisely.
117. S.D.] *This ed.*   118. S.D. DARES *and* SAMIAS] *Baker.*   122. S.D. SIR
TOPHAS *with* EPITON] *Baker, subst.*

0.1–2. S.D. *at one door, and . . . at another*] *Baker, subst.*   2. travail] *Q*
(*trauell*).

---

114. *Wisely*] Samias comments wryly on the pleonasm of Tophas's thanking them individually and then *especially* thanking them both.
  116. *dainty*] (*a*) pleasant, debonair (*b*) a choice morsel for their wit.
  121. *fortify*] strengthen myself and arm myself with weapons (i.e. fishing
gear) (*OED*, v. 3b).

  2. *travail*] Q's *trauell* encompasses both 'travel' and 'travail', labour; *travel*
at III.iv.22 and IV.ii.61 is also spelled *trauell* in Q.
  3. *circumstance*] that which is non-essential (*OED*, III).

Tellus. Tush, Floscula, in obtaining of love what impossibilities will I not try? And for the winning of   10
  Endymion what impieties will I not practise?—Dipsas,
  whom as many honour for age as wonder at for cunning,
  listen in few words to my tale and answer in one word to
  the purpose, for that neither my burning desire can afford
  long speech nor the short time I have to stay many delays.   15
  Is it possible by herbs, stones, spells, incantation, enchantment, exorcisms, fire, metals, planets, or any practice, to plant affection where it is not and to supplant it
  where it is?

Dipsas. Fair lady, you may imagine that these hoary hairs are   20
  not void of experience, nor the great name that goeth of
  my cunning to be without cause. I can darken the sun by
  my skill and remove the moon out of her course; I can
  restore youth to the aged and make hills without bottoms.
  There is nothing that I cannot do but that only which you   25
  would have me do, and therein I differ from the gods,
  that I am not able to rule hearts; for, were it in my power

---

16. incantation] *Fairholt;* incantantation *Q.*   20. hairs] *Q (*heares*).*

12. *cunning*] erudition; skill; artifice; deceit, as also at l. 22, III.iv.195,
IV.i.19, and V.ii.87. See also *cunningly* at IV.iii.2.
  14. *for that*] since.
  16. *stones*] minerals.
  17–18. *practice*] artifice, trickery (*OED*, 6a).
  22–4. *darken the sun . . . bottoms*] Medea, as she prepares to restore old
Aeson to youthful vigour in Ovid's *Metamorphoses*, VII.192–219 (LCL, I.356–7),
claims to be able to darken the sun and draw the moon down from the sky,
call up the dead from their graves, and make the mountains shake. Similarly,
in *Heroides*, VI.85–6 (LCL, pp. 74–7), Hypsiple warns Jason about Medea's
witchcraft: '*illa reluctantem cursu deducere lunam / nititur et tenebris abdere solis
equos*', 'She is one to strive to draw down from its course the unwilling moon,
and to hide in shadows the steeds of the sun' (Edge, 'Sources', pp. 179–80).
These powers are not uncommon in magicians both black and white;
Prospero makes similar claims in a passage indebted to *Metamorphoses*
(*Temp.*, V.i.33–50). On removing the moon from her course (l. 23), Bond
quotes Virgil, *Eclogues*, VIII.69 (LCL, I.60–1): '*carmina vel caelo possunt deducere
lunam*', 'songs can even draw the moon down from heaven'. Compare
Gonzalo's remark to Antonio and Sebastian in *Temp.*, II.i.183–4: 'you would
lift the moon out of her sphere'. The Astronomer in *Gallathea* makes similar
claims: he can 'set a trap for the sun, catch the moon with lime-twigs', etc.
(III.iii.42–79).
  26–7. *therein . . . hearts*] Compare *Euphues*, II.114, 7–9: 'Do you think,
gentleman, that the mind, being created of God, can be ruled by man, or that
anyone can move the heart but he that made the heart?'

to place affection by appointment, I would make such evil
appetites, such inordinate lusts, such cursed desires, as all
the world should be filled both with superstitious heats   30
and extreme love.

Tellus. Unhappy Tellus, whose desires are so desperate that
they are neither to be conceived of any creature nor to be
cured by any art!

Dipsas. This I can: breed slackness in love, though never root   35
it out. What is he whom you love, and what she that he
honoureth?

Tellus. Endymion, sweet Endymion, is he that hath my heart;
and Cynthia, too too fair Cynthia, the miracle of nature,
of time, of fortune, is the lady that he delights in, and   40
dotes on every day, and dies for ten thousand times a day.

Dipsas. Would you have his love, either by absence or sickness, aslaked? Would you that Cynthia should mistrust
him, or be jealous of him without colour?

Tellus. It is the only thing I crave, that, seeing my love to   45
Endymion, unspotted, cannot be accepted, his truth to
Cynthia, though it be unspeakable, may be suspected.

Dipsas. I will undertake it and overtake him, that all his love
shall be doubted of and therefore become desperate. But
this will wear out with time, that treadeth all things down   50
but truth.

Tellus. Let us go.

Dipsas. I follow.   *Exeunt.*

---

30. *superstitious heats*] passionate credulities.

34. *art*] skill, artifice, stratagem (*OED*, sb. 1, 14), as also at II.i.51, II.iii.32,
33, and 48, IV.iii.154 and 170, and v.iv.7, 13, 20, 27, 92, and 270.

43. *aslaked*] slackened; compare l. 35.

44. *without colour*] without reason or excuse; without dissembling, openly.
Compare *colour* at III.iv.55, IV.i.42, IV.iii.53, and v.iv.67.

46. *truth*] steadfast allegiance.

47. *unspeakable*] inexpressible; beyond what can be spoken.
suspected] doubted.

48. *overtake*] overcome the will of, ensnare, overpower (*OED*, 7); with a
play of antithesis on *undertake.*

49. *desperate*] in despair.

50. *wear out*] (*a*) fade (*b*) come to pass, stand the test of experience (*OED*,
wear, v.^{1} 15, 16).

50–1. *time . . . truth*] A proverbial sentiment (see Dent T326, 336, 338).
Compare *Veritas filia temporis*, Truth is the daughter of time (Dent T580).

Act II

Actus Secundus, Scaena Prima

[*Enter*] ENDYMION.

Endymion. O fair Cynthia, O unfortunate Endymion! Why
was not thy birth as high as thy thoughts, or her beauty
less than heavenly? Or why are not thine honours as rare
as her beauty? Or thy fortunes as great as thy deserts?
Sweet Cynthia, how wouldst thou be pleased, how pos-   5
sessed? Will labours, patient of all extremities, obtain thy
love? There is no mountain so steep that I will not climb,
no monster so cruel that I will not tame, no action so
desperate that I will not attempt. Desirest thou the
passions of love, the sad and melancholy moods of per-   10
plexed minds, the not-to-be-expressed torments of
racked thoughts? Behold my sad tears, my deep sighs, my
hollow eyes, my broken sleeps, my heavy countenance.
Wouldst thou have me vowed only to thy beauty and
consume every minute of time in thy service? Remember   15
my solitary life, almost these seven years. Whom have I
entertained but mine own thoughts and thy virtues? What
company have I used but contemplation? Whom have I
wondered at but thee? Nay, whom have I not contemned
for thee? Have I not crept to those on whom I might have   20
trodden, only because thou didst shine upon them? Have

---

3. *rare*] excellent, exalted, as also at l. 42.
6. *patient of*] enduring, longsuffering towards.
12. *racked*] pulled one way and another, like victims on the rack.
16. *seven years*] the normal term of apprenticeship (compare *Euphues*,
II.52, 36), here in the service of love and similarly at III.iv.55–6; also a
proverbial phrase denoting a very long time, as at IV.ii.122 (Dent Y25).
19. *contemned*] disdained. Endymion elaborates on this at ll. 44–6: he has
divorced himself 'from the amiableness of all ladies, the bravery of all courts,
the company of all men'.
20. *crept*] abased myself, cringed.

not injuries been sweet to me if thou vouchsafedst I
should bear them? Have I not spent my golden years in
hopes, waxing old with wishing, yet wishing nothing but
thy love? With Tellus, fair Tellus, have I dissembled,   25
using her but as a cloak for mine affections, that others,
seeing my mangled and disordered mind, might think it
were for one that loveth me, not for Cynthia, whose
perfection alloweth no companion nor comparison.

In the midst of these distempered thoughts of mine,   30
thou art not only jealous of my truth, but careless, suspicious, and secure, which strange humour maketh my
mind as desperate as thy conceits are doubtful. I am none
of those wolves that bark most when thou shinest brightest, but that fish—thy fish, Cynthia, in the flood Araris—   35
which at thy waxing is as white as the driven snow and at
thy waning as black as deepest darkness. I am that

---

22. vouchsafedst] *Dilke;* vouchsafest *Q.*   34–5. brightest, but] *Baker;*
brightest. But *Q;* brightest; but *Dilke.*   35. Araris] *Baker; Aranis / Q.*

22. *vouchsafedst*] Cynthia has deigned to allow Endymion to suffer for her
sake. Q's 'vouchsafest' may be a printer's or copying error, one easily made.

30. *distempered*] vexed, troubled.

31–2. *not only jealous . . . secure*] not only mistrustful of my steadfastness,
but indifferent, suspiciously inclined, and overconfidently careless of my
regard. Dipsas's promise to engender mistrust and jealousy in Cynthia
towards Endymion (I.iv.42–51) seems to have been accomplished.

32. *humour*] disposition.

33. *as thy . . . doubtful*] as your fanciful imaginings are hard to fathom.

34. *wolves that bark*] A proverbial image of petty resentment by underlings
that cannot hurt the great figure they howl at; see Dent D449 for other
instances in Renaissance drama. Here the image anticipates Endymion's
dream at V.i.132. In *Euphues,* II.150.12–13, 'eager wolves bark at the moon,
though they cannot reach it'.

35–7. *that fish . . . darkness*] *Euphues* mentions 'the fish *Scolopidus* in the
flood Araris' which 'at the waxing of the moon is as white as the driven snow,
and at the waning as black as the burnt coal' (I.232, 19–21). Bond traces this
inventive bit of unnatural natural history to the *Pseudo-plutarchea—De Fluviis*
VI, 'Arar': '*Nascitur in eo magnus piscis ab indigenis scolopias vocatus, qui
crescente luna albus est, decrescente autem prorsus niger*' (*Geographi Graeci
Minores,* ed. Karl Müller (Paris: Firmin-Didot, 1882), pp. 644–5), and notes
too that in Aelian (XV.4, LCL, III.210–11) a dark-blue fish called *selena* or
'moon-fish' is reported to vary in size and fertilising power with the changing
of the moon. The Araris is either the Aar or Aare River flowing into the Rhine
in northern Switzerland, or the Arar, the Saône River in F   rn France. 'As

Endymion, sweet Cynthia, that have carried my thoughts
in equal balance with my actions, being always as free
from imagining ill as enterprising; that Endymion whose   40
eyes never esteemed anything fair but thy face, whose
tongue termed nothing rare but thy virtues, and whose
heart imagined nothing miraculous but thy government;
yea, that Endymion who, divorcing himself from the
amiableness of all ladies, the bravery of all courts, the   45
company of all men, hath chosen in a solitary cell to live
only by feeding on thy favour, accounting in the world
(but thyself) nothing excellent, nothing immortal. Thus
mayst thou see every vein, sinew, muscle, and artery of
my love, in which there is no flattery nor deceit, error nor   50
art. But soft, here cometh Tellus. I must turn my other
face to her like Janus, lest she be as suspicious as Juno.

              Enter TELLUS, [FLOSCULA, *and* DIPSAS].

Tellus. Yonder I espy Endymion. I will seem to suspect
    nothing, but soothe him, that, seeing I cannot obtain the
    depth of his love, I may learn the height of his dis-   55
    sembling. Floscula and Dipsas, withdraw yourselves out
    of our sight, yet be within the hearing of our saluting.
                    [*Floscula and Dipsas withdraw.*]
    How now, Endymion, always solitary? No company but
    your own thoughts? No friend but melancholy fancies?
Endymion. You know, fair Tellus, that the sweet remem-   60

52.1. S.D. FLOSCULA, *and* DIPSAS] *Placement as in Dilke, subst.; it is implied in Q
by the indication of Tellus's entrance at this point.*   57.1. S.D.] *Baker.*

---

white as the driven snow' is a proverbial comparison (Dent s591), as also at
v.i.115.
    40. *as enterprising*] as from undertaking any imagined ill deed.
    43. *government*] (*a*) conduct (*b*) rule.
    45. *bravery*] splendour.
    49. *every vein, sinew*] Compare *Euphues*, I.254, 22: 'Search every vein and
sinew of their disposition' (Bond), and *Endymion*, v.i.99–100: 'my very veins
to swell and my sinews to stretch'.
    51. *art*] artfulness, stratagem.
    52. *Janus*] In classical mythology, the two faces of Janus represent past
and future or the rising and setting sun, hence gateways and the beginning of
things; proverbially (Dent J37) the two-facedness can also suggest deception,
as in this present instance.

brance of your love is the only companion of my life, and
thy presence my paradise, so that I am not alone when
nobody is with me, and in heaven itself when thou art
with me.

Tellus. Then you love me, Endymion?   65

Endymion. Or else I live not, Tellus.

Tellus. Is it not possible for you, Endymion, to dissemble?

Endymion. Not, Tellus, unless I could make me a woman.

Tellus. Why, is dissembling joined to their sex inseparable, as
heat to fire, heaviness to earth, moisture to water, thin-   70
ness to air?

Endymion. No, but found in their sex as common as spots
upon doves, moles upon faces, caterpillars upon sweet
apples, cobwebs upon fair windows.

Tellus. Do they all dissemble?   75

Endymion. All but one.

Tellus. Who is that?

Endymion. I dare not tell. For if I should say you, then would
you imagine my flattery to be extreme; if another, then
would you think my love to be but indifferent.   80

Tellus. You will be sure I shall take no vantage of your words.
But in sooth, Endymion, without more ceremonies, is it
not Cynthia?

Endymion. You know, Tellus, that of the gods we are

62–4. *I am not . . . with me*] Endymion flatters Tellus by varying the proverbial phrases, 'Never less alone than when alone' (Dent A228) and 'to be in
heaven' (H350).

66. *Or else I live not*] (*a*) I cannot live without your love (*b*) I know what
your vengeance will be if I do not profess to love you. (The latter possible
meaning is of course not intended for Tellus to understand.) Endymion
flatters by ringing changes on a proverb, 'As sure as I live' (Dent L374).

68. *make me a woman*] turn myself into a woman, the type of dissembling.
Endymion may suggest that if he could make another woman he would have
to dissemble with her, but Tellus does not hear this.

69. *inseparable*] inseparably.

70–1. *heat . . . air*] As the embodiment of earth, Tellus speaks with authority about the inherent properties of the four elements.

78. *say you*] say it was you.

81. *You . . . words*] (*a*) you may be sure I won't take unfair advantage of
your speech (*b*) you're making sure, by choosing your words carefully, that I
shall not be able to take advantage of you.

82. *ceremonies*] mere formalities, as in 'don't stand on ceremony' (*OED* 1b
and 3b).

forbidden to dispute, because their deities come not   85
within the compass of our reasons; and of Cynthia we are
allowed not to talk but to wonder, because her virtues are
not within the reach of our capacities.

Tellus. Why, she is but a woman.

Endymion. No more was Venus.   90

Tellus. She is but a virgin.

Endymion. No more was Vesta.

Tellus. She shall have an end.

Endymion. So shall the world.

Tellus. Is not her beauty subject to time?   95

Endymion. No more than time is to standing still.

Tellus. Wilt thou make her immortal?

Endymion. No, but incomparable.

Tellus. Take heed, Endymion, lest, like the wrestler in
Olympia that, striving to lift an impossible weight,   100
catched an incurable strain, thou, by fixing thy thoughts
above thy reach, fall into a disease without all recure. But
I see thou art now in love with Cynthia.

Endymion. No, Tellus. Thou knowest that the stately cedar,
whose top reacheth unto the clouds, never boweth his   105

---

85. deities] *Q (*dieties*).*

92. *Vesta*] This goddess of the hearth and home is often paired with Venus
to represent antithetical qualities found in the same woman, especially
Queen Elizabeth; in *Euphues*, the Queen is praised for being 'adorned with
singular beauty and chastity, excelling in the one Venus, in the other Vesta'
(II.209, 7–8).

96. *No . . . still*] Endymion speaks in paradox: just as time can never stand
still, Cynthia's beauty cannot fade, because she is constantly renewed
through the changes of the moon.

98. *incomparable*] In seeming to concede that Cynthia is mortal,
Endymion hints at much more: she is not only peerless but transcendent and
unique, like the phoenix (with whom Queen Elizabeth was often compared).

99–100. *the wrestler in Olympia*] In his Epistle Dedicatory to *Euphues and
His England*, Lyly compares himself to 'the young wrestler that came to the
games of Olympia, who, having taken a foil, thought scorn to leave till he had
received a fall' (II.6, 3–5). According to Bond, it was the custom for a
wrestler, as he entered the arena, to lift a heavy weight to demonstrate his
powers. The passage anticipates Corsites's inability to lift Endymion in IV.iii.

102. *recure*] recovery, cure, as at III.i.26 and III.iv.22 and 104.

104. *the stately cedar*] The cedar is often a symbol of majesty, as in the 'high
cedar' associated with Alexander in *Campaspe*, v.iv.144, and in the 'stately
cedar' of Posthumus's dream in *Cym.*, v.iv.140 ff.

head to the shrubs that grow in the valley; nor ivy that
climbeth up by the elm can ever get hold of the beams of
the sun. Cynthia I honour in all humility, whom none
ought or dare adventure to love, whose affections are
immortal and virtues infinite. Suffer me therefore to gaze   110
on the moon, at whom, were it not for thyself, I would die
with wondering.   *Exeunt.*

Actus Secundus, Scaena Secunda

[*Enter*] DARES, SAMIAS, SCINTILLA, [*and*] FAVILLA.

Dares. Come, Samias, didst thou ever hear such a sighing, the
   one for Cynthia, the other for Semele, and both for
   moonshine in the water?
Samias. Let them sigh, and let us sing.—How say you, gentlewomen, are not our masters too far in love?   5
Scintilla. Their tongues haply are dipped to the root in amorous words and sweet discourses, but I think their hearts
   are scarce tipped on the side with constant desires.
Dares. How say you, Favilla, is not love a lurcher, that taketh
   men's stomachs away that they cannot eat, their spleen   10
   that they cannot laugh, their hearts that they cannot fight,
   their eyes that they cannot sleep, and leaveth nothing but
   livers to make nothing but lovers?
Favilla. Away, peevish boy! A rod were better under thy

6. haply] *Q* (*happily*).

106–7. *ivy . . . elm*] Proverbial; see Dent 1109.11.

1–2. *the one . . . the other*] Endymion . . . Eumenides.
3. *moonshine in the water*] Dares uses a proverbial phrase for fruitless
longing (Dent M1128), found also in *Mother Bombie*, v.iii.112.
6. *haply*] Q's *happily* catches the double meaning: (*a*) perchance (*b*) bliss-
fully. So too with *haply* (Q: *happilie*) at v.i.85.
8. *tipped on the side*] lightly touched, in contrast with their tongues, which
are wholly immersed in amorous discourse.
9. *lurcher*] petty thief, swindler.
10–12. *men's stomachs . . . eyes*] In addition to their usual meanings, men's
stomachs are their appetite, *spleen* is the locus of the sense of humour (also of
melancholy), *hearts* generate courage, and *eyes* provide wakefulness.
13. *livers*] organs associated with love and violent passions, and also with
cowardice when deprived of blood. See note at i.iii.8.
14–15. *A rod . . . girdle*] you would do better with a caning on your back-
side, below the belt. The phrase occurs in *Euphues*, i.185, 15, and may be

girdle than love in thy mouth. It will be a forward cock   15
that croweth in the shell.

Dares. Alas, good old gentlewoman, how it becometh you to
be grave!

Scintilla. Favilla, though she be but a spark, yet is she fire.

Favilla. And you, Scintilla, be not much more than a spark,   20
though you would be esteemed a flame.

Samias. [*Aside to Dares*] It were good sport to see the fight
between two sparks.

Dares. [*Aside to Samias*] Let them to it, and we will warm us
by their words.   25

Scintilla. You are not angry, Favilla?

Favilla. That is, Scintilla, as you list to take it.

Samias. That, that!

Scintilla. This it is to be matched with girls, who, coming but
yesterday from making of babies, would before tomorrow   30
be accounted matrons.

22, 24. S.D.] *Baker.*

---

proverbial (Dent R156.11). Roosters are proverbially *'forward'*, i.e. presumptuous and obstreperously precocious (Dent c486 ff.).

17–18. *Alas . . . grave*] Dares mocks the pert young Favilla (meaning 'hot
cinders') for acting as a moral authority. 'Good old gentlewoman' is a riposte
to 'peevish boy' (l. 14), and is especially ironic in that it is addressed to the
younger and presumably smaller of the two maids; see ll. 29–31 and note.

19. *spark*] (*a*) a small particle of fire (*b*) a small trace of feeling or sentiment (*c*) a woman of great beauty, elegance, or wit (*OED*, sb.² 1). Scintilla's
own name means 'spark', as Favilla points out in ll. 20–1. The proverbial
idea (Dent s714.11) that small sparks have their heat occurs also in *Euphues*,
II.90, 22–3, and in *Campaspe*, V.iv.144–5.

21. *a flame*] (*a*) a tongue-like ignited vapour (*b*) a love object (*OED*, sb.
6b, though the earliest citation in *OED*, first and second editions, is 1647).
Favilla retorts to Scintilla's witticism (l. 19) with a pun of her own.

23. *sparks*] The word may also suggest 'young men of an elegant or
foppish character', thus pointing to the boy actors, though *OED*, first and
second editions, sb.² 2, gives its earliest citation in this sense from 1600.

27. *as . . . it*] This familiar phrase (Dent T27) appears also in *Mother
Bombie*, IV.ii.51. *List* means 'please, desire'.

28. *That, that!*] Samias eggs on the combatants, or comments on the
bantering exchange; compare 'Good, good' in l. 36. Bond sees the line as
spoken to Scintilla.

29–31. *This . . . matrons*] Scintilla, apparently the older and taller of the
two maids (see ll. 17–18 and note), lords it over her junior.

30. *babies*] children's dolls, as in *Mac.*, III.iv.107. Scintilla may suggest in
ll. 30–1 that Favilla and her kind will be producing real babies soon enough.
At IV.iii.176 in *Endymion*, *babies* are fairies.

Favilla. I cry your matronship mercy. Because your pantables
be higher with cork, therefore your feet must needs be
higher in the insteps. You will be mine elder because you
stand upon a stool and I on the floor.   35
Samias. Good, good.
Dares. [*Aside to Samias*] Let them alone, and see with what
countenance they will become friends.
Scintilla. [*To Favilla*] Nay, you think to be the wiser, because
you mean to have the last word.   40
                         [*The women threaten each other.*]
Samias. Step between them, lest they scratch. In faith, gentle-
women, seeing we came out to be merry, let not your
jarring mar our jests. Be friends. How say you?
Scintilla. I am not angry, but it spited me to see how short she
was.   45
Favilla. I meant nothing, till she would needs cross me.
Dares. Then so let it rest.
Scintilla. I am agreed.
Favilla. [*Weeping*] And I, yet I never took anything so un-
kindly in my life.   50
Scintilla. [*Weeping*] 'Tis I have the cause, that never offered
the occasion.
Dares. Excellent, and right like a woman.

---

35. floor] *Blount;* flowre *Q.*   37. S.D.] *Baker, subst.*   39. S.D.] *This
ed.*   40.1. S.D. *The women ... other*] *This ed.*   49, 51. S.D.] *Baker, subst.*

32. *your matronship*] a mock title on the model of *your majesty*, etc.,
amusing here in that Scintilla (whose name suggests the diminutive) is
played by a boy actor and appears to be young, like all the pages and maids
in this scene. To cry someone mercy is to beg pardon; here said sarcastically.

pantables] pantofles, embroidered slippers for men or women, usually
outfitted with high cork heels, as here. Favilla mocks Scintilla by suggesting
that her height and seeming authority are contrivances of footwear. 'To stand
on one's pantofles' is a proverbial indication of pride and vanity (Dent P43);
so is 'to be high in the instep' (Dent 184), as in l. 34.

34. *will be*] wish to pass yourself off as being.

35. *a stool*] a comic exaggeration of the effect of high heels.

38. *countenance*] bearing, demeanour, manifestation of regard; feigned
appearance (*OED*, sb. 1, 2b, 7).

40. *you mean ... word*] Women proverbially have the last word (Dent
w722).

44. *short*] abrupt, ill-humoured, 'but of course with a Parthian shot at
Favilla's stature, as above' (Bond).

53. *right like a woman*] To weep is proverbially 'to play the woman' (Dent
w637.2).

Samias. A strange sight, to see water come out of fire.

Dares. It is their property to carry in their eyes fire and water, 55
tears and torches, and in their mouths honey and gall.

Scintilla. You will be a good one if you live. But what is
yonder formal fellow?

Enter SIR TOPHAS [*and* EPITON].

Dares. [*Aside, to his friends*] Sir Tophas, Sir Tophas of whom
we told you. If you be good wenches, make as though you 60
love him, and wonder at him.

Favilla. We will do our parts.

Dares. But first let us stand aside and let him use his garb, for
all consisteth in his gracing.

[*The pages and maids-in-waiting stand aside.*]

Tophas. Epi! 65

Epiton. At hand, sir.

Tophas. How likest thou this martial life, where nothing but
blood besprinkleth our bosoms? Let me see, be our enemies fat?

Epiton. Passing fat. And I would not change this life to be a 70

58.1. S.D. *and* EPITON] *Dilke, subst.* 59. S.D.] *This ed.* 64.1. S.D.] *Baker, subst.*

54. *water . . . fire*] i.e. tears being prompted by anger.

55. *fire and water*] The linking of fire and water is proverbial (Dent F267 and *Euphues*, 1.247, 34–5), as also with *honey and gall*, l. 56 (Dent H551.1 and *Euphues*, 1.247, 11).

57. *a good . . . live*] a fine specimen of a man, if you escape the gallows. (Said sardonically.)

58. *formal*] prim or ceremonious in appearance (*OED*, 8)—a wry comment on Sir Tophas's outlandish manner of accoutring himself; with a suggestion also that he is a man in form only.

63. *use his garb*] show his grace, elegance, stylishness of manners or appearance (*OED*, sb.², 1, citing this passage as its earliest instance); but *OED* § 2 is also apposite: 'outward bearing, behaviour, carriage, or demeanour'.

64. *all . . . gracing*] the jest is not simply in his outlandish appearance but in the way he attempts gracefulness in his affected behaviour; or, all depends on honouring him. (*OED*'s first citation of *gracing*.)

69. *fat*] fattened up, ready to be slaughtered as though they were enemies on the field of battle. Tophas refers either to the trout that Epiton might be carrying or to the sheep that Tophas prepares to encounter at ll. 88ff. At I.iii.121, Tophas resolved to 'fortify for fish', but in this present scene his imagined enemy is 'the monster *ovis*' (l. 96).

70. *Passing*] surpassingly, as also at v.i.88.

lord; and yourself passeth all comparison, for other captains kill and beat, and there is nothing you kill but you
also eat.

Tophas. I will draw out their guts out of their bellies, and tear
the flesh with my teeth, so mortal is my hate and so eager   75
my unstanched stomach.

Epiton. [*Aside*] My master thinks himself the valiantest man in
the world if he kill a wren, so warlike a thing he
accounteth to take away life, though it be from a lark.

Tophas. Epi, I find my thoughts to swell and my spirit to take   80
wings, insomuch that I cannot continue within the compass of so slender combats.

Favilla. [*Aside*] This passeth!

Scintilla. [*Aside*] Why, is he not mad?

Samias. [*Aside*] No, but a little vainglorious.   85

Tophas. Epi!

Epiton. Sir?

Tophas. I will encounter that black and cruel enemy that
beareth rough and untewed locks upon his body, whose

77, 83–5. s.d.] *Baker.*   79. accounteth] *Q (*accompteth*).   84. Why, is]
*Q (*Why is*).

71. *yourself passeth all comparison*] (*a*) you are a nonpareil (*b*) you are too
outlandish for words.

72–3. *there is . . . eat*] In *H5*, the Constable remarks wryly of the Dauphin's
resolution to eat the English, 'I think he will eat all he kills' (III.vii.92). Sir
Tophas approaches the burly sport of eating one's enemies with the gour-
mand's perfect solution. Gutting his enemies and tearing their flesh with his
teeth, the gestures of the violent warrior (ll. 74–5), will be for him a gastron-
omic adventure.

75. *eager*] keen of appetite; but also suggesting 'biting', in a continuation
of the metaphor of teeth, and 'fierce', as befits a warrior.

76. *unstanched stomach*] (*a*) unsated appetite (*b*) unrestrained belly (*c*)
unstoppable courage.

81–2. *within the compass*] Compare the joking on Falstaff's fatness as he
attempts to live 'in good compass' (i.e. in orderly fashion) but manages to
live 'out of all compass, out of all reasonable compass' as evidenced by his
excessive girth (*1H4*, III.iii.19–23).

83. *This passeth!*] This is too much, goes beyond belief (as again at
III.iv.82). Compare Page's repeated phrase in *Wiv.*: 'This passes!' (IV.ii.115,
128), and Don Armado in *LLL*, v.i.101–5.

89. *untewed*] uncombed, undressed (*OED*'s sole citation). Tophas's hy-
perbolic language converts the proverbial black sheep (Dent s296) into a
monster from medieval folklore and romance, *black* or 'sinister' in appearance (l. 88), with uncombed hair, four legs, and horns. Such features in a

sire throweth down the strongest walls, whose legs are as   90
many as both ours, on whose head are placed most horrible horns by nature as a defence from all harms.

Epiton. What mean you, master, to be so desperate?

Tophas. Honour inciteth me, and very hunger compelleth me.

Epiton. What is that monster?   95

Tophas. The monster *ovis*. I have said; let thy wits work.

Epiton. I cannot imagine it. Yet let me see. A black enemy
with rough locks—it may be a sheep, and *ovis* is a sheep.
His sire so strong—a ram is a sheep's sire, that being also
an engine of war. Horns he hath, and four legs—so hath   100
a sheep. Without doubt this monster is a black sheep. Is
it not a sheep that you mean?

Tophas. Thou hast hit it. That monster will I kill and sup
with.

Samias. [*To his friends*] Come, let us take him off.   105
                [*The pages and maids come forward.*]
Sir Tophas, all hail!

Tophas. Welcome, children. I seldom cast mine eyes so low as
to the crowns of your heads, and therefore pardon me
that I spake not all this while.

Dares. No harm done. Here be fair ladies come to wonder at   110
your person, your valour, your wit, the report whereof
hath made them careless of their own honours, to glut
their eyes and hearts upon yours.

---

105. s.d.] *This ed.*   105.1. s.d.] *Baker, subst.*

wild giant would be monstrous indeed, though they are perfectly normal in
a sheep. The *sire* that 'throweth down the strongest walls' is a *ram* or
battering ram, as Epiton deduces in ll. 99–100.

92. *all harms*] with a suggestion of cuckoldry.

93. *desperate*] driven to reckless courage in the face of serious risk (*OED*,
4). In Epiton's ironic praise we may hear a suggestion of a more ludicrously
comic sort of desperation.

94. *hunger*] i.e. for honour and for food.

96. ovis] Latin for sheep, as Epiton immediately perceives.

103–4. *sup with*] feed upon.

105. *take him off*] divert or distract him. *OED*'s first citation (*take*, v. 85d)
is from *Mac.*, II.iii.32, in 1605.

112. *careless . . . honours*] i.e. taking risks with their reputations by being
seen in male company without feminine escort.

114. *cannot but injure me*] i.e. can only injure me, since my merits exceed
what report is likely to say.

for that] since.

Tophas. Report cannot but injure me, for that, not knowing   115
    fully what I am, I fear she hath been a niggard in her
    praises.
Scintilla. No, gentle knight. Report hath been prodigal, for
    she hath left you no equal, nor herself credit. So much
    hath she told, yet no more than we now see.   120
Dares. [*Aside*] A good wench.
Favilla. If there remain as much pity toward women as there
    is in you courage against your enemies, then shall we be
    happy, who, hearing of your person, came to see it, and,
    seeing it, are now in love with it.   125
Tophas. Love me, ladies? I easily believe it, but my tough
    heart receiveth no impression with sweet words. Mars
    may pierce it; Venus shall not paint on it.
Favilla. A cruel saying.
Samias. [*Aside*] There's a girl.   130
Dares. [*To Sir Tophas*] Will you cast these ladies away, and all
    for a little love? Do but speak kindly.
Tophas. There cometh no soft syllable within my lips. Cus-
    tom hath made my words bloody and my heart barbar-
    ous. That pelting word 'love', how waterish it is in my   135
    mouth! It carrieth no sound. Hate, horror, death are

120, 129. S.D.] *Bond.*   130. S.D.] *This ed.*

117. *gentle*] well-born, honourable, and generous—all of which qualities
are inverted in Sir Tophas.

117–19. *Report . . . see*] Scintilla ambiguously praises Sir Tophas in such a
way as to suggest that he is without parallel in human history and more
outlandish than ordinary belief could possibly credit. Compare l. 71 and
note.

120. *A good wench*] Dares quietly applauds Scintilla's wit, undetected by
Sir Tophas. Samias similarly comments on Favilla's cleverness at l. 129.

121–2. *If . . . enemies*] Since Favilla regards Sir Tophas as a person of no
courage whatsoever, this seeming praise of his pity towards women amounts
to no praise at all.

124. *in love with it*] (*a*) full of admiring affection for your person (*b*)
delighted with the comedy you unintentionally provide.

126–7. *Mars . . . Venus*] On the antithetical pairing of this amorous twain,
see note at IV.iii.127. Pyrgopolynices in Plautus's *Miles Gloriosus* (ll. 985,
1257, 1264, 1413–14; LCL, III.226–7, 260–3, 282–3) boasts that he is the pupil
of Mars and the darling of Venus (Boughner, pp. 967–73).

130–1. *and . . . love*] when all they ask is a little affection.

134. *pelting*] paltry.
waterish] thin, tasteless, insipid (*OED*, 5).

speeches that nourish my spirits. I like honey, but I care
not for the bees; I delight in music, but I love not to play
on the bagpipes; I can vouchsafe to hear the voice of
women, but to touch their bodies I disdain it as a thing
childish and fit for such men as can disgest nothing but   140
milk.

Scintilla. A hard heart. Shall we die for your love and find no
remedy?

Tophas. I have already taken a surfeit.

Epiton. Good master, pity them.   145

Tophas. Pity them, Epi? No, I do not think that this breast
shall be pestered with such a foolish passion. What is that
the gentlewoman carrieth in a chain?

Epiton. Why, it is a squirrel.

Tophas. A squirrel? O gods, what things are made for money!   150
[*The pages and maids speak confidentially to one another.*]

Dares. Is not this gentleman overwise?

Favilla. I could stay all day with him if I feared not to be
shent.

Scintilla. Is it not possible to meet again?

150.1. s.d.] *This ed.; Bond instead provides a stage direction, 'to the ladies', in
line 151; Baskervill provides 'asides' in ll. 151–6.*

136–7. *I like . . . bees*] Sir Tophas paraphrases the proverb, 'Honey is
sweet but the bee stings' (Dent H553), suggesting his wariness of women.

138. *bagpipes*] For other testimonials as to the irritating quality of this
instrument, see *MV*, IV.i.49–50, where some men 'cannot contain their urine'
in hearing it sing 'i'the nose', and *1H4*, I.ii.75, where 'the drone of a Lincoln-
shire bagpipe' is associated with melancholy. The figurative meaning of
'windbag' dates from 1827, according to the *OED*.

140. *disgest*] digest, as also at l. 159. The two words are parallel forms but
historically separate.

144. *a surfeit*] i.e. of love or women.

148. *in*] on.

150. *A squirrel . . . money*] Sir Tophas paraphrases a proverb: 'What pretty
things are made for money, quoth the woman when she saw a monkey (or
squirrel)' (Dent T215). Sir Tophas appears to take offence at the vapidity and
idle decadence of keeping such a pet. Baker suggests that Sir Tophas may be
thinking of *squirrel* as a cant term for 'prostitute'. Fairholt notes an instance
of a lady of rank portrayed in a tapestry (the Tapestry of Nancy, after 1476)
with a favourite squirrel attached by a chain to her wrist. Perhaps one of the
young ladies in this scene is to be outfitted thus.

153. *shent*] scolded, disgraced (for being so idle and being seen in men's
company); see l. 112 and note above.

154. *meet*] i.e. meet each other, or meet with Sir Tophas.

Dares. Yes, at any time.   155
Favilla. Then let us hasten home.
Scintilla. [*Aloud*] Sir Tophas, the god of war deal better with
    you than you do with the god of love.
Favilla. Our love we may dissemble, disgest we cannot; but I
    doubt not but time will hamper you and help us.   160
Tophas. I defy time, who hath no interest in my heart.—
    Come, Epi, let me to the battle with that hideous beast.
    Love is pap, and hath no relish in my taste because it is
    not terrible.   [*Exeunt* SIR TOPHAS *and* EPITON.]
Dares. Indeed, a black sheep is a perilous beast. But let us in   165
    till another time.
Favilla. I shall long for that time.   *Exeunt.*

Actus Secundus, Scaena Tertia

[*Enter*] ENDYMION, [*near the lunary bank; and, unseen
    by him,*] DIPSAS [*and*] BAGOA.

Endymion. No rest, Endymion? Still uncertain how to settle
    thy steps by day or thy thoughts by night? Thy truth is

157. S.D.] *This ed.*   164. S.D.] *Baker.*

0.1–2. S.D. *near . . . by him*] *This ed.; A Grove . . . Dipsas [and] Bagoa [in the
background] Bond.*

---

157. *the . . . deal*] may the god of war deal.
159. *disgest we cannot*] we cannot stomach (this indifference to our love).
Scintilla and Favilla fool Sir Tophas by pretending to be disappointed at his
rejection of them. *Disgest* is a parallel form to *digest* still much used in the
Renaissance.
161. *interest in*] claim upon.
163. *pap*] pulpy, infantile fare, as in Lyly's *Pap with a Hatchet*, but perhaps
also associated here with a woman's breast, since the subject is love. Compare Hotspur in *1H4*, II.iii.91–2: 'This is no world / To play with mammets
and to tilt with lips', where *mammets* plays on 'dolls' and 'breasts'.
165. *a black sheep . . . beast*] Dares sardonically quotes a proverb (Dent
S296); cited also in Lyly, *Speeches Delivered to Her Majesty This Last Progress*
(Oxford, 1592), 'The Entertainment at Sudeley' (Bond, 1.477, 19).

0.1–2. S.D.] *Lunary* is moonwort or some similar fern, to which magical
properties are attributed; a symbol of Endymion's constancy of affection to
Cynthia. Compare *Euphues*, II.172, 18, where the herb lunaris, 'as long as the
moon waxeth, bringeth forth leaves, and in the waning shaketh them off'.
Telusa, in *Gallathea*, III.i.20–2, reports of the leaves of lunary that 'the further
they grow from the sun, the sooner they are scorched with his beams'. In

measured by thy fortune, and thou art judged unfaithful
because thou art unhappy. I will see if I can beguile
myself with sleep; and, if no slumber will take hold in my   5
eyes, yet will I embrace the golden thoughts in my head
and wish to melt by musing, that as ebony, which no fire
can scorch, is yet consumed with sweet savours, so my
heart, which cannot be bent by the hardness of fortune,
may be bruised by amorous desires. On yonder bank   10
never grew anything but lunary, and hereafter I will never
have any bed but that bank. O Endymion, Tellus was fair!

Sappho and Phao, we learn that lunary, 'being bound to the pulses of the sick,
causeth nothing but dreams of weddings and dances' (III.iii.45–7). The herb
is still known today in England as 'honesty', and was once thought to have
the power of making locks fly open. (See John Gerard, *The Herball* (London,
1633), pp. 405–7, 464–6, and 1132; and Knapp, 'The Monarchy of Love', p.
358.) Compare the 'flower of the moon' called '*selenetropium*' that opens and
closes with the moon in Drayton's 'The Man in the Moon' (ed. Hebel, II.582,
ll. 316–18), and the flowers that weep whenever the moon 'looks with a
watery eye' in *MND*, III.i.193–4; also the 'little western flower' called 'love-in-
idleness' and associated with 'the chaste beams of the watery moon' (II.i.162–
8). Croll and Clemons, p. 395, n. 8, cite Cornelius Agrippa, *De Occulta
Philosophia*, Book I, ch. xxiv (translated as *Occult Philosophy or Magic* and
edited by Willis F. Whitehead (New York: Samuel Weiser, 1897, rpt 1975)),
and a Latin treatise by Konrad Gesner—presumably his *De raris et admirandis
herbis, quae sive quod noctu luceant, sive alias ob causas, Lunariae nominantur*
(Tiguri: Apud Andream Gesnerum, 1555). On 'discovery' as a possible
staging method used to reveal the lunary bank, which may also feature a
young tree, see Introduction, pp. 51–5.
    The entrance of Dipsas and Bagoa could come as late at l. 27; they are
named at the scene heading in Q, but as a literary convention of grouping
characters' names at each scene heading even when some of them enter later.
Dipsas's speech at ll. 28–30 may perhaps indicate that Dipsas has overheard
at least part of what he has said, but not indisputably so. Bond and Daniel
bring Dipsas and Bagoa on at l. 1, Baskervill at l. 27.
    2–4. *Thy truth . . . unhappy*] i.e. the destiny that decrees your separation
from Cynthia has the effect of making you seem disloyal to her, and breeds
in her mistrust and and jealousy (as Dipsas promised to bring about at
I.iv.42–51; see II.i.31–2 and note). *Unhappy* means 'unfortunate, unlucky'
(*OED*, 2).
    7–8. *as ebony . . . savours*] Lyly adapts an item from Pliny, XII.ix.20 (LCL,
IV.14–15): '[*Ebenum*] *accendi Fabianus negat; uritur tamen odore iucundo*',
'According to Fabius ebony does not give out a flame, yet burns with an
agreeable scent' (Bond).
    12–20. *O Endymion . . . comprehend it*] Endymion combines the rhetorical
figures of *altercatio* and *deliberatio*, alternating assertions and replies in a

But what availeth beauty without wisdom? Nay,
Endymion, she was wise. But what availeth wisdom without honour? She was honourable, Endymion, belie her   15
not. Ay, but how obscure is honour without fortune? Was
she not fortunate, whom so many followed? Yes, yes, but
base is fortune without majesty. Thy majesty, Cynthia, all
the world knoweth and wondereth at, but not one in the
world that can imitate it or comprehend it. No more,   20
Endymion! Sleep or die. Nay, die, for to sleep it is
impossible; and yet, I know not how it cometh to pass, I
feel such a heaviness both in mine eyes and heart that I
am suddenly benumbed, yea, in every joint. It may be
weariness, for when did I rest? It may be deep melan-   25
choly, for when did I not sigh? Cynthia, ay so, I say,
Cynthia!   *He falls asleep.*
Dipsas. [*Advancing*] Little dost thou know, Endymion, when
thou shalt wake; for, hadst thou placed thy heart as low in
love as thy head lieth now in sleep, thou mightest have   30
commanded Tellus, whom now instead of a mistress
thou shalt find a tomb. These eyes must I seal up by art,
not nature, which are to be opened neither by art nor
nature. Thou that layest down with golden locks shalt not
awake until they be turned to silver hairs; and that chin,   35
on which scarcely appeareth soft down, shall be filled

---

24. joint] *Q* (*iont*).   27. s.d.] *Bond.*   34. layest] *Q* (*laist*).

---

dialogue of the mind with itself, with that of ladder or climax (Puttenham,
The Art of English Poesie, III.xix.217, where it is called *auxesis*, or 'the
avancer'), in which each item in a series rises out of the previous one, from
beauty to wisdom, thence to honour and fortune, and finally to majesty. The
ascent is by a Neoplatonic chain of being to Cynthia's highest perfections
and, by implication, those of Queen Elizabeth. Examples of *altercatio* are
common in Lyly. See for example *Euphues*, I.205, 17–21 ('Why, Euphues
doth perhaps desire my love, but Philautus hath deserved it. Why, Euphues'
feature is worthy as good as I, but Philautus his faith is worthy a better. Aye,
but the latter love is most fervent. Aye, but the first ought to be most faithful',
etc.) and I.233, 3–5; *Campaspe*, II.ii.52–5; and *Endymion*, III.iv.111–28. The
device is also a kind of *sorites*, a logical sophism formed by an accumulation
of arguments. For an example of ladder, see Kyd's *The Spanish Tragedy*,
II.i.111–29.
    19. *not one*] there is no one.
    31–2. *whom . . . tomb*] i.e. instead of enjoying whom as a mistress you shall
now find yourself entombed as it were in a deep sleep.

with bristles as hard as broom. Thou shalt sleep out thy
youth and flowering time and become dry hay before
thou knewest thyself green grass, and ready by age to step
into the grave when thou wakest, that was youthful in the   40
court when thou laidst thee down to sleep. The malice of
Tellus hath brought this to pass, which, if she could not
have entreated of me by fair means, she would have
commanded by menacing; for from her gather we all our
simples to maintain our sorceries. [*To Bagoa*] Fan with   45
this hemlock over his face, and sing the enchantment for
sleep, whilst I go in and finish those ceremonies that are
required in our art. Take heed ye touch not his face, for
the fan is so seasoned that whoso it toucheth with a leaf
shall presently die, and over whom the wind of it   50
breatheth, he shall sleep for ever.   *Exit.*
Bagoa. Let me alone, I will be careful. [*She fans Endymion as
she sings.*] What hap hadst thou, Endymion, to come
under the hands of Dipsas? O fair Endymion, how it
grieveth me that that fair face must be turned to a with-   55
ered skin and taste the pains of death before it feel the
reward of love! I fear Tellus will repent that which the
heavens themselves seemed to rue.—But I hear Dipsas
coming. I dare not repine, lest she make me pine, and

---

39. knewest] *Q;* knowest *Dilke.*   45. S.D. *To Bagoa*] *Baker.*   52–3. S.D.]
This ed.   59. lest] *Q (*least*).*

37–9. *Thou shalt... grass*] Dipsas appeals to proverbial wisdom, 'Green
grass must turn to dry hay' (Dent G415.11), found also in *Euphues*, II.134, 21,
and *Campaspe*, IV.i.54, and based ultimately on the New Testament 'All flesh
is as grass' (1 Peter i.24) and its Old Testament antecedents in Ecclesiastes
and elsewhere.

39. *knewest... grass*] will have known yourself to be green grass, i.e. in the
prime of youth. (The grammatical construction appears to be future perfect.)
Dilke's emendation to 'knowest' is possible; a copying error of this sort
would be easy.

45. *simples*] uncompounded medicinal plants, as also at V.iv.5.

46–7. *sing... sleep*] Although Blount provides no song, Bagoa presumably
does sing at l. 52, since Endymion falls under enchantment.

52. *Let me alone*] leave it to me; as also at III.iv.79, IV.ii.71 and 81, and
V.ii.84. Said to the departing Dipsas, or in a reflective speech after her
departure. On this staging option, compare I.ii.90 and note. Baker places
Dipsas's exit after 'Let me alone, I will be careful'.

53. *hap*] misfortune.

rock me into such a deep sleep that I shall not awake to   60
my marriage.

Enter Dipsas.

Dipsas. How now, have you finished?
Bagoa. Yea.
Dipsas. Well, then, let us in, and see that you do not so much
   as whisper that I did this; for if you do, I will turn thy   65
   hairs to adders and all thy teeth in thy head to tongues.
   Come away, come away.

Exeunt[, leaving Endymion asleep].

A Dumb Show

Music sounds. Three Ladies *enter, one with a knife and a
looking-glass, who, by the procurement of one of the other two,
offers to stab Endymion as he sleeps, but the third wrings her
hands, lamenteth, offering still to prevent it, but dares not. At
last, the first lady, looking in the glass, casts down the knife.
Exeunt [the* Ladies]. *Enters an ancient* Man *with books with
three leaves, offers the same twice. Endymion refuseth. He*

---

60. awake] *Blount;* awakd *Q.*   67.1. S.D. *leaving Endymion asleep] This ed.;*
DIPSAS *and* BAGOA / *Baker.*   67.2–12. S.D. A Dumb Show . . . *Exit] Blount;
not in Q.*

67.2. *A Dumb Show*] Bond speculates that this dumb show is missing from
Q because Lyly, as his own stage manager, could have instructed the boy
actors in what they were to do. The dumb show presents visually the
substance of the dream Endymion narrates at v.i.88 ff. Stylistically it resembles the dumb shows of *Gorboduc*, 1561, and *The Misfortunes of Arthur*,
1588, both Inns of Court plays. On the three ladies as projections of
Endymion's ambivalent feelings about Cynthia and Tellus, see v.i.82 ff. and
the Introduction, p. 25.
   67.4. procurement] instigation.
   67.5. offers] attempts, shows her intention, as also at v.i.90 (*offered*) and 98
(*offer*).
   67.6. offering still] continually making as though.
   67.9. He] the old Man (see v.i.114–29). This dream, as Baker notes, bears
a resemblance to the story of Tarquin and the Sibyl. According to old
legends about the Roman republic (as in Lucan, v.138, LCL, I–X, pp. 248–9),
one of the Sibyls offered to sell nine volumes to Tarquin II (Tarquinius
Superbus) at a very high price. When he refused, she disappeared and
returned when she had burned three volumes; refused once again, she
burned three more, still demanding the original price. Tarquin was so
astonished by this that he paid the price. The Sibyl disappeared, never to be

rendeth two and offers the third, where he stands a while, and
then Endymion offers to take it. Exit [the old Man. *Endymion*
remains sleeping on the lunary bank, curtained off from view.]

67.10. S.D. *rendeth*] *Dilke; readeth / Blount.*   67.11. S.D. *the old* Man]
Baker.   67.11–12. S.D. *Endymion . . . bank*] *Daniel.*   67.12. S.D. *curtained*
off from view] *This ed.*

seen again by any mortal. The book, preserved as the Sibylline verses and
guarded by a college of priests, became a sacred prophetic text for Rome.
When the verses perished in a fire at the capitol in the time of Sulla, attempts
were made to reconstruct them from different parts of Greece; some eight
books are now extant, but their spuriousness is demonstrable by their references to the martyrdom of Christ.

67.11–12. Endymion . . . bank] See Introduction, pp. 51–5, on possible
ways of staging the sleeping Endymion during scenes in which he is not
required. He is not needed in the stage action until IV.iii; perhaps he and the
lunary bank are concealed by a curtain in the interim, their presence felt in
the theatre though they are not actually seen.

Act III

Actus Tertius, Scaena Prima

[*Enter*] CYNTHIA, *three lords* [CORSITES, ZONTES, *and*
PANELION,] TELLUS, [SEMELE, *and* EUMENIDES].

Cynthia. Is the report true that Endymion is stricken into
such a dead sleep that nothing can either wake him or
move him?

Eumenides. Too true, madam, and as much to be pitied as
wondered at.   5

Tellus. As good sleep and do no harm as wake and do no
good.

Cynthia. What maketh you, Tellus, to be so short? The time
was, Endymion only was.

Eumenides. It is an old saying, madam, that a waking dog doth   10
afar off bark at a sleeping lion.

Semele. It were good, Eumenides, that you took a nap with
your friend, for your speech beginneth to be heavy.

Eumenides. Contrary to your nature, Semele, which hath been
always accounted light.   15

Cynthia. What, have we here before my face these unseemly
and malapert overthwarts? I will tame your tongues and

0.1–2. S.D.] *Bracketed material, Baker, subst.*   16. What, have . . . face
these] *Baker;* What haue . . . face, these *Q.*

6–7. *As . . . good*] Compare the proverb, 'As good be fast asleep as idle
awake' (Dent A347.01), and *LLL*, I.i.44, 'When I was wont to think no harm
all night'.

8. *short*] curt, irascible.

9. *Endymion only was*] no one mattered to you but Endymion (with
wordplay on *was . . . was*).

10–11. *It is . . . lion*] The proverbial sentiment (Dent D515) is presumably
a variant of Dent H165: 'Hares may pull dead lions by the beard'.

13. *heavy*] sleep-inducing, ponderous; sententious.

15. *light*] light-hearted, gay; frivolous, wanton.

16–17. *What, have . . . overthwarts?*] The Q punctuation, 'What
have . . . face, these' etc., is perhaps defensible and indicative of a rhetorical
pause, especially since the phrase 'What (Whom) have we here?' is commonplace (Dent W280.2, occurring also in *Sappho and Phao*, V.ii.76), but the

your thoughts, and make your speeches answerable to
your duties and your conceits fit for my dignity; else will
I banish you both my person and the world.   20
Eumenides. Pardon, I humbly ask; but such is my unspotted
faith to Endymion that whatsoever seemeth a needle to
prick his finger is a dagger to wound my heart.
Cynthia. If you be so dear to him, how happeneth it you
neither go to see him nor search for remedy for him?   25
Eumenides. I have seen him, to my grief, and sought recure
with despair, for that I cannot imagine who should restore him that is the wonder to all men. Your Highness,
on whose hands the compass of the earth is at command
(though not in possession), may show yourself both wor-   30
thy your sex, your nature, and your favour, if you redeem
that honourable Endymion, whose ripe years foretell rare
virtues and whose unmellowed conceits promise ripe
counsel.
Cynthia. I have had trial of Endymion, and conceive greater 35
assurance of his age than I could hope of his youth.
Tellus. But timely, madam, crooks that tree that will be a
cammock, and young it pricks that will be a thorn; and

---

28. wonder] *Blount;* wounder *Q.*

---

sentence as a whole seems to mean: 'Are these unseemly and impudent
wranglings being uttered in my very presence?' *Overthwarts,* i.e. wranglings
or contradictions, occurs also as a noun in *Campaspe,* III.ii.39–40, and *Love's
Metamorphosis,* v.iv.141.
    19. *conceits*] thoughts (completing the parallelism of 'tongues'/'speeches'
and 'thoughts'/'conceits').
    26. *recure*] remedy, succour.
    27. *for that*] since.
    29. *on*] in.
    the compass of the earth] all that is bound within the earth's circumference.
Compass also hints at the moon's circuitous course around the earth. The
moon commands all that is sublunary or beneath the moon, including the
tides, but does not enjoy absolute possession (l. 30).
    31. *favour*] beauty of feature; compare v.i.61.
    redeem] buy back, ransom, rescue, deliver from sinful durance.
    32–4. *whose . . . counsel*] whose ripening years will bring excelling virtues
and whose thoughts, though now callow, will mature into wise counsel. (The
syntax is proleptic.)
    37–8. *timely . . . thorn*] as the young plant is bent, so grows the tree; so too,
the thorn tree reveals at an early age its disposition to be prickly. On this
proverbial wisdom, compare *Euphues,* II.23, 21–2 ('crooked trees prove good

therefore he that began without care to settle his life, it is
a sign without amendment he will end it.   40

Cynthia. Presumptuous girl, I will make thy tongue an example of unrecoverable displeasure.—Corsites, carry her to
the castle in the desert, there to remain and weave.

Corsites. Shall she work stories or poetries?

Cynthia. It skilleth not which. Go to, in both; for she shall   45
find examples infinite in either, what punishment long
tongues have.

[*Exeunt* CORSITES *and* TELLUS.]

Eumenides, if either the soothsayers in Egypt, or the
enchanters in Thessaly, or the philosophers in Greece, or
all the sages of the world can find remedy, I will procure   50
it. Therefore dispatch with all speed: you, Eumenides,
into Thessaly; you, Zontes, into Greece (because you
are acquainted in Athens); you, Panelion, to Egypt,
saying that Cynthia sendeth and, if you will,
commandeth.   55

Eumenides. On bowed knee I give thanks, and with wings on
my legs I fly for remedy.

Zontes. We are ready at Your Highness' command, and hope
to return to your full content.

47.1. s.d. *Exeunt . . .* TELLUS] *Daniel.*   53. Panelion] *Baker; Pantlion / Q;
Pantalion / Blount.*

cammocks'); *Sappho and Phao*, II.iv.123 ('Cammocks must be bowed with
sleight, not strength'); *Mother Bombie*, I.iii.108 ('as crooked as a cammock');
John Heywood, *A Dialogue of Proverbs*, originally published in 1546 and
expanded in 1549, ed. Rudolph E. Habenicht (Berkeley: University of California Press, 1963), l. 2505, p. 172; and Dent T493 and T232. A *cammock* is a
crooked staff or club.
    40. *without amendment*] that without improvement.
    44. *stories or poetries*] truths (histories) or fictions. Tellus's needlework
might embody pictorial illustrations of instructive fictions, or didactic mot-
toes, or both. *Story* is used in a similar sense at Prologue l. 10.
    45. *skilleth*] matters.
    Go to] An expression of impatience.
    both] both stories and poetries.
    49. *enchanters in Thessaly*] Thessaly was fabled for skill in the use of
potions and philters. Bond cites Ovid, *Amores*, III.vii.27 (LCL, pp. 476–7);
Horace, *Odes*, I.xxvii.21–2 (LCL, pp. 74–5); Juvenal, *Satire* VI.610 (LCL, pp.
132–3); and Apuleius, *Metamorphoses (Golden Ass)*, II.21 (LCL, I.100–1), where
Fotis is a Thessalian enchantress.

Cynthia. It shall never be said that Cynthia, whose mercy and   60
   goodness filleth the heavens with joys and the world with
   marvels, will suffer either Endymion or any to perish if he
   may be protected.

Eumenides. Your Majesty's words have been always deeds,
   and your deeds virtues.   *Exeunt.*   65

Actus Tertius, Scaena Secunda

[*Enter*] CORSITES [*and*] TELLUS.

Corsites. Here is the castle, fair Tellus, in which you must
   weave, till either time end your days or Cynthia her
   displeasure. I am sorry so fair a face should be subject to
   so hard a fortune, and that the flower of beauty, which is
   honoured in courts, should here wither in prison.   5

Tellus. Corsites, Cynthia may restrain the liberty of my body;
   of my thoughts she cannot. And therefore do I esteem
   myself most free, though I am in greatest bondage.

Corsites. Can you then feed on fancy, and subdue the malice
   of envy by the sweetness of imagination?   10

Tellus. Corsites, there is no sweeter music to the miserable
   than despair; and therefore the more bitterness I feel, the
   more sweetness I find. For so vain were liberty, and so
   unwelcome the following of higher fortune, that I choose
   rather to pine in this castle than to be a prince in any   15
   other court.

Corsites. A humour contrary to your years and nothing agreeable to your sex, the one commonly allured with delights,
   the other always with sovereignty.

Tellus. I marvel, Corsites, that you, being a captain, who   20
   should sound nothing but terror and suck nothing but

---

62. marvels] *Q (*meruailes*).*

64. *Your . . . deeds*] you have always fulfilled what you promised.

1. *Here is the castle*] Corsites's words may indicate a fixed locus onstage. See Introduction, pp. 51–3.

17. *humour*] attitude, disposition.
nothing] not at all, as also at III.iii.49.

21–2. *sound . . . blood*] The figure recurs in *Midas*, II.i.102–3: 'thee, Martius, that soundest but blood and terror' (Bond). To *suck blood* is to drain the life out of something or someone (*OED, suck*, v. 1c).

blood, can find in your heart to talk such smooth words,
for that it agreeth not with your calling to use words so
soft as that of love.

Corsites. Lady, it were unfit of wars to discourse with women,   25
into whose minds nothing can sink but smoothness. Be-
sides, you must not think that soldiers be so rough-hewn
or of such knotty metal that beauty cannot allure, and
you, being beyond perfection, enchant.

Tellus. Good Corsites, talk not of love, but let me to my   30
labour. The little beauty I have shall be bestowed on my
loom, which I now mean to make my lover.

Corsites. Let us in, and what favour Corsites can show, Tellus
shall command.

Tellus. The only favour I desire is now and then to walk.   35

Exeunt.

Actus Tertius, Scaena Tertia

[*Enter*] SIR TOPHAS [*armed as before*], *and* EPITON[, *with a
gown and other paraphernalia*].

Tophas. Epi!
Epiton. Here, sir.
Tophas. Unrig me. Heighho!
Epiton. What's that?
Tophas. An interjection, whereof some are of mourning, as   5
eho, vah.

28. metal] *Q* (*mettle*).

0.1–2. S.D. *armed as before . . . with . . . paraphernalia*] *Bracketed material, this
ed.*

---

22. *smooth*] (*a*) pleasant, polite (*b*) specious, insinuating. Corsites's
smoothness in l. 26 picks up a similar ambiguity.

23. *for that*] since.

25. *of wars to discourse*] to discourse of wars.

28. *metal*] Q's *mettle* suggests both 'metallic substance' (metal) and 'disposition' (mettle), as also at V.iv.72; often thus in Renaissance literature.

3. *Unrig*] undress (*OED*, 2, citing this as its first example).

6. eho, vah] *Eho!* is an interjection meaning ha? ho! holla! etc., but Tophas
presumably means *eheu*, 'alas!' or, as he has put it in l. 3, 'Heighho!' *Vah!* is
an exclamation of astonishment, joy, anger, like 'ah! oh!' William Lilly and
John Colet's *A Short Introduction of Grammar* introduces interjections to the
reader as follows: 'Some are of mirth, as *Evax, vah*. [Some are of] sorrow, as
Heu, hei' (1577 ed., sig. Ciii, cited by Bond). Compare *Midas*, III.ii.12–14.

Epiton. I understand you not.

Tophas. Thou seest me.

Epiton . Ay.

Tophas. Thou hearst me.   10

Epiton. Ay.

Tophas. Thou feelest me.

Epiton. Ay.

Tophas. And not understandst me?

Epiton. No.   15

Tophas. Then am I but three quarters of a noun substantive.
        But alas, Epi, to tell thee the troth I am a noun adjective.

Epiton. Why?

Tophas. Because I cannot stand without another.

Epiton. Who is that?   20

Tophas. Dipsas.

Epiton. Are you in love?

Tophas. No, but love hath, as it were, milked my thoughts and
        drained from my heart the very substance of my accus-
        tomed courage. It worketh in my head like new wine, so   25
        as I must hoop my sconce with iron, lest my head break

---

16. *Then am I . . . substantive*] Tophas's witticism plays on a traditional definition of a noun, as in Lilly and Colet's *A Short Introduction of Grammar*, sig. A5: 'A noun is the name of a thing, that may be seen, felt, heard, or understande[d].' Because he has not been understood, Tophas is defective in the most important of these four attributes.

17. *troth*] truth.

19. *Because . . . another*] Another schoolboy jest about definitions as phrased in Lilly and Colet's well-known grammer, A5: 'A noun substantive is that standeth by himself. . . . A noun adjective is that cannot stand by himself, but requireth to be joined with another word.' *OED, noun,* 2, *noun substantive,* cites Stephen Hawes, *The Pastime of Pleasure,* Chap. v, p. 24: 'A noun substantive / Might stand without help of an adjective.' Examples of noun adjectives are 'body *politic*' and 'a *black* coat', in which the italicised word, standing for the name of an attribute, is added to describe the chief noun of the phrase more fully (see *OED,* sv. adjective *B*). We would call these noun adjectives simply adjectives.

stand] Tophas applies the grammatical meaning, 'stand alone in a sentence', to other suggested meanings: (*a*) survive, get on (*b*) be erect.

23-4. *love hath . . . heart*] Each sigh of love or sadness was thought to drain the heart of a drop of blood. Compare *2H6,* III.ii.61: 'blood-consuming sighs'.

25. *worketh*] ferments (*OED, work,* v. 32).

25-6. *so as . . . iron*] so that I must fasten an iron hoop tightly around my head. S*conce* is a jocose term for the head (*OED,* sb.²), taking its metaphorical meaning evidently from the literal meanings of a lantern in a protective screen (*OED,* sb.¹) or a fortification (*OED,* sb.³).

and so I bewray my brains. But I pray thee, first discover
me in all parts, that I may be like a lover, and then will I
sigh and die. Take my gun, and give me a gown. *Cedant
arma togae.* 30
Epiton. [*Helping Sir Tophas to disarm*] Here.
Tophas. Take my sword and shield, and give me beard-brush
and scissors. *Bella gerant alii; tu, Pari, semper ama.*
Epiton. Will you be trimmed, sir?
Tophas. Not yet, for I feel a contention within me whether I 35
shall frame the bodkin beard or the bush. But take my
pike and give me pen. *Dicere quae puduit, scribere jussit
amor.*

---

29. *Cedant*] Dilke; *Cædant* / Q. 31. S.D.] This ed. 32–3. beard-brush
and] *Dilke;* beard, brush, and Q. 33. scissors] Q *(*Cyssers*)*. 33. *alii; tu,
Pari, semper*] Daniel; *alii tu pari semper* / Q; *alij, tu Pari semper* / Blount.
37. *quae*] Q *(que)*.

---

27. *bewray*] expose (with a suggestion of divulging the secret as to what
little brain Tophas has); compare *bewraying* at v.ii.86 and *bewrayed* at v.iii.5.
But an Elizabethan audience is sure to hear the word also as *beray*, dirty or
befoul oneself. Compare Francis Beaumont, *The Knight of the Burning Pestle,*
II.i.239: 'Unless it were by chance I did beray me' (*Drama of the English
Renaissance,* ed. R. Fraser and N. Rabkin (New York: Macmillan, 1976),
II.528); see also *The First Part of The Return from Parnassus,* ed. J. B.
Leishman, l. 1239, and *The Second Part,* ll. 1693 ff. and especially 1772 ff.
Modern spelling disguises the Lylyan wordplay, whether one prints *bewray* or
beray in the text.
 discover] (*a*) disarm, dis-cover (*b*) uncover, make known, as also at
III.iv.201 and v.i.157.
 29–30. Cedant arma togae] let military life give way to civil life, to the toga
that a wooer might wear (Cicero, *de Officiis,* I.xxii.77, LCL, pp. 78–9).
 32–3. *Take . . . scissors*] As at ll. 29–30 above and at ll. 36–7, where he
surrenders the *pike* or iron-pointed staff for the *pen* of the sonneteer who is
in love, Tophas here proposes to turn from soldier to wooer.
 33. Bella . . . ama] let others wage war; do thou, O Paris, love always.
From Ovid, *Heroides,* XVII.254 (LCL, pp. 242–3), '*bella gerant fortes: tu, Pari,
semper ama*', alluded to also in *Midas,* IV.iv.28–9 (Bond). Paris's reputation
for cowardice and sensuality redounds ill to Tophas's credit, even if the
comparison to Paris were not ludicrous to begin with.
 34. *trimmed*] The expected meaning of 'have your beard trimmed' shades
satirically into other ideas of being clipped, shorn, reproved, trounced (*OED,*
trim, v. 9–10).
 36. *the bodkin . . . bush*] Tophas considers two styles of beard, dagger-
shaped and bushy-untrimmed.
 37–8. Dicere . . . amor] Love bids one write what one is ashamed to speak
(Ovid, *Heroides,* IV.10, LCL, pp. 44–5). Many of the citations to classical
authors in this scene have been identified by George Pierce Baker in his
edition of the play.

Epiton. I will furnish you, sir.

Tophas. Now for my bow and bolts, give me ink and paper;   40
for my smiter, a penknife. For *scalpellum, calami,
atramentum, charta, libelli, sint semper studiis arma parata
meis.*

Epiton. Sir, will you give over wars and play with that bauble
called love?   45

Tophas. Give over wars? No, Epi. *Militat omnis amans, et habet
sua castra Cupido.*

Epiton. Love hath made you very eloquent, but your face is
nothing fair.

Tophas. Non formosus erat, sed erat facundus Ulysses.   50

Epiton. Nay, I must seek a new master if you can speak
nothing but verses.

Tophas. Quicquid conabar dicere versus erat. Epi, I feel all Ovid
de Arte Amandi lie as heavy at my heart as a load of logs.
O, what a fine thin hair hath Dipsas! What a pretty low   55

---

44. bauble] *Q* (bable).   47. *castra*] *Blount; castea / Q.*

---

41. *smiter*] (*a*) a weapon with which one smites (*b*) a scimitar—a word of
French and possibly Persian derivation whose sound however lends itself to
wordplay, as at I.iii.93–4.

41–3. scalpellum . . . meis] may penknife, quills, black ink, paper, and
booklets always be ready weapons for my literary exertions. Adapted from
Lilly and Colet's *A Short Introduction of Grammar* (1577 ed., sig. D4), as
demonstrated by Donald Edge, 'The Source of Some Latin Lines in John
Lyly's *Endimion*', *N&Q*, CCXVIII, n.s. XX (1973), 453.

44. *bauble*] plaything, trifle; often with phallic suggestion. Q's *bable* is an
obsolete form of *bauble* and also of *babble*, affording a possible wordplay.

46–7. Militat . . . Cupido] every lover goes to war, and Cupid has a camp
of his own, or has his consecrated season (Ovid, *Amores*, I.ix.1, LCL, pp. 354–
5). Q's *castea* can be justified, but it an easy compositorial error for *castra*,
which makes better sense and is true to the Ovidian text.

49. *nothing*] not at all.

50. Non . . . Ulysses] Ulysses wasn't handsome, but he was eloquent
(Ovid, *Ars Amatoria*, II.123, LCL, pp. 74–5).

53. Quicquid . . . erat] whatever I ventured to say came out as poetry
(Ovid, *Tristia*, IV.x.26, LCL, pp. 198–9): '*et quod tentabam dicere [scribere] versus
erat*'). The first edition of Sidney's *Apology for Poetry* (1595) reads '*conabor*',
later corrected to '*conabar*'—a reading that occurs only in the Codex
Bernensis of Ovid, the other MSS. having '*tentabam*' (Baker, Bond).

54. de Arte Amandi] concerning the art of love, known also as the *Artis
Amatoriae libri tres* and the *Ars Amatoria*.

55–64. *O, what . . . jealous*] This sort of misogynistic burlesque of the
Petrarchan blazon, or heraldic cataloguing of one's mistress's charms,

forehead! What a tall and stately nose! What little hollow
eyes! What great and goodly lips! How harmless she is,
being toothless! Her fingers fat and short, adorned with
long nails like a bittern! In how sweet a proportion her
cheeks hang down to her breasts like dugs, and her paps   60
to her waist like bags! What a low stature she is, and yet
what a great foot she carrieth! How thrifty must she be in
whom there is no waste! How virtuous is she like to be,
over whom no man can be jealous!

---

56. tall] *Blount;* tale *Q.*   59. bittern] *Q (Bytter).*   61. waist] *Q (*waste*).*

---

became a trope in its own right during the Renaissance; an instance is to be
found in Francesco Berni's *Rime,* 31 (23), '*Sonetto alla sua donna*'. See Alison
Saunders, *The Sixteenth Century Blason Poetique* (Bern: Peter Lang, *c.* 1981),
Ilse Garnier, *Blason du Corps Feminin* (Paris: A. Silvaire, 1979), and Jan
Ziolkowski, 'Avatars of Ugliness in Medieval Literature', *MLR,* 79 (1984), 1–
20.

   In *Midas,* the page Licio undertakes to 'unfold every wrinkle of my mistress' disposition', praising her head 'as round as a tennis ball', her parrot's
tongue, her mole-like ears, her sow's nose, and the like (I.ii.19–87). See also
The Woman in the Moon, I.i.113–17. Shakespeare has parodic fun with the
blazon in Dromio of Syracuse's recital of the charms (sooty complexion,
unwieldy girth, dripping nose, discoloured teeth, etc.) of his kitchen wench
(*CE,* III.ii.101–38) and in Lance's memorandum about his milkmaid's good
and bad qualities (*TGV,* III.i.262–361). In both these early Shakespeare plays,
written when Lyly's influence was strong, the parody comments wryly on the
wooing in the serious scenes. See also Shakespeare's Sonnet 130, 'My mistress' eyes are nothing like the sun.' The parodic blazon reappears in
Endymion at v.ii.65ff. and 101–7.

   55–6. *low forehead*] a damning detail, according to conventional Renaissance standards of beauty. Compare the Messenger's description of Octavia
to Cleopatra, who has every reason to wish Octavia unhandsome: her hair is
'Brown, madam, and her forehead / As low as she would wish it' (*Ant.,*
III.iii.35–6). The jest in Tophas's description is that Dipsas has her attributes
in the wrong places: thin hair and wide girth, little eyes and fat lips, a stately
nose and a low forehead, small stature and big feet, etc., not unlike Pyramus
in Thisbe's lament for him: 'These lily lips, / This cherry nose, / These yellow
cowslip cheeks' (*MND,* v.i.327–9).

   59. *bittern*] a heron-like bird with pronounced claws. Q's *Bytter* is a variant
spelling.

   63. *waste*] with a pun on 'waist' (l. 61), as in *2H4,* I.ii.139–42: 'CHIEF
JUSTICE. Your means are very slender, and your waste is great. FALSTAFF. I
would it were otherwise; I would my means were greater, and my waist
slenderer.' The Q spelling, *waste* at both ll. 61 and 63, underscores the
homonym.

Epiton. Stay, master, you forget yourself.   65

Tophas. O Epi, even as a dish melteth by the fire, so doth my
    wit increase by love.

Epiton. Pithily, and to the purpose. But what, begin you to
    nod?

Tophas. Good Epi, let me take a nap. For as some man may   70
    better steal a horse than another look over the hedge, so
    divers shall be sleepy when they would fainest take rest.

                                    He sleeps.

Epiton. Who ever saw such a woodcock? Love Dipsas? With-
    out doubt all the world will now account him valiant, that
    ventureth on her whom none durst undertake. But here   75
    cometh two wags.

                Enter DARES *and* SAMIAS.

Samias. [*To Dares*] Thy master hath slept his share.

Dares. [*To Samias*] I think he doth it because he would not
    pay me my board wages.

Samias. It is a thing most strange, and I think mine will never   80
    return; so that we must both seek new masters, for we
    shall never live by our manners.

Epiton. [*To Samias and Dares*] If you want masters, join with

---

77, 78, 83. s.d.] *This ed.*

  65. *you forget yourself*] (*a*) you're letting yourself get carried away (*b*)
you're forgetting that you yourself might be jealous of Dipsas.

  68. *Pithily . . . purpose*] Epiton jibes sardonically at the utter pointlessness
of comparing a melting dish to increasing wit—a vapidity that is all the more
noticeable in a play renowned for its apposite, recondite, and rhetorically
antithetical conceits.

  70–2. *as some men . . . rest*] Again, Tophas applies a proverbial idea (found
in John Heywood's *A Dialogue of Proverbs*, ll. 2438–9, p. 170; Dent H692) with
extraordinary ineptitude. The proverb contrasts the resolute thief with the
passive onlooker. Tophas applies this idea to the self-evident proposition that
when people are sleepy they want to sleep.

  73. *woodcock*] a proverbially stupid bird, easily trapped, as in *Shr.*, I.ii.159.

  75. *ventureth . . . undertake*] Knapp ('The Monarchy of Love', pp. 357–8)
suggests a Latinate pun on 'belly' (*venter* in Latin), and notes a parody here
of Endymion and Cynthia.

  79. *board wages*] wages paid to servants to keep themselves in victual
(*OED*).

  80. *mine*] i.e. Eumenides.

  81–2. *we shall . . . manners*] Samias despairs of fulfilling the proverb:
'Manners make often fortunes' (Dent M630).

  83. *want*] (*a*) lack (*b*) desire. Compare the nominative *want* at v.iv.148.

me and serve Sir Tophas, who must needs keep more
men because he is toward marriage.   85
Samias. What, Epi, where's thy master?
Epiton. Yonder sleeping in love.
Dares. Is it possible?
Epiton. He hath taken his thoughts a hole lower, and saith,
seeing it is the fashion of the world, he will vail bonnet to   90
beauty.
Samias. How is he attired?
Epiton. Lovely.
Dares. Whom loveth this amorous knight?
Epiton. Dipsas.   95
Samias. That ugly creature? Why, she is a fool, a scold, fat,
without fashion, and quite without favour.
Epiton. Tush, you be simple. My master hath a good
marriage.
Dares. Good? As how?   100
Epiton. Why, in marrying Dipsas, he shall have every day
twelve dishes of meat to his dinner, though there be none
but Dipsas with him. Four of flesh, four of fish, four of
fruit.
Samias. As how, Epi?   105
Epiton. For flesh, these: woodcock, goose, bittern, and rail.
Dares. Indeed, he shall not miss if Dipsas be there.
Epiton. For fish, these: crab, carp, lump, and pouting.

---

98. master] *Q (Ma.).*   106. bittern] *Q (bitter).*

89. *a hole lower*] i.e. down a peg in self-humiliation (*OED, hole*, sb. 11).
The idea of taking someone a buttonhole lower is proverbial (Dent P181).
The erotic possibilities of the image recall Tophas's voyeuristic interest in
Dipsas's body at ll. 55–64.
90. *vail bonnet*] take off his hat in a respectful salute. Tophas has disarmed
himself and sleeps bareheaded.
93. *Lovely*] beautifully, lovingly, amorously (*OED*, adv.). As a lover,
Tophas has dedicated his absurd appearance to love.
97. *without fashion . . . favour*] lacking fashionable shape and facial
features.
98. *simple*] simpleminded, as also at IV.i.79 and v.iv.5.
106. *rail*] a small crane-like wading bird, like the *bittern*, invoked at l. 59 to
suggest Dipsas's long, scratching nails. *Rail* puns of course on her railing; she
is a *scold* at l. 96. *Woodcock* and *goose* suggest foolishness.
108. *lump*] a spiny and unattractive fish, commonly supposed to have been
so named because of its bulky appearance (*OED*, sb.² 1–2).
pouting] a small fish, chosen here for the obvious pun on its name. 'Powt

Samias. Excellent! For, of my word, she is both crabbish,
    lumpish, and carping.   110
Epiton. For fruit, these: fretters, medlers, hart-i-chockes, and
    lady-longings. Thus you see he shall fare like a king,
    though he be but a beggar.
Dares. Well, Epi, dine thou with him, for I had rather fast
    than see her face. But see, thy master is asleep. Let us   115
    have a song to wake this amorous knight.
Epiton. Agreed.
Samias. Content.

                            Song.

Epiton.   Here snores Tophas,
                 That amorous ass,   120
                 Who loves Dipsas,

---

111. hart-i-chockes] *Q (*hartichockes*).*   115. master] *Q (*Ma.*).*   119–
37. *Epiton.* Here . . . wise] *Blount; not in Q. The song is labelled 'The First Song'
in Blount.*

---

or eel-powt' (John Minsheu, *Ductor in Linguas, The Guide into Tongues*
(London: I. Browne, 1617), p. 378). *Crab* and *carp* invoke a similar double
meaning, as Samias points out.
    109. *of*] on.
    111–12. *fretters . . . lady-longings*] *OED* sb.¹ 2 lists 'fritter' as a nonce-word
in this meaning. The Q spelling (*fretters*) plays on the idea of a fretting,
scolding woman. The *OED* speculative definition, '? A species of apple.
Obs.', is plainly derived from this present sole instance. *Medlars* are pear-like
fruit eaten in a soft pulpy state, and hence a slang term for the female sexual
organ, as in *Rom.*, II.i.37; the Q spelling here, *medlers*, may also suggest sexual
meddling. The Q spelling *hartichockes* for artichokes suggests a derivation
either from the plant's choking the garden or having a 'chock' or 'choke' at
its heart; perhaps the suggestion is that Dipsas is a heart-choker. *Lady-
longings*, listed in *OED* as *lady's longing*, are a variety of apple; this is *OED*'s
earliest citation. The name has an erotic suggestion.
    112–13. *fare . . . beggar*] To fare like a prince or king or emperor is prover-
bial for living well (Dent P592). In the contrast of king and beggar, Epiton
seems to recall stories of a beggar turned king for a day, as in the Induction
to *Shr.*, and possibly the ballad of King Cophetua and the beggar wench (as
in *Rom.*, II.i.15 and elsewhere).
    119–37. *Here . . . wise*] Like other songs in this and other Lyly plays, this
one first appears in Blount's edition of *Six Court Comedies* of 1632. They seem
authentic and by Lyly.
    120. *ass*] absurd, conceited fellow; but see also note at I.iii.97.

| | With face so sweet, |
| | Nose and chin meet. |

All Three. At sight of her each Fury skips
                And flings into her lap their whips.   125
Dares.   Holla, holla in his ear.
Samias.   The witch sure thrust her fingers there.
Epiton.   Cramp him, or wring the fool by th'nose.
Dares.   Or clap some burning flax to his toes.
Samias.   What music's best to wake him?   130
Epiton.   Bow-wow! Let bandogs shake him.
Dares.   Let adders hiss in's ear.
Samias.   Else earwigs wriggle there.
Epiton.   No, let him batten; when his tongue
                Once goes, a cat is not worse strung.   135
All Three. But if he ope nor mouth nor eyes,
                He may in time sleep himself wise.
Tophas. [*To himself, as he wakens*] Sleep is a binding of the
   senses, love a loosing.
Epiton. [*Aside to Samias and Dares*] Let us hear him awhile.   140
Tophas.   There appeared in my sleep a goodly owl, who,

---

138. s.d.] *Baskervill, subst.*   140. s.d.] *Bond.*

___

123. *Nose and chin meet*] A commonplace gag about ugliness in older women (Dent c349.11).

124–5. *At . . . whips*] The avenging deities of Greek mythology yield their power to Dipsas.

128–9. *Cramp . . . toes*] The pages propose to waken Tophas from a trance-like state by wringing him by the nose, a common first-aid remedy to restore consciousness, as in *Venus and Adonis*, l. 475, and *2H6*, III.ii.34. At the same time they will torment him with cramps and touch him with trial-fire by applying burning flax to his toes as a test or trial—the sorts of pinches and plaguings that the 'fairies' use in *Wiv.*, v.v.84–101, to find out tainted desire in an amorous mortal, Falstaff. Thus will these pages counter the magical effects of the witch's fingers in l. 127.

131. *bandogs*] tied-up or chained watchdogs.

133. *Else earwigs*] or else let crawling insects.

134. *batten*] be left there at his ease; literally, thrive, grow fat.

135. *goes*] gets started.

a cat . . . strung] Cats' guts are commonly used for musical strings. Tophas will caterwaul (*cat + waul,* said of cats and squalling children) as volubly as a fiddle.

136. *nor . . . nor*] neither . . . nor.

141–3. *There . . . Dipsas*] Tophas's dream vision spoofingly anticipates that of Endymion in Act IV. The owl's note, 'Tu-whit, to-whoo' (*LLL,*

sitting upon my shoulder, cried 'Twit, twit', and before
mine eyes presented herself the express image of Dipsas.
I marvelled what the owl said, till at the last I perceived
'Twit, twit', 'To it, to it', only by contraction admonished   145
by this vision to make account of my sweet Venus.

Samias. [*Loudly*] Sir Tophas, you have overslept yourself.

Tophas. No, youth, I have but slept over my love.

Dares. Love? Why, it is impossible that into so noble and
unconquered a courage, love should creep, having first a   150
head as hard to pierce as steel, then to pass to a heart
armed with a shirt of mail.

Epiton. [*Aside to Samias and Dares*] Ay, but my master yawn-
ing one day in the sun, love crept into his mouth before
he could close it, and there kept such a tumbling in his   155
body that he was glad to untruss the points of his heart
and entertain Love as a stranger.

---

144. marvelled] *Q* (meruailed).   147, 153. s.d.] *This ed.*

---

v.ii.908), is ambiguously emblematic of death and wisdom, love and folly.
See Alciato or Alciati (Andreas Alciatus), *Index Emblematicus*, ed. Peter M.
Daly, assisted by Simon Cuttler, 3 vols (University of Toronto Press, 1985),
vol. II: *Emblems and Translations*, Emblem 65; and Knapp, 'The Monarchy of
Love', p. 358. M. C. Bradbrook sees wordplay in the *LLL* passage on the
hunter's cry, 'To it!', and the lover's cry, 'To it! to woo!' (*SQ*, XXXIII (1982),
94–5). In a similar vein, Michael Cameron Andrews wonders if the owl's call
was not associated with wooing 'long before Sir Tophas—or modern critics—noted the connection' (*N&Q*, CCXXIX, n.s. XXXI.2 (1984), 187–8). See
next note.

144–6. *I perceived . . . Venus*] I perceived that 'Twit, twit' meant 'To it, to
it', and that I was being admonished in a vision by means of this gnomic
contraction to esteem my sweet mistress, the veritable goddess of Love. (See
OED, account, sb. 12.) Tophas's fatuous interpretation of *twit* as an encouragement to him to go 'To it, to it' overlooks a meaning of *twit* that applies
better to him: to blame, censure, taunt, or, as a noun, a taunt or reproach.

148. *I have. . . . love*] Tophas strains at wordplay (*overslept, slept over*) to
suggest that he has dreamt of love as he slept, and perhaps that he has slept
in his mistress's arms, but the idea is ridiculously imprecise.

150. *courage*] (*a*) brave temperament (said ironically) (*b*) young man of
spirit, as in Q2 of *Ham.*, I.iii.64–5: 'But do not dull thy palm with entertainment / Of each new-hatched, unfledged courage' (see *OED, courage*, sb. 1c).

150–1. *a head . . . steel*] (*a*) the armed head of a warrior (*b*) the thick head
of a dunce. Steel is proverbially strong (Dent s839).

152. *mail*] armour.

156. *untruss the points*] undo the metal-tagged laces used to fasten clothes
in lieu of buttons.

157. *entertain*] welcome.

Tophas. If there remain any pity in you, plead for me to
Dipsas.

Dares. Plead? Nay, we will press her to it. [*Aside to Samias*] 160
Let us go with him to Dipsas, and there shall we have
good sport.—But Sir Tophas, when shall we go? For I
find my tongue voluble, and my heart venturous, and all
myself like myself.

Samias. [*Aside to Dares*] Come, Dares, let us not lose him till 165
we find our masters, for as long as he liveth, we shall lack
neither mirth nor meat.

Epiton. We will traverse.—Will you go, sir?

Tophas. I prae, sequar. *Exeunt.*

Actus Tertius, Scaena Quarta

[*Enter*] EUMENIDES [*and*] GERON [*near the fountain.
Geron sings.*]

Eumenides. Father, your sad music, being tuned on the same
key that my hard fortune is, hath so melted my mind that
I wish to hang at your mouth's end till my life end.

Geron. These tunes, gentleman, have I been accustomed with
these fifty winters, having no other house to shroud my- 5
self but the broad heavens; and so familiar with me hath
use made misery that I esteem sorrow my chiefest solace.
And welcomest is that guest to me that can rehearse the
saddest tale or the bloodiest tragedy.

160, 165. S.D.] *Baker.* 165. lose] *Q* (loose). 168. traverse] *Baker;*
trauice *Q.*

0.1–2. S.D. *near . . . sings*] Bracketed material, Bond, subst.

---

168. *traverse*] proceed. The word can also mean thwart, affirm, dispute
(*OED*, v. 11–13)—all potentially relevant to the wit combat of these pert
servants. Q's *trauice* is an obsolete form.

169. I prae, sequar] go ahead; I'll follow. As in Terence, *Andria*, I.i.171
(LCL, I.18–19), *Mother Bombie*, II.4.20, etc. (Bond).

0.1. the fountain] Perhaps a fixed stage location; see Introduction, pp. 51–3.

0.2. Geron sings] Blount does not provide the song to which Eumenides
seemingly alludes in ll. 1–3. Compare II.iii.46–52.

1. *Father*] old man, as throughout this scene.
sad] solemn.

3. *hang . . . end*] To hang on someone's mouth or lips is a commonplace
metaphor; see Dent H129.11, *Sappho and Phao*, II.iv.59–60, etc.

8. *rehearse*] relate. Compare IV.iii.98 and V.i.82.

Eumenides. A strange humour. Might I enquire the cause?   10

Geron. You must pardon me if I deny to tell it, for, knowing
    that the revealing of griefs is, as it were, a renewing of
    sorrow, I have vowed therefore to conceal them, that I
    might not only feel the depth of everlasting discontent-
    ment, but despair of remedy. But whence are you? What   15
    fortune hath thrust you to this distress?

Eumenides. I am going to Thessaly to seek remedy for
    Endymion, my dearest friend, who hath been cast into a
    dead sleep almost these twenty years, waxing old and
    ready for the grave, being almost but newly come forth of   20
    the cradle.

Geron. You need not for recure travel far, for whoso can
    clearly see the bottom of this fountain shall have remedy
    for anything.

Eumenides. That, methinketh, is unpossible. Why, what virtue   25
    can there be in water?

Geron. Yes, whosoever can shed the tears of a faithful lover
    shall obtain anything he would. Read these words
    engraven about the brim.

Eumenides. [*Reading*] Have you known this by experience, or   30
    is it placed here of purpose to delude men?

Geron. I only would have experience of it, and then should
    there be an end of my misery. And then would I tell the
    strangest discourse that ever yet was heard.

Eumenides. [*To himself*] Ah, Eumenides!   35

Geron. What lack you, gentleman? Are you not well?

Eumenides. Yes, father, but a qualm that often cometh over
    my heart doth now take hold of me. But did never any
    lovers come hither?

---

15. remedy.] *Q (*remedie?*).   22. travel] *Q* (*trauell*).   30. s.d.] *This ed.*

---

10. *humour*] disposition, mood.

12–13. *the revealing . . . sorrow*] A proverbial-sounding idea, though Dent
R89 cites no other instances.

22. *recure*] remedy.

travel] with suggestion of 'travail' also (Q: *trauell*); see note at I.iv.2.

30. *Have . . . experience*] i.e. do you know from experience that the tears of
a faithful lover will in fact be rewarded?

32. *I only . . . of it*] All I want is to have experience of it.

35. *Ah, Eumenides*] This aside is evidently 'caused by the sudden thought
that he may win Semele by sacrificing his friend' (Bond).

Geron. Lusters, but not lovers. For often have I seen them　　40
　　weep, but never could I hear they saw the bottom.
Eumenides. Came there women also?
Geron. Some.
Eumenides. What did they see?
Geron. They all wept, that the fountain overflowed with tears,　　45
　　but so thick became the water with their tears that I could
　　scarce discern the brim, much less behold the bottom.
Eumenides. Be faithful lovers so scant?
Geron. It seemeth so, for yet heard I never of any.
Eumenides. Ah, Eumenides, how art thou perplexed! Call to　　50
　　mind the beauty of thy sweet mistress and the depth of
　　thy never-dying affections. How oft hast thou honoured
　　her, not only without spot, but suspicion of falsehood!
　　And how hardly hath she rewarded thee without cause or
　　colour of despite! How secret hast thou been these seven　　55
　　years, that hast not, nor once darest not, to name her for
　　discontenting her! How faithful, that hast offered to die
　　for her to please her! Unhappy Eumenides!
Geron. Why, gentleman, did you once love?
Eumenides. Once? Ay, father, and ever shall.　　60
Geron. Was she unkind, and you faithful?
Eumenides. She of all women the most froward, and I of all
　　creatures the most fond.
Geron. You doted, then, not loved. For affection is grounded
　　on virtue, and virtue is never peevish; or on beauty, and　　65
　　beauty loveth to be praised.
Eumenides. Ay, but if all virtuous ladies should yield to all that
　　be loving, or all amiable gentlewomen entertain all that
　　be amorous, their virtues would be accounted vices and
　　their beauties deformities, for that love can be but be-　　70

---

55. *colour of despite*] any pretext for her scorn. Compare I.iv.44.
secret] silent, protective of her honour (*OED*, 2).
55–6. *these seven years*] At II.i.16, Endymion complains of his solitary life
'almost these seven years'. The phrase proverbially denotes a long time and
also a conventional term of apprenticeship; see Dent Y25 and note at II.i.16.
56. *for*] for fear of.
62. *froward*] perverse, ill-humoured, as also at IV.i.29.
63. *fond*] foolish, doting, as also at 118 and 198 and at IV.iii.124.
69–70. *their . . . their*] the ladies' . . . the gentlewomen's.
70–2. *for that . . . fortunate*] The phrase *for that love* can either mean 'since
love', preceded by a comma as in Q, or 'because *that* love, the love we

tween two, and that not proceeding of him that is most
faithful, but most fortunate.

Geron. I would you were so faithful that your tears might
make you fortunate.

Eumenides. Yea, father, if that my tears clear not this fountain,   75
then may you swear it is but a mere mockery.

Geron. So, 'faith, everyone yet that wept.

Eumenides. [*Looking into the fountain*] Ah, I faint, I die! Ah,
sweet Semele, let me alone, and dissolve by weeping into
water!   80

Geron. [*Aside*] This affection seemeth strange. If he see nothing, without doubt this dissembling passeth, for nothing
shall draw me from the belief.

Eumenides. Father, I plainly see the bottom, and there in
white marble engraven these words: 'Ask one for all, and   85
but one thing at all.'

Geron. O fortunate Eumenides (for so have I heard thee call
thyself), let me see.   [*He looks into the fountain.*]

---

78. S.D.] *Bond, subst. (at l. 80.1).*   81. S.D.] *This ed.*   85. one] *Q; once /
Dilke.*   88. S.D.] *Bond, subst.*

---

are talking about', preceded by a semicolon. The sentence is difficult.
Eumenides defends monogamous attachment, and insists that a virtuous
lady will encourage one wooer only, but seems also to concede that the
successful man wins the lady more readily than does the devoted and faithful
type of lover we see in Eumenides. His point is that Geron's advice hasn't
worked in his case; Eumenides has worshipped virtue and beauty in Semele,
but to no effect.

75. *if that*] if. Compare *for that* meaning 'for', 'since', at I.i.48 and elsewhere.

77. *So . . . wept*] i.e. the tears of all lovers who have wept heretofore into
this fountain have made a mockery of their oaths, as shown by their failure
to see the bottom. *'faith* = in faith.

79. *and dissolve*] and let me dissolve. Compare 'Slow, slow, fresh font' in
Act I of Jonson's *Cynthia's Revels*, where Echo's song compares a lover
weeping to a spring fed by melting snow.

81. *affection*] (*a*) expression of passion (*b*) affectation.

82. *passeth*] is excessive, goes beyond belief.

83. *the belief*] i.e. 'in the magic properties of the fountain' (Bond).

85–6. *Ask one . . . at all*] Possibly, as Dilke proposes, this should read 'Ask
once for all', etc., i.e. 'make but one wish, only this once'; but the Q reading
preserved in this text may mean, tautologously, 'Make one wish in place of
all you might ask.' Compare IV.i.56–7 and note.

87–8. *O fortunate . . . call thyself*] Geron has heard Eumenides name
himself at l. 58, and, though Eumenides there called himself 'unhappy

I cannot discern any such thing. I think thou dreamest.

Eumenides. Ah, father, thou art not a faithful lover and there-   90
fore canst not behold it.

Geron. Then ask, that I may be satisfied by the event, and
thyself blessed.

Eumenides. Ask? So I will. And what shall I do but ask, and
whom should I ask but Semele, the possessing of whose   95
person is a pleasure that cannot come within the compass
of comparison, whose golden locks seem most curious
when they seem most careless, whose sweet looks seem
most alluring when they are most chaste, and whose
words, the more virtuous they are, the more amorous   100
they be accounted. I pray thee, Fortune, when I shall first
meet with fair Semele, dash my delight with some light
disgrace, lest, embracing sweetness beyond measure, I
take surfeit without recure. Let her practise her accustomed coyness, that I may diet myself upon my desires.   105
Otherwise the fullness of my joys will diminish the sweetness, and I shall perish by them before I possess them.

Why do I trifle the time in words? The least minute
being spent in the getting of Semele is more worth than
the whole world; therefore let me ask.—What now,   110
Eumenides? Whither art thou drawn? Hast thou forgotten both friendship and duty, care of Endymion and the
commandment of Cynthia? Shall he die in a leaden sleep

---

103. lest] *Q (*least*).*   112. duty, care of Endymion and] *Q (*duetie? Care of
Endimion*, and).*

Eumenides', Geron now renames him 'happy Eumenides' since he claims to
have seen the bottom of the fountain.

95. *ask*] ask for. Compare *asked* at v.i.16 and v.iv.229.

97. *curious*] fastidious, delicate, artfully arranged. Semele's charms are
oxymoronic, like those of Cleopatra.

101–4. *I pray . . . recure*] Eumenides's fear of ruinous surfeit in pleasure
conjures up, with a reversal of sexual roles, Semele's mythological encounter
with Zeus in all his majesty; she was consumed by fire, whereas Eumenides
hopes by 'some light disgrace' to be restrained from a sweetness that would
destroy him. Compare *Pericles*, v.i.195–9, where Pericles asks to be given a
painful hurt lest his happiness at finding Marina overwhelm and even kill him.

110–26. *What now . . . Semele*] Compare this use of the rhetorical figures
of *altercatio* and *deliberatio* with II.iii.12–20 and note.

113–14. *leaden sleep . . . golden dream*] Lead and gold are at opposite ends
of the achemical hierarchy of metals, lead being the basest and gold the most

because thou sleepest in a golden dream?—Ay, let him
sleep ever, so I slumber but one minute with Semele.   115
Love knoweth neither friendship nor kindred.

    Shall I not hazard the loss of a friend, for the obtaining
of her for whom I would often lose myself?—Fond
Eumenides, shall the enticing beauty of a most disdainful
lady be of more force than the rare fidelity of a tried   120
friend? The love of men to women is a thing common,
and of course; the friendship of man to man infinite, and
immortal.—Tush, Semele doth possess my love.—Ay,
but Endymion hath deserved it. I will help Endymion; I
found Endymion unspotted in his truth.—Ay, but I shall   125
find Semele constant in her love. I will have Semele.—
What shall I do? Father, thy grey hairs are ambassadors of
experience. Which shall I ask?

Geron. Eumenides, release Endymion; for all things, friendship excepted, are subject to fortune. Love is but an eye-   130
worm, which only tickleth the head with hopes and
wishes; friendship the image of eternity, in which there is
nothing movable, nothing mischievous. As much difference as there is between beauty and virtue, bodies and
shadows, colours and life, so great odds is there between   135

---

118. lose] *Q (loose).*

---

refined and noble. Lead is often associated with bad sleep, as in *R3*, v.iii.105:
'leaden slumber'. Gold is conversely associated with good sleep, as in Virgil's
Aeneid (Dent D585.11).

    115. *so*] so long as.

    116. *Love . . . kindred*] A proverbial idea (Dent L505, L549).

    118. *lose myself*] (*a*) risk my life (*b*) forget who I am.
Fond] foolish.

    121–2. *common, and of course*] in the regular run of things. Compare l. 154.

    130–1. *an eye-worm*] *OED* cites this line as its sole instance (*eye*, sb.[1] 28),
and take the word to mean a worm in the eye, here figuratively applied. Love
conventionally enters at the eye with the distracting and illusory results that
Geron describes here; perhaps an eyeworm might produce similar
symptoms.

    135. *shadows*] In this context and in opposition to *bodies*, *shadows* must
refer to things spiritual. The antithesis also plays on the contrast between a
solid body and its shadow.

    colours] mere outward appearance, as opposed to essence (*life*). The Pla-
tonic commonplace antithesis of illusion and reality is often applied by Lyly
and other Renaissance writers to the difference between eros and friendship,

love and friendship. Love is a chameleon, which draweth
nothing into the mouth but air, and nourisheth nothing in
the body but lungs. Believe me, Eumenides, desire dies in
the same moment that beauty sickens, and beauty fadeth
in the same instant that it flourisheth. When adversities   140
flow, then love ebbs, but friendship standeth stiffly in
storms. Time draweth wrinkles in a fair face but addeth
fresh colours to a fast friend, which neither heat, nor cold,
nor misery, nor place, nor destiny can alter or diminish.
O friendship, of all things the most rare, and therefore   145
most rare because most excellent, whose comforts in
misery is always sweet and whose counsels in prosperity
are ever fortunate! Vain love, that only coming near to
friendship in name, would seem to be the same, or better,
in nature!   150
Eumenides. Father, I allow your reasons and will therefore
conquer mine own. Virtue shall subdue affections, wisdom lust, friendship beauty. Mistresses are in every place,

---

136. Love] *No paragraph as in Dilke; Q introduces a new paragraph
here.*   136. chameleon] *Q (Camelion).*

---

as for example in Richard Edwards's *Damon and Pythias* and in Shakespeare's *TGV*, v.iv.62–83.

136–8. *Love . . . lungs*] The supposed ability of the chameleon to live on
air alone is a commonplace in Renaissance literature (Dent M226) that may
be derived from Bartholomew (Berthelet), 1535, who however points to an
older tradition: 'It is said that the chameleon liveth only by air'
(XVIII.xxi.353). Pliny, VIII.li.122 (LCL, III.86–7), says that the animal sustains
itself without food or drink or anything other than what it gets from the air
('*solus animalium nec cibo nec potu alitur nec alio quam aeris alimento*'). *Euphues*,
I.194, 21–6, uses the chameleon as an emblem of 'shadows without substance', since the chameleon, 'though he have most guts, draweth least
breath' (Bond).

142–3. *Time . . . friend*] Another Renaissance commonplace about love
and friendship, as for instance in Shakespeare's Sonnets 108 and 116 among
many others. Geron's tribute to friendship in this speech owes many of its
ideas ultimately to Aristotle's *Nicomachean Ethics*, Book VIII and IX, esp. VIII.i–
iii, 1155a–1156a (LCL, pp. 450–61).

145–6. *rare . . . rare*] with conscious wordplay on the idea of (*a*) uncommon and (*b*) excellent. See note at I.i.89.

147. *is*] On the use of singular verbs with plural nouns in Elizabethan
English, see I.iii.57 and Abbott 333.

148–50. *Vain . . . nature*] how frivolous of love to trade on the nominal
similarity of *amor* and *amicitia*, and how absurd to claim a higher status in the
nature of things!

and as common as hares in Athos, bees in Hybla, fowls in
the air; but friends to be found are like the phoenix in   155
Arabia, but one, or the philadelphi in Arays, never above
two. I will have Endymion.

> [*He looks into the fountain again.*]

Sacred fountain, in whose bowels are hidden divine secrets, I have increased your waters with the tears of
unspotted thoughts, and therefore let me receive the re-   160
ward you promise. Endymion, the truest friend to me,
and faithfullest lover to Cynthia, is in such a dead sleep
that nothing can wake or move him.

---

154. Athos] *Baker; Atho* / *Q.*   155. phoenix] *Q* (*Phænix*).   157.1. S.D.]
Bond, subst.

---

154. *common*] (*a*) frequently occurring (*b*) vulgar, cheap, whorish, belong-
ing to anyone. See ll. 121–2 above, and compare *Ham.* I.ii.74: 'Ay, madam,
it is common.'

hares . . . Hybla] Lyly couples these allusions also in *Euphues*, I.221, 23–5,
to suggest vast quantity: 'I have not been used to the court of Cupid, wherein
there be more slights than there be hares in Athon, than bees in Hybla, than
stars in heaven.' Lyly's source appears to be Ovid's *Ars Amatoria*, II.517 (LCL,
pp. 100–1): '*Quot lepores in Atho, quot apes pascuntur in Hybla*', 'As many as
the hares that feed on Athos or the bees on Hybla' (Mustard), and III.150
(LCL, pp. 128–9): '*Nec quot apes Hyblae, nec quot in Alpe ferae*' (Bond). Hybla
in Sicily, noted for its honey, is mentioned also in *Euphues*, I.314, 19–20, and
in *Sappho and Phao*, The Prologue at the Court, l. 2. Mount Athos is in
north-eastern Greece, on the Aegean.

155–6. *the phoenix in Arabia*] The phoenix was a type not only of rarity and
reincarnation but also of fidelity in love and friendship, as in Shakespeare's
Phoenix and Turtle and in proverbial lore (Dent F688, P256). Pliny reports of
the phoenix that it is '*unum in toto orbe nec visum magno opere*', 'the only one
in the entire world and scarcely ever seen' (x.ii.3, LCL, III.292–3).

156. *the philadelphi in Arays*] Perhaps Lyly invented this legend as a parallel to that of the phoenix, for no source has been found in Pliny, Aelian, or
Bartholomew (Bertelet). 'The philadelphi' suggests 'loving brothers', from
the Greek, *philadelphos*, 'loving one's sibling', as exemplified by Damon and
Pythias and in other legends. *Arays* has not been located, unless it possibly
points to Araya or Aranjuez in Spain, where Philip II maintained famous
gardens. The paradox of two in one is the central idea of Shakespeare's
Phoenix and Turtle. Donald Edge argues that Lyly's phrase is the equivalent
of *philadelphi ad aras*, 'friendship at the altar (or pillar, in this case a wishing
well)', varying the proverb *amicus usque ad aras*, 'a friend as far as the altar (as
far as conscience permits)' (Dent F690), changing *amicus* to *philadelphi* for
the alliteration with *Phoenix* (Edge, 'A Crux', pp. 439–40).

157. *I will have Endymion*] Eumenides's choice of Endymion over Semele
reflects a medieval and Renaissance commonplace on the primacy of friendship over erotic love; see ll. 148–50 n. above and Introduction, pp. 38–40.

Geron. Dost thou see anything?

Eumenides. I see in the same pillar these words: 'When she,   165
    whose figure of all is the perfectest and never to be
    measured, always one yet never the same, still inconstant
    yet never wavering, shall come and kiss Endymion in his
    sleep, he shall then rise; else, never.' This is strange.

Geron. What see you else?   170

Eumenides. There cometh over mine eyes either a dark mist,
    or upon the fountain a deep thickness, for I can perceive
    nothing. But how am I deluded? Or what difficult, nay,
    impossible, thing is this?

Geron. Methinketh it easy.   175

Eumenides. Good father, and how?

Geron. Is not a circle of all figures the perfectest?

Eumenides. Yes.

Geron. And is not Cynthia of all circles the most absolute?

Eumenides. Yes.   180

Geron. Is it not impossible to measure her, who still worketh
    by her influence, never standing at one stay?

Eumenides. Yes.

Geron. Is she not always Cynthia, yet seldom in the same
    bigness, always wavering in her waxing or waning, that   185

---

165. *the same pillar*] i.e. the 'white marble' of ll. 85–6 on which is engraved,
'Ask one for all, and but one thing in all.'

165–8. *she . . . wavering*] These paradoxes of perfection that cannot be
circumscribed and of inconstant constancy, reflecting medieval and Renaissance commonplaces about *concordia discors*, characterise the moon as the
boundary between heavenly perfection and the impermanence of the
sublunary world; see Introduction, p. 16. Geron explicitly applies these
paradoxes to Cynthia in ll. 177–92.

181. *still*] continually.

182. *influence*] An astrological term connoting 'the supposed flowing or
streaming from the stars or heavens of an etherial fluid acting upon the
character and destinies of men, and affecting sublunary things generally'
(*OED*, sb. 2). See I.i.44 and n.

stay] fixed abode (referring to the heavenly 'houses' of the zodiac; see
previous note).

184. *Is she . . . Cynthia*] Perhaps a reference to Elizabeth's motto, *Semper
eadem*, ever the same. (The feminine ending of '*eadem*' in the Latin has a
resonance here that is untranslatable.)

185–6. *that our . . . governed*] The idea that the moon governs human
health, including eyesight, may be derived from Bartholomew (Bertelet),
VIII.xxx.135, who quotes Ptolemy ('Ptolomeus') as his source (Bond).

our bodies might the better be governed, our seasons the
dailier give their increase, yet never to be removed from
her course as long as the heavens continue theirs?

Eumenides. Yes.

Geron. Then who can it be but Cynthia, whose virtues, being   190
all divine, must needs bring things to pass that be miraculous? Go humble thyself to Cynthia; tell her the success,
of which myself shall be a witness. And this assure thyself:
that she that sent to find means for his safety will now
work her cunning.   195

Eumenides. How fortunate am I, if Cynthia be she that may do
it!

Geron. How fond art thou, if thou do not believe it!

Eumenides. I will hasten thither, that I may entreat on my
knees for succour, and embrace in mine arms my friend.   200

Geron. I will go with thee, for unto Cynthia must I discover all
my sorrows, who also must work in me a contentment.

Eumenides. May I now know the cause?

Geron. That shall be as we walk, and I doubt not but the
strangeness of my tale will take away the tediousness of   205
our journey.

Eumenides. Let us go.

Geron. I follow.   *Exeunt.*

186–7. *our seasons . . . increase*] i.e. the days of our spring season grow
longer day by day as summer approaches (with a suggestion too that our lives
become more fruitful until eventually we wane).

192. *the success*] (*a*) the sequel, upshot, result (*b*) your good fortune at the
well.

195. *cunning*] skill, craft.

201. *discover*] reveal, declare.

207–8. *Let . . . follow*] Compare the endings of I.iv ('Let us go'; 'I follow')
and of III.iii: '*I prae, sequar.*'

Act IV

[*Enter*] TELLUS.

Tellus. I marvel Corsites giveth me so much liberty—all the
world knowing his charge to be so high and his nature to
be most strange, who hath so ill entreated ladies of great
honour that he hath not suffered them to look out of
windows, much less to walk abroad. It may be he is in   5
love with me, for, Endymion, hardhearted Endymion,
excepted, what is he that is not enamoured of my beauty?
But what respectest thou the love of all the world?
Endymion hates thee. Alas, poor Endymion, my malice
hath exceeded my love, and thy faith to Cynthia   10
quenched my affections. Quenched, Tellus? Nay, kindled
them afresh, insomuch that I find scorching flames for
dead embers, and cruel encounters of war in my thoughts
instead of sweet parleys. Ah, that I might once again see
Endymion! Accursed girl, what hope hast thou to see   15
Endymion, on whose head already are grown grey hairs,
and whose life must yield to nature before Cynthia end
her displeasure? Wicked Dipsas, and most devilish
Tellus, the one for cunning too exquisite, the other for
hate too intolerable! Thou wast commanded to weave the   20
stories and poetries wherein were showed both examples
and punishments of tattling tongues, and thou hast only
embroidered the sweet face of Endymion, devices of love,

---

23. embroidered] *Q* (*imbrodered*).

---

2. *his charge . . . high*] his commission (to act as my keeper) to be of such
magnitude.

3. *strange*] distant, reserved (*OED*, 1, 11).

8. *thou*] Tellus herself.

19. *the one . . . exquisite*] Dipsas, consummate in deceitful spells.

20–2. *Thou . . . tongues*] Tellus addresses herself, self-accusingly recollect-
ing how Cynthia has banished her to 'the castle in the desert' and assigned
her the penance of embroidering 'stories or poetries' (i.e. histories or fictions)
intended as moral warnings against 'long tongues' (III.i.41–7).

melancholy imaginations, and what not out of thy work,
that thou shouldst study to pick out of thy mind. But here   25
cometh Corsites. I must seem yielding and stout, full of
mildness yet tempered with a majesty. For if I be too
flexible I shall give him more hope than I mean; if too
froward, enjoy less liberty than I would. Love him I
cannot, and therefore will practise that which is most   30
contrary to our sex, to dissemble.

Enter CORSITES.

Corsites. Fair Tellus, I perceive you rise with the lark, and to
    yourself sing with the nightingale.
Tellus. My lord, I have no playfellow but fancy. Being barred
    of all company, I must question with myself and make my   35
    thoughts my friends.
Corsites. I would you would account my thoughts also your
    friends, for they be such as are only busied in wondering
    at your beauty and wisdom, and some such as have
    esteemed your fortune too hard, and divers of that kind   40
    that offer to set you free if you will set them free.
Tellus. There are no colours so contrary as white and

---

36. friends] *Q* (frindes).   39. beauty and wisdom, and some such] *Q*
(beautie, & wisdome: & some such).

24–6. *melancholy . . . mind*] melancholy fancies, and so on in your embroi-
dery when you should have been endeavouring to extirpate Endymion from
your mind.

25. *study . . . out of*] endeavour to extirpate from.

26. *stout*] proud, arrogant, unyielding. '*Yielding and stout*' is an oxymoron.

29. *froward*] hard to please, ungovernable.

30–1. *that which . . . dissemble*] Tellus jests about women's notorious reputation for dissembling. Bond's emendation of *contrarie* in Q to *customarie* is
unnecessary if Tellus is speaking ironically.

32–3. *you rise . . . nightingale*] Though Tellus rises in proverbial fashion
with the lark (Dent B186), she also stays awake to sing with the nightingale
(compare Dent N182.11). The emblematic contrast of these two birds is a
staple for poets, as in *Rom.*, III.v.1–7.

39–40. *some such . . . kind*] Corsites refers to his *thoughts* (l. 37) that pity
Tellus and are ready to befriend her. Compare *R2*, v.v.9–30.

42–3. *There . . . water*] Tellus trades proverbs in a battle of wits with
Corsites, invoking the proverbial oppositions of black and white (Dent B435,
B438, B440) and of fire and water (Dent F246) to charge men with the same
dissembling that supposedly characterises women (ll. 30–1).

42. *colours*] (*a*) hues (*b*) fair pretences. Compare I.iv.44 and III.iv.55.

black, nor elements so disagreeing as fire and water,
nor anything so opposite as men's thoughts and their
words.   45
Corsites. He that gave Cassandra the gift of prophesying, with
the curse that, spake she never so true, she should never
be believed, hath, I think, poisoned the fortune of men,
that, uttering the extremities of their inward passions, are
always suspected of outward perjuries.   50
Tellus. Well, Corsites, I will flatter myself and believe you.
What would you do to enjoy my love?
Corsites. Set all the ladies of the castle free and make you the
pleasure of my life. More I cannot do; less I will not.
Tellus. These be great words, and fit your calling, for captains   55
must promise things impossible. But will you do one
thing for all?
Corsites. Anything, sweet Tellus, that am ready for all.
Tellus. You know that on the lunary bank sleepeth Endymion.
Corsites. I know it.   60
Tellus. If you will remove him from that place by force and
convey him into some obscure cave by policy, I give you
here the faith of an unspotted virgin that you only shall
possess me as a lover and, in spite of malice, have me for
a wife.   65
Corsites. Remove him, Tellus? Yes, Tellus, he shall be re-

46–8. *He . . . believed*] The story of Apollo's love for the daughter of Priam
and Hecuba, his granting her prophetic knowledge as a gift to win her favour
and then, when she refused to yield to him, his denying her the power to be
believed, was widely available in the Renaissance—in Hyginus's *Fabulae*, 93
and 117 (*Myths*, trans. and ed. Mary Grant, pp. 83 and 98–9), in Virgil's
Aeneid, II.246 (LCL, I.310–11), in Homer's *Iliad*, XIII.366 ff. (LCL, II.28–31), etc.

51. *flatter myself*] deceive myself (to gratify my own vanity by believing, or
pretending to believe, that your praise is genuine).

53. *all . . . castle*] presumably Tellus and her ladies-in-waiting. See l. 87,
'the other ladies'.

55. *fit*] fit for.

56–7. *one thing for all*] Tellus's request ironically recalls the first inscription that Eumenides reads in the fountain: 'Ask one for all, and but one thing
at all' (III.iv.85–6).

58. *that . . . for all*] I who am ready to do anything for you. Corsites plays
on Tellus's 'will you do one thing for all'.

62. *policy*] artfulness, cunning. Compare *policies* at V.i.118.

64. *malice*] malicious gossip.

moved, and that so soon as thou shalt as much commend
my diligence as my force. I go.   [*He starts to leave.*]

Tellus. Stay. Will yourself attempt it?

Corsites. Ay, Tellus. As I would have none partaker of my   70
sweet love, so shall none be partners of my labours. But
I pray thee go at your best leisure, for Cynthia beginneth
to rise, and if she discover our love we both perish, for
nothing pleaseth her but the fairness of virginity. All
things must be not only without lust but without suspi-   75
cion of lightness.

Tellus. I will depart, and go you to Endymion.

Corsites. I fly, Tellus, being of all men the most fortunate.

                                                                Exit.

Tellus. Simple Corsites! I have set thee about a task, being but
a man, that the gods themselves cannot perform. For   80
little dost thou know how heavy his head lies, how hard
his fortune. But such shifts must women have to deceive
men, and, under colour of things easy, entreat that which
is impossible. Otherwise we should be cumbered with
importunities, oaths, sighs, letters, and all implements of   85
love, which, to one resolved to the contrary, are most
loathsome. I will in and laugh with the other ladies at
Corsites' sweating.   *Exit.*

---

68. s.d.] *This ed.*

---

72. *go . . . leisure*] Corsites may simply mean that she is free to go where
she likes at his 'castle in the desert' while he attempts to move Endymion at
her behest; she offers to 'depart' from him, l. 77, in the sense of leaving him
to his devices. At l. 87 she resolves to go 'in' and share with 'the other
ladies'—presumably her retinue—a scornful laugh at Corsites. She has already commented at ll. 1–6 on the large degree of 'liberty' Corsites has given
her in her royal confinement (which is not unlike that provided for Mary
Queen of Scots).

72–3. *Cynthia . . . rise*] (*a*) the queen awakes, or, possibly, rises from table
(*b*) the moon rises, signifying nighttime.

74. *nothing . . . virginity*] A flattering remark presumably intended for
Queen Elizabeth, as in *Gallathea*, III.iv.1–12 and 16–53, in which Diana
deplores unchasteness in her 'nymphs', with a seeming allusion to Elizabeth's jealousy about marriages involving persons in her entourage (Bond).

76. *lightness*] wantonness, levity.

Actus Quartus, Scaena Secunda

[Enter] SAMIAS *[and]* DARES.

Samias. Will thy master never awake?

Dares. No, I think he sleeps for a wager. But how shall we
    spend the time? Sir Tophas is so far in love that he pineth
    in his bed and cometh not abroad.

Samias. But here cometh Epi, in a pelting chafe.   5

[Enter] EPITON.

Epiton. A pox of all false proverbs! And, were a proverb a
    page, I would have him by the ears.

Samias. Why art thou angry?

Epiton. Why? You know it is said, the tide tarrieth no man.

Samias. True.   10

Epiton. A monstrous lie; for I was tied two hours, and tarried
    for one to unloose me.

Dares. Alas, poor Epi!

---

4. abroad.] *Q* (abroade?).   5.1. s.d. *[Enter]* EPITON] *Placement as in Baker;
grouped with other names at the head of the scene in Q.*   6. proverbs! And,
were] *This ed.*; Prouerbes, and were *Q.*   9. tide] *Q* (tyde).   11. tied] *Q*
(tide).   12. unloose] *Q* (vnlose).

---

5. *a pelting chafe*] a pet, a childish rage. *Pelting*, 'paltry, petty, worthless', is
appropriate both to Epiton's diminutive size (as Bond points out) and to a
tempest in a teacup.

6. *A pox*] An exclamation of irritation or impatience, meaning, in effect, 'A
plague'.

And, were] Perhaps this should read *An were*, 'were'.

7. *have . . . ears*] attack him, fight with him. To set combatants together
'by the ears', i.e. to put them at variance, is a proverb (Dent E23), usually
applied to two contestants. Epiton may mean simply that he intends to grab
any proverb by the ears as a teacher might grab a refractory pupil, or else
plans to deliver a box on the ears.

9. *the . . . man*] Epiton presumably chooses this well-known proverb
(Dent T323, *Euphues*, II.185, 35) for the wordplay it provides on *tide*. See next
note.

11. *tied*] A favourite outlandish pun on *tide* (l. 9), as in *TGV*, II.iii.35–40:
'PANTHINO. You'll lose the tide if you tarry any longer. LANCE. It is no matter
if the tied were lost, for it is the unkindest tied that ever any man tied', etc.
Evidently Epiton, who went with Samias and Dares at the end of III.iii to have
sport in witnessing Sir Tophas with Dipsas, has been detained by his master
and scolded for failing to help Tophas fall into a prolonged sleep like
Endymion's.

Epiton. Poor? No, no, you base-conceited slaves, I am a most
   complete gentlemen, although I be in disgrace with Sir   15
   Tophas.
Dares. Art thou out with him?
Epiton. Ay, because I cannot get him a lodging with
   Endymion. He would fain take a nap for forty or fifty
   years.   20
Dares. A short sleep, considering our long life.
Samias. Is he still in love?
Epiton. In love? Why, he doth nothing but make sonnets.
Samias. Canst thou remember any one of his poems?
Epiton. Ay, this is one: 25
      The beggar Love that knows not where to lodge,
      At last within my heart when I slept,
         He crept.
      I waked, and so my fancies began to fodge.
Samias. That's a very long verse.   30
Epiton. Why, the other was short. The first is called from the

---

14. base-conceited] *Q* (*base conceited*).   26–9. The beggar . . . fodge]
Verse lineation as in Fairholt; first arranged as verse, Dilke.

---

14. *Poor?*] Epiton plays on the word. Dares meant only 'deserving of pity',
but Epiton takes it in the sense of 'poor-spirited' and 'impoverished'.
   base-conceited] base-minded, thinking low thoughts.
   15. *complete*] accomplished, perfect.
   17. *out*] out of favour.
   21. *A short sleep*] Dares speaks ironically; he and his fellows have not lived
a half of forty or fifty years.
   29. *fodge*] fadge, suit, fit in, fit together; or, possibly, 'trudge', though *OED*
gives a first date for *fadge* in this sense in 1658. With this desperate word
choice, and the chime of 'slept' and 'crept', Lyly parodies bad sonneteering
and verse writing in his day.
   30–1. *That's . . . short*] Samias and Epiton amusedly explain the length of
the poem's last line by pointing to the shortness of the preceding one.
Compare Rosalind's objecting to the verses by Orlando that Celia has found
posted on a tree: 'some of them had in them more feet than the verses would
bear' (*AYLI*, III.ii.163–4). The metrical irregularity of Tophas's verse, especially in length of lines, continues to amuse the pages. Donald Edge sees
a parody here of the controversy over quantitative Latin verse, advocated by
Lyly's enemy Gabriel Harvey. Ovid too comments on his own use of elegaics
in *Amores*, I.i.1–30 (esp. 3–4), II.xvii.21–2, III.i.5–68 (esp. 5–8, 35–8, 66),
III.xii.19–20 (LCL, pp. 318–21, 434–5, 444–9, 500–1), and *Heroides*, xv.5–8
(LCL, pp. 180–1; Edge, 'Prosody', pp. 178–9).
   31–3. *The first . . . elbow*] Epiton continues to joke about the absurd un-
evenness of length in Tophas's verses by measuring them literally. The

thumb to the little finger, the second from the little finger
to the elbow, and some he hath made to reach to the
crown of his head and down again to the sole of his foot.
It is set to the tune of the Black Saunce, *ratio est*, because   35
Dipsas is a black saint.

Dares. Very wisely. But pray thee, Epi, how art thou complete? And, being from thy master, what occupation wilt
thou take?

Epiton. Know, my hearts, I am an absolute microcosmos, a   40
petty world of myself. My library is my head, for I have no
other books but my brains; my wardrobe on my back, for
I have no more apparel than is on my body; my armoury

---

34. sole] *Q* (soule). 40. Know, my] *Baker;* No my *Q.*
40. microcosmos] *Q* (Microcosmus). 42. wardrobe] *Q* (wardrope).

---

distance from the outstretched thumb to the tip of the little finger is a span
(*OED*, sb.[1] 1); from the tip of the little finger to the elbow is an ell (Latin
ulna, OE *eln* = forearm), sometimes reckoned as two spans. *Span* is a term
of physical measurement and of metrics (Edge, 'Prosody', pp. 178–9).

33–4. *the crown . . . foot*] A commonplace expression of a measure from
top to bottom or start to finish (Dent c864). A distance of about eight spans;
see previous note.

35. *Black Saunce*] Black Sanctus, a parodic hymn to Satan in ridicule of
the monks. The term was sometimes used of any discord of harsh sounds or
profane ditty such as might be used to serenade a faithless wife (*OED*,
sanctus, 3). Here, Epiton makes a more literal application, since Dipsas is a
sorceress and hence the antithesis of a saint—a black saint (l. 36). Bond
quotes, from Nashe's *Have With You to Saffron Walden*, a recollection of
Lyly's animosity towards Gabriel Harvey: 'With a black sant he means
shortly to be at his chamber window for calling him the fiddlestick of Oxford'
(ed. McKerrow, III.138). See n. 30–1 above on Lyly and Harvey.

ratio est] with good reason, the reason is. A formal statement in a dispu-
tation, like *sic probo, nego argumentum*, etc.

37–8. *how art thou complete?*] Dares challenges Epiton's claim in l. 15 of
being a 'complete gentleman' by asking how he intends to survive now that
Tophas has sent him away.

41. *of*] unto.

42. *my wardrobe on my back*] A proverbial sign of poverty (Dent w61), as
with Christopher Sly's having 'no more doublets than backs' etc. (*Shr.*,
Induction ii.8–9).

43–4. *my armoury . . . nails*] the only weapons I need to fight with are my
nails. The conventional phrase *at one's fingers' ends* denotes having something
within one's convenient grasp (Dent F245); here it is also comically literal, for
Epiton's fingernails are indeed at his fingers' ends.

at my fingers' ends, for I use no other artillery than my
nails; my treasure in my purse. *Sic omnia mea mecum porto.*   45

Dares. Good.

Epiton. Now, sirs, my palace is paved with grass and tiled with
stars; for *caelo tegitur qui non habet urnam*, he that hath no
house must lie in the yard.

Samias. A brave resolution. But how wilt thou spend thy   50
time?

Epiton. Not in any melancholy sort. For mine exercise I will
walk horses.

Dares. Too bad.

Epiton. Why, is it not said, 'It is good walking when one hath   55
his horse in his hand'?

Samias. Worse and worse. But how wilt thou live?

Epiton. By angling. O,'tis a stately occupation to stand four
hours in a cold morning and to have his nose bitten with
frost before his bait be mumbled with a fish.   60

---

44. fingers'] *Q* (fingers).   47. Now] *Q; Know Baker.*   48. *caelo*] *Q*
(*celo*).

---

45. *Sic . . . porto*] The motto of the snail: Thus I carry with me all that I
have. From Cicero, *Paradoxa Stoicorum*, I.4–5, 'nam omnia mecum porto mea'
(ed. Michele V. Ronnick (Frankfurt: Peter Lang), 1991), p. 108, and ascribed
by Cicero to Bias. Compare Phaedrus, *Fabularum Aesopiarum*, IV.21 (numbered 22 or 23 in some editions), '*De Simonide*', in which Simonides is asked,
'Do you need nothing?' and he replies, 'All that I have is here with me'
('*Mecum . . . mea sunt cuncta*', LCL, pp. 338–9, *The Fables of Phaedrus*, trans. P.
F. Widdows (Austin: University of Texas Press, 1992), p. 111; see Baker).

48. caelo . . . urnam] he who has no burial urn is sheltered by the heavens.
From Lucan, *Pharsalia*, VII.819 (LCL, I–X, 428–9), but Bond speculates that
Lyly had recourse to some collection of *Sententiae*. In any event the idea had
become proverbial: 'Heaven covereth him that hath no burial' (Kyd, *Spanish
Tragedy*, III.xiii.19; Dent H347.11). Epiton goes on to quote a closely related
proverb: 'He that has no house must lie in the yard' (Dent H760).

54. *Too bad*] i.e. not a very good joke. Compare 'Worse and worse' in l. 57.

55–6. *It is . . . hand*] Epiton deliberately uses a proverb (Dent W10, 'It is
good walking with a horse in one's hand') out of context. The proverb
deals with the idea of being safe and prosperous, not of being in need of
employment.

58. *angling*] (*a*) fishing (*b*) using wily and artful means to catch something
or someone.

stately] (*a*) noble (*b*) stationary.

60. *mumbled with a fish*] bitten on with toothless gums by a fish.

Dares. A rare attempt. But wilt thou never travel?

Epiton. Yes, in a western barge, when, with a good wind and
    lusty pugs, one may go ten miles in two days.

Samias. Thou art excellent at thy choice. But what pastime
    wilt thou use? None?   65

Epiton. Yes, the quickest of all.

Samias. What, dice?

Epiton. No. When I am in haste, one-and-twenty games at
    chess to pass a few minutes.

Dares. A life for a little lord, and full of quickness.   70

Epiton. Tush, let me alone. But I must needs see if I can find
    where Endymion lieth, and then go to a certain fountain
    hard by, where they say faithful lovers shall have all things
    they will ask. If I can find out any of these, *ego et magister*
    meus erimus in tuto, I and my master shall be friends. He   75

---

68. one-and-twenty] *Q (*xxj.*).*

---

61. *A rare attempt*] (*a*) a noble enterprise (*b*) something to be undertaken
as seldom as possible.

travel] See note at I.iv.2.

62. *a western barge*] i.e. one travelling westward on the Thames, as in
'Westward, ho!' Travelling west was slow work, pulling against the flow of
the river. All of Epiton's imagined adventures turn anticlimactically to attempts at part-time gainful employment: walking horses for exercise, fishing
on a cold morning, operating a barge on the Thames, playing games of
chance (perhaps in order to gamble on the outcome). Thames barges were
evidently known for their slow movement to westward, as in Thomas
Nashe's *Epistle* preceding *Astrophel and Stella* (1591): 'Indeed, to say the
truth, my style is somewhat heavy-gaited ... Only I can keep pace with
Gravesend barge' (ed. McKerrow, III.332; Baker).

63. *lusty pugs*] strong bargemen (*OED*, sb.[1] 3, citing this passage as its
earliest example). More generally, *pug* is a term of endearment for a good
fellow or a whore, or an impish companion, a Puck.

66. *quickest*] (*a*) liveliest (*b*) soonest played. Epiton thus sets up his feeble
jest about playing twenty-one games of chess, a notoriously time-consuming
game, in a few minutes.

70. *quickness*] (*a*) vitality (*b*) keeping a sharp eye out for an opportunity.

71. *let me alone*] i.e. don't worry about me, leave me to fend for myself.
(Also at l.81; compare l. 99.)

74–5. ego ... tuto] I and my master will be in a safe place. (Cardinal
Wolsey was accused of arrogance because he wrote *ego et rex meus*, putting his
name before that of the king, though in fact the Latin construction requires
'ego' to precede any nouns parallel with it; see *Henry VIII*, III.ii.315.)

is resolved to weep some three or four pailfuls to avoid
the rheum of love that wambleth in his stomach.

Enter the watch [two WATCHMEN *and the* CONSTABLE].

Samias. Shall we never see thy master, Dares?

Dares. Yes, let us go now, for tomorrow Cynthia will be there.

Epiton. I will go with you. But how shall we see for the watch?   80

Samias. Tush, let me alone. I'll begin to them.—Masters,
    God speed you.

First Watchman. Sir boy, we are all sped already.

Epiton. [*Aside to Samias and Dares*] So methinks, for they
    smell all of drink like a beggar's beard.   85

Dares. But I pray, sirs, may we see Endymion?

Second Watchman. No, we are commanded in Cynthia's
    name that no man shall see him.

Samias. No man? Why, we are but boys.

---

77. rheum] *Q (*rume*).*   77.1. S.D. two WATCHMEN *and the* CONSTABLE]
Baker, subst.   84. S.D.] *Baker, subst.*

76–7. *to avoid . . . wambleth*] Love is a *rheum* because it produces watery
discharges, especially tears, and is a contagious affliction. Absurdly adopting
the theory of humours to his condition, Tophas hopes to cure his love
melancholy by voiding (*avoiding*) through tears the excess fluid that *wambleth*
or rolls about nauseatingly in his digestive system.

77.1. *Enter the watch*] This is the guard set by Cynthia to watch over the
sleeping Endymion, as we learn at ll. 87–8 and IV.iii.9–10; see also III.i.60–3.
The men stand near the place where Endymion has been sleeping since the
end of Act II, quite possibly curtained off from view, until the pages approach them at ll. 78 ff. of the present scene, in a stage movement signifying
metonymically their journey to the place 'where Endymion lieth', 'hard by'
to 'a certain fountain' (ll. 72–3).

80. *for the watch*] considering that the watch will attempt to prevent our
seeing or approaching Endymion.

81. *Masters*] Said to persons of inferior social rank. The First Watchmen
replies in l. 83 with an oxymoronic mock title for the page: 'Sir boy'.

83. *sped*] done for, as in *Shr.*, v.ii.189: 'We three are married, but you two
are sped.' The First Watchman plays sardonically on Samias's conventional
greeting, 'God speed you' (i.e. God prosper you), by answering, in effect,
'We've had it.' Epiton, borrowing a proverbial phrase ('Drunk as a beggar',
Dent B225), responds *sotto voce* in ll. 84–5 with a quip that puts yet another
spin on *sped*: the watchmen are far gone in drink.

89. *we are but boys*] Samias quibbles on *no man* in l. 88: (*a*) no one (*b*) no
adult male. Quibbling of this sort appeals at once to the First Watchman's
experience as a drinking man (ll. 90–3). His comic analogy is reinforced by
the fact that 'pint-pot' and 'half-pint' are common ways of referring to young
lads. The joke is fitting for juvenile actors.

First Watchman. [*To his fellow watchmen*] Mass, neighbours,   90
    he says true. For if I swear I will never drink my liquor by
    the quart, and yet call for two pints, I think with a safe
    conscience I may carouse both.
Dares. [*Aside to Samias and Epiton*] Pithily, and to the pur-
    pose.   95
Second Watchman. [*To his fellow watchmen*] Tush, tush, neigh-
    bours, take me with you.
Samias. [*Aside to Dares and Epiton*] This will grow hot.
Dares. [*Aside to Samias and Epiton*] Let them alone.
Second Watchman. [*To his fellow watchmen*] If I say to my wife,   100
    'Wife, I will have no raisins in my pudding', she puts in
    currants. Small raisins are raisins, and boys are men.
    Even as my wife should have put no raisins in my pud-
    ding, so shall there no boys see Endymion.
Dares. [*Aside*] Learnedly.   105
Epiton. Let Master Constable speak; I think he is the wisest
    among you.
Constable. You know, neighbours, 'tis an old said saw, 'Chil-
    dren and fools speak true.'

90, 94, 96, 100, 105. S.D.]   *This ed.*   98, 99. S.D.]   *Baker, subst.*
102. currants. Small raisins are raisins] *Q* (Corance, smal Reysons are
Reysons*)*.   108, 111, 114. S.P. *Constable*] *Q* (*Ma. Const.*).   108. an]
Blount; an an *Q*.   108–9. 'Children . . . true'] *Q* (children . . . true*)*.

    90. *Mass*] by the Mass.
    93. *carouse*] drink off, swill.
    94–5. *Pithily . . . purpose*] As at III.iii.68, this phrase expresses the pages'
ironic view that the analogy just offered by the First Watchman is anything
but pithy and to the purpose. 'Learnedly' at l. 105 has the same ironic effect.
Between them, the two watchmen demonstrate how argument by analogy
can prove that boys are not men (pints are not quarts) or that boys are men
(small raisins are still raisins).
    97. *take me with you*] let me be part of this, let me be sure I understand
you. Compare Capulet in *Rom.*, III.v.141: 'Soft, take me with you, take me
with you, wife.'
    98. *This will grow hot*] we're going to have a heated argument.
    106–7. *he . . . you*] Epiton's irony plays on the proverb, 'You might be a
constable for your wit' (Dent c616), as does *Ado*, III.v.32–41 and *The
Changeling*, I.ii.125–6: 'I'll undertake to wind him up to the wit of constable'
(Revels edition, giving still further citations).
    108. *said saw*] commonly repeated proverb (or, perhaps, 'serious prov-
erb'). For the proverb itself, see Dent c328.

All. True.   110

Constable. Well, there you see the men be the fools, because it
　　is provided from the children.

Dares. Good.

Constable. Then say I, neighbours, that children must not see
　　Endymion, because children and fools speak true.   115

Epiton. O, wicked application!

Samias. Scurvily brought about.

First Watchman. Nay, he says true; and therefore till Cynthia
　　have been here he shall not be uncovered. Therefore
　　away.   120

Dares. [*Aside to Samias and Epiton*] A watch, quoth you? A
　　man may watch seven years for a wise word and yet go
　　without it. Their wits are all as rusty as their bills.—But
　　come on, Master Constable, shall we have a song before
　　we go?   125

Constable. With all my heart.

　　　　　　　　　　　　Song.

Watch.　　　　Stand. Who goes there?

110. S.P. *All*] *Dilke; All say. / Q.*　121. S.D.] *Bond.*　122. seven] *Q (7.).*
124. Master Constable,] *Q (Ma. Const.)*　127–48. *Watch.* Stand . . . to
bed] *Blount; not in Q. The song is labelled 'The Second Song' in Blount.*

───────────────────────────

　　110. All. *True*] The Q rendition, '*All say. True.*', underscores the joke: by
speaking 'True', the watchmen put themselves in the proverbial category of
children and fools (Bond).

　　111–12. *Well . . . children*] Having enticed the watchmen into proclaiming
themselves fools, the Constable proceeds with his inversion of folly and
wisdom; the folly provided by children becomes the property of the grown
men. That being the case, the overly wise and clever children must not be
allowed to outwit the watch and get to see Endymion (ll. 114–15). Q.E.D.

　　116. *application*] bringing a fable or proverb to bear on present circumstances. The term often suggests the disclosing of covert allegorical meaning,
especially in a political context. Compare *apply* in the Prologue, ll. 7–8, and
note.

　　119. *shall not be uncovered*] The phrase indicates that Endymion, asleep
since the end of Act II, is partly or wholly concealed, and yet Corsites must
be able to find him in the next scene and attempt to lift him. If Endymion is
to be curtained off, the effect is easily produced in the theatre.

　　121. *quoth you?*] i.e. is that what you call yourselves, forsooth?

　　122. *seven years*] the length of an apprenticeship, or simply a very long
time; see notes at II.i.16 and III.iv.55–6. See Dent Y25.

　　123. *bills*] long-handled halberds terminating in a spike, an axe, and a
spear-head. Often brown from rust or paint, as at l. 146.

　　127–48. *Stand . . . bed*] The song is from Blount's 1632 edition, as at
III.iii.119–37. Presumably adult singers (the Constable and watch) join with

                      We charge you appear
                      'Fore our constable here.
               In the name of the Man in the Moon,   130
                      To us billmen relate
                      Why you stagger so late,
               And how you come drunk so soon.
Pages.   What are ye, scabs?
Watch.   The watch;
                      This is the constable.
Pages.   A patch.   135
Constable. Knock 'em down unless they all stand.
                      If any run away,
                      'Tis the old watchman's play
               To reach him a bill of his hand.
Pages.   O gentlemen, hold.   140
                      Your gowns freeze with cold,
               And your rotten teeth dance in your head.
Epiton.   Wine nothing shall cost ye,
Samias.   Nor huge fires to roast ye.
Dares.   Then soberly let us be led.   145
Constable.   Come, my brown bills, we'll roar,
                      Bounce loud at tavern door,
Omnes.   And i'th'morning steal all to bed.   Exeunt.

---

juvenile choristers; see Introduction, pp. 57–9. This is an exit-song and a
drinking song, of a type familiar in morality plays of the mid century. *Stand*
means 'halt', as also at l. 136.

   131. *billmen*] nightwatchmen armed with bills, long-handled weapons terminating in a blade or axe and spear.

   134. *scabs*] scoundrels, 'scurvy' fellows.

   135. *A patch*] a fool.

   138. *play*] ploy, role, trick.

   139. *reach . . . hand*] detain him with a halberd (with perhaps a play on the
idea of handing over a handwritten bill).

   141. *gowns*] long garments supplied to the watch as uniforms.

   142. *dance in your head*] chatter with cold.

   143–4. *Wine . . . roast ye*] The pages offer to stand the watch to a round of
drinks in a warm tavern, perhaps to lure them off duty; they are not present
in the next scene when Corsites approaches the sleeping Endymion.

   145. *soberly*] quietly, gravely; but with paradoxical wordplay in anticipation of all the drinking that will take place.

   146. *bills*] watchmen armed with long-handled, rust-coloured weapons;
see n. 131.

   roar] revel boisterously, carouse.

   147. *Bounce*] knock loudly.

Actus Quartus, Scaena Tertia

[*Enter*] CORSITES *solus.* [*Endymion lies asleep on the lunary bank.*]

Corsites. I am come in sight of the lunary bank. Without doubt
  Tellus doteth upon me; and cunningly, that I might not
  perceive her love, she hath set me to a task that is done
  before it is begun. Endymion, you must change your
  pillow, and, if you be not weary of sleep, I will carry you   5
  where at ease you shall sleep your fill. It were good that
  without more ceremonies I took him, lest, being espied, I
  be entrapped and so incur the displeasure of Cynthia,
  who commonly setteth watch that Endymion have no
  wrong.   *He lifts.*   10
    What now, is your mastership so heavy? Or are you
  nailed to the ground? Not stir one whit?—Then use all
  thy force, though he feel it and wake.—What, stone still?
  Turned, I think, to earth, with lying so long on the earth.
  Didst not thou, Corsites, before Cynthia pull up a tree   15
  that forty years was fastened with roots and wreathed in
  knots to the ground? Didst not thou with main force pull
  open the iron gates which no ram or engine could move?
  Have my weak thoughts made brawnfallen my strong
  arms? Or is it the nature of love or the quintessence of the 20
  mind to breed numbness, or litherness, or I know not

0.1. S.D. *Endymion . . . bank*] *Baker.*   7. lest] *Q (*least*).*

  0.1. Endymion . . . bank] If the sleeping Endymion has been curtained off
from view since the end of II.iii, when he was left asleep by Dipsas and Bagoa
(see IV.ii.119 and note), he must now be 'discovered' again to view. The
nearby tree (see V.i.57–8 and note, and V.iii.15–16) is alleged to be old by
now, for Endymion has now aged (see ll. 158–63), and with apparent
symbolic fitness Corsites speaks here of uprooting a forty-year-old tree in
Cynthia's presence (ll. 15–17).
  9. *commonly*] Corsites notes to his delight that the watch, normally there,
is absent. See IV.ii.143–4, note.
  11. *is your mastership*] are you. See IV.ii.81, note.
  13. *stone still*] a proverbial phrase (Dent S879.1).
  19. *brawnfallen*] shrunken in flesh, thin, skinny, unnerved, as in *Euphues*,
I.307, 29–30: 'Milo, that great wrestler, began to weep when he saw his arms
brawnfallen and weak.'
  20–1. *Or is it . . . numbness*] Corsites wonders if the lassitude of lovesickness is inherent in the nature of love or is bred in the mind.
  21. *litherness*] languor, listlessness, as in *Euphues*, II.50, 30–1: 'they that
angle for the tortoise, having once caught him, are driven into such a
litherness that they lose all their sprightes, being benumbed'.

what languishing in my joints and sinews, being but the
base strings of my body? Or doth the remembrance of
Tellus so refine my spirits into a matter so subtle and
divine that the other fleshy parts cannot work whilst they   25
muse? Rest thyself, rest thyself; nay, rend thyself in
pieces, Corsites, and strive, in spite of love, fortune, and
nature, to lift up this dulled body, heavier than dead and
more senseless than death.

Enter FAIRIES.

But what are these so fair fiends that cause my hairs to   30
stand upright and spirits to fall down? Hags—out, alas!
Nymphs, I crave pardon. Ay me, out! What do I here?
              The fairies dance, and with a song
              pinch him, and he falleth asleep.

                        [*Song.*]

All.   Pinch him, pinch him, black and blue.

22. what languishing] *Dilke;* what, languishing *Q.*   26. rend] *Q* (rent).
31–2. Hags—out, alas! Nymphs, I crave pardon. Ay me, out! What do I
here?] *Q* (hags, out alas, Nymphes I craue pardon. Aye me, out what doe I
heere.).   33–45. [*Song. All.* Pinch him . . . hay-de-guise] *Blount; not in Q.*
The song is labelled 'The Third Song by Fairies' in Blount.   33. S.P.] *All*]
Blount (Omnes).

23. *base strings*] (*a*) the basest, lowest, most purely physical part of the
body's structure (*b*) bass strings on a musical instrument.
    25. *they*] the 'refined spirits'.
    28. *heavier than dead*] The phrase suggests 'heavier than lead' (cf. Dent
L134), and 'deade' in Q may simply represent the compositor's anticipation
of 'death' at the end of the sentence, but conceivably Lyly intends some kind
of wordplay, the phrase meaning 'heavier than as if dead'. *Dulled* suggests (*a*)
'as dull as lead' (Dent L133.1) and (*b*) rendered insensible (*OED, dull,* a. 2).
Lyly may have had in mind old Aeson's body, lying heavily like one dead
('*exanimi similem*') as Medea prepares to restore his youth (Ovid, *Metamorphoses,* VII.254, LCL, I.360–1; Edge, 'Sources', pp. 179–80).
    29. *senseless*] (*a*) deprived of sensation, unconscious (playing on *dulled,*
'rendered insensible') (*b*) meaningless.
    32. *Nymphs*] Corsites instantly regrets having called these powerful spirits
'Hags' (i.e. witches, as in *Euphues,* I.255, 3, and in *Mac.,* IV.1.48: 'How now,
you secret, black, and midnight hags?'), and tries to atone with a euphemism—a common stratagem, as in calling the Furies 'Eumenides' or Puck
'Robin Goodfellow'. The fairies are already pinching him.
    33. *Pinch him*] A torment commonly inflicted by fairies as a punishment
for illicit sensual desire, as in *Wiv.,* V.v.44–102. Bond prints a song from *Old*

Saucy mortals must not view
What the Queen of Stars is doing,   35
Nor pry into our fairy wooing.

First Fairy.   Pinch him blue
Second Fairy.   And pinch him black.
Third Fairy.   Let him not lack
Sharp nails to pinch him blue and red,   40
Till sleep has rocked his addle head.

Fourth Fairy. For the trespass he hath done,
Spots o'er all his flesh shall run.
Kiss Endymion, kiss his eyes;
Then to our midnight hay-de-guise.   45

They kiss Endymion and depart[,
leaving him and the spotted Corsites asleep].

---

45. hay-de-guise] *Blount (Heidegyes).*   45.1. S.D. *They kiss Endymion and
depart] Placement, this ed.; placed before the song, at the end of the s.d. at 32.1–
2, in Blount.*   45.2. S.D. *leaving him . . . asleep] This ed.;* CORSITES *sleeping /
Dilke*   45.4. S.D. GYPTES] *Gyptes, Corsites / Q.*

Ballads, Historical and Narrative, ed. Thomas Evans (London, 1810), I.145,
corresponding closely to the present song; in that song, fairies bid each other
'Pinch him black, and pinch him blue, / That seeks to steal a lover true.' The
version in this play differs, however, in specifically mentioning Endymion
and in poking fun at Corsites's spots, suggesting that Lyly wrote this song for
or at least adapted it to his dramatic text. See Dent, B160, for other uses of
the proverbial phrase, 'to beat (pinch) one black and blue'.

41. *addle*] empty, vain, confused, muddled, like the contents of a decom-
posing egg.

43. *Spots*] The fairies may actually paint Corsites with spots in their dance,
as happens to the protagonist of John Redford's *Wit and Science* (1531–47)
while he lies asleep in the lap of Idleness. There the spots betoken Wit's
ignorance; here they are signs of Corsites's trespass against Cynthia and his
sensual infatuation with Tellus. See ll. 125–6, where Cynthia speaks of
wantonness as deserving such a change in appearance.

45. *hay-de-guise*] a country dance, presumably a kind of *hay* or reel dance,
though the etymology is uncertain. It is mentioned by John Skelton, 'Against
Venomous Tongues' (*The Complete Poems of John Skelton, Laureate*, ed.
Philip Henderson (London: Dent, 1959), p. 247); by Spenser, *Shepheardes
Calendar*, June, ll. 25–7 ('But friendly Faeries . . . can chace the lingring
Night / With Heydeguyes, and trimly trodden traces'); by Michael Drayton,
Polyolbion, The Argument to the Fifth Song (ed. Hebel, IV.97), and elsewhere
(*OED, hay*, sb.⁴ 2).

[*Enter*] CYNTHIA, FLOSCULA, SEMELE, PANELION,
ZONTES, PYTHAGORAS, [*and*] GYPTES.

Cynthia. You see, Pythagoras, what ridiculous opinions you
hold, and I doubt not but you are now of another mind.

Pythagoras. Madam, I plainly perceive that the perfection of
your brightness hath pierced through the thickness that
covered my mind, insomuch that I am no less glad to be   50
reformed than ashamed to remember my grossness.

Gyptes. They are thrice fortunate that live in your palace,
where truth is not in colours but life, virtues not in
imagination but execution.

Cynthia. I have always studied to have rather living virtues   55
than painted gods, the body of truth than the tomb. But
let us walk to Endymion; it may be it lieth in your arts to
deliver him. As for Eumenides, I fear he is dead.

Pythagoras. I have alleged all the natural reasons I can for
such a long sleep.   60

Gyptes. I can do nothing till I see him.

Cynthia. Come, Floscula, I am sure you are glad that you
shall behold Endymion.

Floscula. I were blessed if I might have him recovered.

Cynthia. Are you in love with his person?   65

Floscula. No, but with his virtue.

Cynthia. What say you, Semele?

Semele. Madam, I dare say nothing for fear I offend.

Cynthia. Belike you cannot speak except you be spiteful. But

46–54.] In *Campaspe*, Diogenes presents an effectively contrastive point of
view to that of Alexander, casting doubt on the idea of monarch as philosopher; here, the criticism has all but disappeared.

53. *in colours*] in feigned imagination or specious appearance (*OED*, *colour*,
sb. II and 12).

57. *let us walk*] Cynthia and the rest move across the playing area to
represent their going from Cynthia's palace to Endymion's lunary bank,
where he has remained visible to the audience but unseen by these new
arrivals until l. 77; Gyptes says, at l. 61, 'I can do nothing till I see him.' See
Introduction, pp. 50–4.

58. *deliver*] release.

59. *alleged*] cited (*OED*, 2).

69. *except you be*] without being (*OED*, *except*, conj. C2).

as good be silent as saucy. Panelion, what punishment   70
were fit for Semele, in whose speech and thoughts is only
contempt and sourness?

Panelion. I love not, madam, to give any judgement. Yet sith
Your Highness commandeth: I think, to commit her
tongue close prisoner to her mouth.   75

Cynthia. Agreed. Semele, if thou speak this twelvemonth,
thou shalt forfeit thy tongue.—Behold Endymion. Alas,
poor gentleman, hast thou spent thy youth in sleep, that
once vowed all to my service? Hollow eyes? Grey hairs?
Wrinkled cheeks? And decayed limbs? Is it destiny or   80
deceit that hath brought this to pass? If the first, who
could prevent thy wretched stars? If the latter, I would I
might know thy cruel enemy. I favoured thee, Endymion,
for thy honour, thy virtues, thy affections; but to bring thy
thoughts within the compass of thy fortunes, I have   85
seemed strange, that I might have thee stayed. And now
are thy days ended before my favour begin. But whom
have we here? Is it not Corsites?

Zontes. It is, but more like a leopard than a man.

Cynthia. Awake him.   [*Corsites is awakened.*]   90
How now, Corsites, what make you here? How came you
deformed? Look on thy hands, and then thou seest the
picture of thy face.

Corsites. Miserable wretch, and accursed! How am I deluded?
Madam, I ask pardon for my offence, and you see my   95
fortune deserveth pity.

Cynthia. Speak on. Thy offence cannot deserve greater pun-

---

73. s.p. *Panelion*] Q *(Pane.)*.   86. stayed] Q *(staied)*.   90. s.d.] *This ed.;*
Zontes awakens Corsites / Baker.

70. *as good . . . saucy*] A proverbial bit of advice (Dent s448).

73. *sith*] since.

84. *but*] only (with a resonance also of the more normal adversative
meaning).

86. *strange*] distant, reserved—the 'strange humour' of suspiciousness
lamented by Endymion in II.i.30–3 and II.iii.3.

stayed] (*a*) prevented from too great familiarity, brought emotionally under control (*b*) supported, sustained (*OED*, *stay*, v.¹ 28 and v.² 1). Compare
I.i.3.

91. *make*] do.

ishment; but see thou rehearse the truth, else shalt thou
not find me as thou wishest me.

Corsites. Madam, as it is no offence to be in love, being a man	100
mortal, so I hope can it be no shame to tell with whom,
my lady being heavenly. Your Majesty committed to my
charge fair Tellus, whose beauty in the same moment
took my heart captive that I undertook to carry her body
prisoner. Since that time have I found such combats in	105
my thoughts between love and duty, reverence and affection, that I could neither endure the conflict nor hope for
the conquest.

Cynthia. In love? A thing far unfitting the name of a captain,
and, as I thought, the tough and unsmoothed nature of	110
Corsites. But forth.

Corsites. Feeling this continual war, I thought rather by parley
to yield than by certain danger to perish. I unfolded to
Tellus the depth of my affections, and framed my tongue
to utter a sweet tale of love, that was wont to sound	115
nothing but threats of war. She, too fair to be true and too
false for one so fair, after a nice denial practised a notable
deceit, commanding me to remove Endymion from this
cabin and carry him to some dark cave, which I, seeking
to accomplish, found impossible, and so by fairies or	120
fiends have been thus handled.

Cynthia. How say you, my lords, is not Tellus always practising of some deceits?—In sooth, Corsites, thy face is now
too foul for a lover and thine heart too fond for a soldier.
You may see, when warriors become wantons, how their	125
manners alter with their faces. Is it not a shame, Corsites,

---

98. *rehearse*] recite, tell.

106–7. *reverence and affection*] reverent duty towards Queen Cynthia and
passionate desire for Tellus.

112. *parley*] negotiation of terms under a truce.

114. *framed*] directed, shaped.

115. *that was wont*] I who (or, my tongue that) was accustomed.

117. *nice*] coy.

118–19. *from this cabin*] i.e. from this sheltering lunary bank, spoken of
here as a fixed stage location, a locus. Diogenes's tub in *Campaspe*, v.iv.79
and 82, is similarly called a 'cabin'. See Introduction, pp. 50–4.

124. *fond*] foolish, as also at III.iv.118 and 198.

that, having lived so long in Mars his camp, thou shouldst
now be rocked in Venus' cradle? Dost thou wear Cupid's
quiver at thy girdle, and make lances of looks? Well,
Corsites, rouse thyself and be as thou hast been, and let   130
Tellus, who is made all of love, melt herself in her own
looseness.

Corsites. Madam, I doubt not but to recover my former state,
for Tellus' beauty never wrought such love in my mind as
now her deceit hath despite; and yet to be revenged of a   135
woman were a thing than love itself more womanish.

Gyptes. These spots, gentleman, are to be worn out if you rub
them over with this lunary, so that in place where you
received this maim you shall find a medicine.

Corsites. I thank you for that. The gods bless me from love   140
and these pretty ladies that haunt this green!

Floscula. Corsites, I would Tellus saw your amiable face.

[*Corsites rubs out his spots with lunary from the bank.*
Semele laughs.]

Zontes. How spitefully Semele laugheth, that dare not speak!

Cynthia. Could you not stir Endymion with that doubled
strength of yours?   145

Corsites. Not so much as his finger with all my force.

Cynthia. Pythagoras and Gyptes, what think you of
Endymion? What reason is to be given, what remedy?

139. maim] *Blount;* maine *Q.*   142.1. s.d. *Corsites . . . bank*] *This ed.*
142.2. s.d. *Semele laughs*] *Baker.*

127. *Mars his*] Mars's. The monitory image of Mars as a soldier enslaved
by his lust to Venus goes back at least to the *Odyssey,* VIII.266–366 (LCL, I.276–
85), and is used by Lyly in *Campaspe,* II.ii.68–9.

135. *hath despite*] has wrought scorn and anger in my mind.

136. *than love . . . womanish*] even more womanish than being in love.
Revenge too is proverbially womanish; see Dent R91.

138–9. *so that . . . medicine*] The proverbial idea of seeking one's salve
where one got one's sore (Dent S83) is often connected to the idea of the
lover who can be cured only by his beloved's favour; that idea resonates here,
since lunary is associated with the moon and with Cynthia.

140. *bless*] protect.

141. *these pretty ladies*] the fairies, whom Corsites again appeases with an
euphemistic avoidance of their more dangerous name. Compare l. 32 and
note.

142. *amiable*] lovable, lovely, but here with the ironic suggestion that
Corsites's face has been disfigured by love. The wry jest draws a laugh from
Semele.

Pythagoras. Madam, it is impossible to yield reason for things
    that happen not in compass of nature. It is most certain   150
    that some strange enchantment hath bound all his senses.
Cynthia. What say you, Gyptes?
Gyptes. With Pythagoras, that it is enchantment, and that so
    strange that no art can undo it, for that heaviness argueth
    a malice unremovable in the enchantress, and that no   155
    power can end it till she die that did it or the heavens
    show some means more than miraculous.
Floscula. O Endymion, could spite itself devise a mischief so
    monstrous as to make thee dead with life, and living
    being altogether dead? Where others number their years,   160
    their hours, their minutes, and step to age by stairs, thou
    only hast thy years and times in a cluster, being old before
    thou rememberest thou wast young.
Cynthia. No more, Floscula; pity doth him no good. I would
    anything else might, and I vow by the unspotted honour   165
    of a lady he should not miss it. But is this all, Gyptes, that
    is to be done?
Gyptes. All as yet. It may be that either the enchantress shall
    die or else be discovered. If either happen I will then
    practise the utmost of my art. In the mean season, about   170
    this grove would I have a watch, and the first living thing
    that toucheth Endymion to be taken.
Cynthia. Corsites, what say you, will you undertake this?
Corsites. Good madam, pardon me; I was overtaken too late.
    I should rather break into the midst of a main battle than   175
    again fall into the hands of those fair babies.

---

157. than] *Q* (then*).*   175. midst] *Q* (middest*).*

149–50. *it is . . . nature*] Compare *Campaspe*, I.iii.30–57, where Plato, Aristotle, and other philosophers debate the relationship between 'natural
causes and supernal effects'.

154. *for that heaviness argueth*] either (*a*) since heaviness evinces, or (*b*)
because that heaviness which we see evinces. The second *that* in l. 155
supports (*a*).

169. *discovered*] divulged, identified.

170. *mean season*] meantime.

174. *overtaken too late*] overpowered by the fairies all too recently. Corsites
plays on the opposition of *undertake* (l. 173) and *overtake*.

176. *babies*] Corsites refers euphemistically to the fairies by their diminutive size. Compare ll. 32 and 141, notes. At II.ii.30, *babies* are children's dolls.

Cynthia. Well, I will provide others. Pythagoras and Gyptes,
     you shall yet remain in my court till I hear what may be
     done in this matter.
Pythagoras. We attend.   180
Cynthia. Let us go in.

>   *Exeunt.* [*Endymion continues asleep on his lunary
>   bed, near a tree, but perhaps curtained off during the
>   entr'acte music.*]

181.1–3. S.D. *Endymion . . . music*] *This ed.*

Act V

Actus Quintus, Scaena Prima

[*Enter*] SAMIAS [*and*] DARES.

Samias. Eumenides hath told such strange tales as I may well
wonder at them but never believe them.

Dares. The other old man, what a sad speech used he, that
caused us almost all to weep! Cynthia is so desirous to
know the experiment of her own virtue, and so willing to   5
ease Endymion's hard fortune, that she no sooner heard
the discourse but she made herself in a readiness to try
the event.

1–2. *strange . . . believe them*] In choosing to report rather than stage a
scene of reunion that the observers reckon to be wholly unbelievable, in
order not to upstage a still more highly charged scene of reconciliation, Lyly
has anticipated Shakespeare's *The Winter's Tale* by more than two decades.
The present speakers, Samias and Dares, are at the lunary bank where
Endymion still lies in his ageing sleep (having perhaps been curtained off
from view during the entr'acte music). Presumably he is now guarded, in
accordance with Cynthia's determination at iv.iii.177. Whether a watch stays
with him at the end of Act IV or now enters unobtrusively is not clear.

3. *The other old man*] Geron, the other man besides Eumenides, and who
is old (as Eumenides is not; the play employs a double sense of time). Geron
has been married fifty years (iii.iv.5, v.ii.91). At iii.iv.201–2, he promises to
accompany Eumenides to court so that he may discover unto Cynthia 'all my
sorrows, who also must work in me a contentment'. Earlier in that scene (ll.
8–15), Geron has hinted at having the saddest tale imaginable to tell about
himself, but has vowed to conceal his grief until there is hope of remedy.
Cynthia represents that hope, and so he has now told her his tale. Although
we never learn the details, they presumably have to do with his wife Dipsas's
'vile art of enchanting', which, when she promises to renounce it, Geron
forgives and happily receives her back (v.iv.269–82). Geron and Eumenides
have evidently told Endymion's story also, for it is this 'discourse' (l. 7),
confirming no doubt what she has learned in iv.iii by her visit to the lunary
bank, that prompts Cynthia to see if she is signified by the sacred fountain to
be the deliverer of Endymion.

5. *know . . . virtue*] make trial of her power.

8. *event*] outcome.

Samias. We will also see the event. But whist! Here cometh
Cynthia with all her train. Let us sneak in amongst them.   10

> *Enter* CYNTHIA, FLOSCULA, SEMELE, PANELION *etc.*
> [EUMENIDES, ZONTES, GYPTES, *and* PYTHAGORAS.
> *Samias and Dares join the throng.*]

Cynthia. Eumenides, it cannot sink into my head that I
should be signified by that sacred fountain, for many
things are there in the world to which those words may be
applied.

Eumenides. Good madam, vouchsafe but to try, else shall I   15
think myself most unhappy that I asked not my sweet
mistress.

Cynthia. Will you not yet tell me her name?

Eumenides. Pardon me, good madam, for if Endymion awake
he shall. Myself have sworn never to reveal it.   20

Cynthia. Well, let us to Endymion. [*They approach the sleeping
Endymion.*] I will not be so stately, good Endymion, not
to stoop to do thee good; and if thy liberty consist in a kiss
from me, thou shalt have it. And although my mouth
hath been heretofore as untouched as my thoughts, yet   25
now to recover thy life (though to restore thy youth it be
impossible) I will do that to Endymion which yet never
mortal man could boast of heretofore, nor shall ever hope
for hereafter.   *She kisseth him.*

Eumenides. Madam, he beginneth to stir.   30

Cynthia. Soft, Eumenides. Stand still.

Eumenides. Ah, I see his eyes almost open.

---

9. will] *Q* (will)).   10.2. S.D. [EUMENIDES . . . *and* PYTHAGORAS] *Baker,
subst.*   10.3. S.D. *Samias . . . throng*] *This ed.*   21–2. S.D.] *This ed.*

9. *whist*] be silent.

16–17. *asked . . . mistress*] asked not for Semele instead of for Endymion
(at III.iv.94–157).

29. S.D. She kisseth him] Among classical authorities on the story of
Endymion, only Cicero, in *Tusculan Disputations*, I.xxxviii.92 (LCL, pp. 110–
11), links the Endymion beloved by the moon to the sleeping man whom
Luna 'put to sleep so that she might kiss him while he was unawares' ('*a qua
consopitus putatur, ut eum dormientem oscularetur*'). Renaissance mythographers made much of the kiss (Thomas, '*Endimion* and Its Sources', pp.
48–9). See Introduction, p. 11.

Cynthia. I command thee once again, stir not. I will stand
    behind him.
       [*She stands where Endymion will not see her at first.*]
Panelion. What do I see, Endymion almost awake?   35
Eumenides. Endymion, Endymion, art thou deaf or dumb? Or
    hath this long sleep taken away thy memory? Ah, my
    sweet Endymion, seest thou not Eumenides, thy faithful
    friend, thy faithful Eumenides, who for thy safety hath
    been careless of his own content? Speak, Endymion,   40
    Endymion, Endymion!
Endymion. Endymion? I call to mind such a name.
Eumenides. Hast thou forgotten thyself, Endymion? Then
    do I not marvel thou rememberest not thy friend. I tell
    thee thou art Endymion and I Eumenides. Behold also   45
    Cynthia, by whose favour thou art awaked, and by whose
    virtue thou shalt continue thy natural course.
Cynthia. Endymion, speak, sweet Endymion. Knowest thou
    not Cynthia?
Endymion. O heavens, whom do I behold? Fair Cynthia, di-   50
    vine Cynthia?
Cynthia. I am Cynthia, and thou Endymion.
Endymion. Endymion? What do I hear? What, a grey beard?
    Hollow eyes? Withered body? Decayed limbs? And all in
    one night?   55
Eumenides. One night? Thou hast here slept forty years, by

34.1. s.d.] *This ed.*   53. hear] *Dilke;* heere *Q.*

47. *continue thy natural course*] live in the normal human way.
53. *hear*] The Q spelling, *heere*, could mean 'hear' or 'here'.
53–4. *grey beard . . . limbs*] The details seem to recall those of Jason's
father, old Aeson, as he is rejuvenated by Medea: '*barba comaeque / canitie
posita nigrum rapuere colorem, / pulsa fugit macies, abeunt pallorque situsque, /
adiectoque cavae supplentur corpore rugae, / membraque luxuriant*', 'his beard
and hair lost their grey colour and quickly became black again; his leanness
vanished, away went the pallor and the look of neglect, the deep wrinkles
were filled out with new flesh, his limbs had the strength of youth' (Ovid,
Metamorphoses, VII.288–92, LCL, I.362–3).
56. *forty years*] The discrepancy between this figure and 'almost these
twenty years' at III.iv.19 may be owing to the dependence of the present
passage on Ovid (see previous note), in which Medea restores to Aeson the
strength of his youth forty years earlier by means of magical herbs.

what enchantress as yet it is not known. And behold, the
twig to which thou laidst thy head is now become a tree.
Callest thou not Eumenides to remembrance?

Endymion. Thy name I do remember by the sound, but thy   60
favour I do not yet call to mind. Only divine Cynthia, to
whom time, fortune, destiny, and death are subject, I
see and remember, and in all humility I regard and
reverence.

Cynthia. You have good cause to remember Eumenides, who   65
hath for thy safety forsaken his own solace.

Endymion. Am I that Endymion who was wont in court to
lead my life, and in jousts, tourneys, and arms to exercise
my youth? Am I that Endymion?

Eumenides. Thou art that Endymion and I Eumenides. Wilt   70
thou not yet call me to remembrance?

Endymion. Ah, sweet Eumenides, I now perceive thou art he,
and that myself have the name of Endymion. But that this
should be my body I doubt; for how could my curled
locks be turned to grey hairs and my strong body to a   75
dying weakness, having waxed old and not knowing it?

---

68. jousts] *Q* (Iustes).

57–8. *the twig . . . tree*] The language may call for some staging illusion,
even though the metaphor is an Ovidian commonplace about a love that
matures (*Ars Amatoria*, II.342, LCL, pp. 88–9, '*Sub qua nunc recubas arbore,
virga fuit*', 'The tree under which you lie was once a sapling', as noted by
Edge, 'Sources', pp. 179–80). At I.i.50, Endymion has referred to 'twigs that
become trees' as parallel to 'children that become men'. Onstage, the sapling
perhaps seen earlier at the lunary bank (even as early as II.iii) is now a mature
tree. Quite possibly it is the tree that is turned into Bagoa at the end of the
play (v.iv.297.1). Similarly, Endymion's hair is now visibly grey (l. 75). The
actor portraying Endymion is to mime the effect of 'hollow eyes', 'withered
body', and 'decayed limbs'. Presumably he kneels to Cynthia, then arises at
her command at l. 77 and sits. Perhaps she is herself enthroned when he sits.

61. *favour*] aspect, face.

63. *remember*] recall; commemorate.

regard] gaze upon (parallel to 'see' in l. 63); give heed to; value, have
respect for.

68. *jousts, tourneys*] In a joust or just, two knights on horseback tilt at each
other with lances; a tourney or tournament is a spectacular multiplication of
such encounters (*OED*, *joust*, sb. and *just*, sb.¹, citing among others Joseph
Strutt, *Sports and Pastimes of the People of England* (London: Bensley, 1801,
rpt Methuen, 1903, reissued Detroit: Singing Tree Press, 1968), Bk III, chap.
i, p. 113, for this distinction).

74–6. *my curled . . . it*] Compare Peele's song from *Polyhymnia*: 'His
golden locks time hath to silver turned'—particularly significant perhaps in

Cynthia. Well, Endymion, arise. A while sit down, for that thy
    limbs are stiff and not able to stay thee, and tell what hast
    thou seen in thy sleep all this while? What dreams, vi-
    sions, thoughts, and fortunes? For it is impossible but in   80
    so long time thou shouldst see things strange.

Endymion. Fair Cynthia, I will rehearse what I have seen,
    humbly desiring that when I exceed in length, you give
    me warning, that I may end. For to utter all I have to
    speak would be troublesome, although haply the strange-   85
    ness may somewhat abate the tediousness.

Cynthia. Well, Endymion, begin.

Endymion. Methought I saw a lady passing fair but very mis-
    chievous, who in the one hand carried a knife with which
    she offered to cut my throat, and in the other a looking   90
    glass, wherein, seeing how ill anger became ladies, she
    refrained from intended violence. She was accompanied
    with other damsels, one of which, with a stern counte-
    nance, and as it were with a settled malice engraven in her
    eyes, provoked her to execute mischief. Another with   95
    visage sad, and constant only in sorrow, with her arms
    crossed, and watery eyes, seemed to lament my fortune,
    but durst not offer to prevent the force. I started in my
    sleep, feeling my very veins to swell and my sinews to
    stretch with fear, and such a cold sweat bedewed all my   100
    body that death itself could not be so terrible as the
    vision.

Cynthia. A strange sight. Gyptes at our better leisure shall
    expound it.

---

85. haply] *Q* (*happilie*).

the context of '*jousts, tourneys, and arms*' (l. 68), since the Peele song was sung
at the farewell tourney for Sir Henry Lee as Queen's champion.

    77. *for that*] since.

    78. *stay*] support (*OED*, v.² 1).

    82. *rehearse*] recite, tell.

    85. *haply*] (*a*) perhaps (*b*) happily, fortunately (Q: *happilie*). See also at
II.ii.6.

    88. *passing*] surpassingly. On possible allegorical meanings of Endymion's
dream, see Introduction, pp. 24–7.

    90. *offered*] proposed; made a move as if. As also at l. 98.

    96–7. *with her arms crossed*] A conventional sign of melancholy, as in *LLL*,
III.i.18 and IV.iii.131–2. *Sad* at l. 96 connotes both seriousness and sorrow.

    103–4. *Gyptes . . . it*] In fact, Gyptes never does expound the dream. The
audience is left to interpret for itself.

Endymion. After long debating with herself, mercy overcame   105
anger, and there appeared in her heavenly face such a
divine majesty, mingled with a sweet mildness, that I was
ravished with the sight above measure, and wished that I
might have enjoyed the sight without end. And so she
departed with the other ladies, of which the one retained   110
still an unmovable cruelty, the other a constant pity.

Cynthia. Poor Endymion, how wast thou affrighted! What
else?

Endymion. After her immediately appeared an aged man with
a beard as white as snow, carrying in his hand a book with   115
three leaves, and speaking, as I remember, these words:
'Endymion, receive this book with three leaves, in which
are contained counsels, policies, and pictures.' And with
that, he offered me the book, which I rejected; wherewith
moved with a disdainful pity, he rent the first leaf in a   120
thousand shivers. The second time he offered it, which I
refused also; at which, bending his brows and pitching his
eyes fast to the ground as though they were fixed to the
earth and not again to be removed, then suddenly casting
them up to the heavens, he tore in a rage the second leaf   125
and offered the book only with one leaf. I know not
whether fear to offend or desire to know some strange
thing moved me; I took the book, and so the old man
vanished.

Cynthia. What didst thou imagine was in the last leaf?   130

Endymion. There—ay, portrayed to life—with a cold quaking

---

131. There—ay, portrayed to life—with] *Baskervill;* There I portraid to life,
with *Q;* There, pourtrayed to life, with *Dilke.*

118. *policies*] political strategies and cunning, statecraft; courses of action
to be adopted. See Introduction, p. 25.

121. *shivers*] fragments.

122. *pitching*] setting, fixing, implanting *OED, pitch,* v.[1] 6).

131. *There . . . life*—] Editors variously interpret Q's 'There I portraid to
life,' as a typographical error in which the 'I' is the compositor's erroneous
anticipation of 'I' in l. 134, and should thus be omitted (Dilke), or a
compositorial inversion that should read 'There I, portrayed to life,'
(Daniel). Baskervill's reading, adopted here, regards the 'I' as a defensible
rendition of 'ay', a common meaning. The play on 'ay' and 'I' is plausibly like
Lyly.

in every joint, I beheld many wolves barking at thee,
Cynthia, who, having ground their teeth to bite, did with
striving bleed themselves to death. There might I see
Ingratitude with an hundred eyes, gazing for benefits, and   135
with a thousand teeth gnawing on the bowels wherein she
was bred. Treachery stood all clothed in white, with a
smiling countenance but both her hands bathed in blood.
Envy, with a pale and meagre face, whose body was so
lean that one might tell all her bones, and whose garment   140
was so tattered that it was easy to number every thread,
stood shooting at stars, whose darts fell down again on
her own face. There might I behold drones, or beetles, I

---

132. joint, I] *Blount*; ioynt. I *Q*.   141. tattered] *Q* (totterd).

132. *wolves barking*] For a political interpretation, see Introduction, p. 26.
135. *with an hundred eyes*] Argus, a herdsman with eyes all over his body,
was set by Hera to watch Io and prevent Zeus from seducing this princess
whom Zeus had turned into a heifer to escape Hera's watchfulness. See
I.ii.73–4 and note, and Ovid, *Metamorphoses*, 1.567–746 (LCL, 1.42–55).
Virgil's Fama (*Aeneid*, IV.179–90, LCL, 1.408–9) is fitted out with many eyes,
ears, and tongues; compare Chaucer's *Hous of Fame*, ll. 1389–92.
gazing for benefits] fixedly looking for promotion and reward.
136–7. *a thousand teeth ... bred*] For a famous instance of this conventional image of Ingratitude as a serpent or monster (Dent 166.1) gnawing its
parent's bowels with its sharp teeth, see *Lear*, I.iv.257–88, I.v.39, and
III.vii.61; and compare *1H6*, III.i.72–3, where civil dissension 'is a viperous
worm / That gnaws the bowels of the commonwealth'.
137. *white*] The colour, betokening innocence, contrasts vividly with
Treachery's true nature as revealed by the red blood on her hands. Ingratitude, Treachery, and Envy are all female in Endymion's dream allegory.
139. *meagre*] emaciated.
140. *tell*] count.
141. *tattered*] Q's *totterd* is originally a common variant of *tattered* that
came also to be associated with the verb *totter*, to swing to and fro, vacillate
(*OED*, *tottered*, ppl. a). Here it seems to mean simply 'torn and hanging in
tatters'.
142–3. *stood ... face*] This proverbial idea that an arrow shot straight
upwards falls on the shooter's head (Dent A324) is an object lesson against
presumption, and is part of a larger proverbial mythology about 'even-
handed justice' that 'Commends th' ingredience of our poisoned chalice / To
our own lips' (*Mac.*, I.vii.10–12), about 'purposes mistook / Fall'n on th'
inventors' heads' (*Ham.*, v.ii.386–7), about being a 'woodcock' caught in
one's own 'springe' and thus 'justly killed' with one's 'own treachery' (*Ham.*,
v.ii.309–10), etc.
143–6. *drones ... the eagle*] The image is repeated, with a more uncertain
resolution, from *Euphues*, II.215, 19–24: 'This is that mighty eagle ... into

know not how to term them, creeping under the wings of
a princely eagle, who, being carried into her nest, sought   145
there to suck that vein that would have killed the eagle. I
mused that things so base should attempt a fact so barba-
rous or durst imagine a thing so bloody. And many other
things, madam, the repetition whereof may at your better
leisure seem more pleasing; for bees surfeit sometimes   150
with honey, and the gods are glutted with harmony, and
Your Highness may be dulled with delight.
Cynthia. I am content to be dieted; therefore let us in.
Eumenides, see that Endymion be well tended, lest, either eating immoderately or sleeping again too long, he   155

---

154. lest] *Q* (*least*)

---

whose wings although the blind beetle would have crept, and so, being
carried into her nest, destroyed her young ones, yet hath she with the virtue
of her feathers consumed that fly in his own fraud.' The image is derived
from Aesop's *Fables*, no. 56, 'Of the Eagle and the Beetle' (1665 ed., pp. 139–
41), where a beetle vengefully invades an eagle's nest and destroys its eggs.
See also Pliny, x.iv.15 (LCL, III.302–3), where an eagle's feathers are said to be
able to consume those of other birds (Bond, II.535). Lyly's more direct
source may have been Erasmus's long satire against bad princes as part of his
gloss for the adage, *Scarabaeus aquilam quaerit* (*Adagia*, chiliad III, century 7,
first proverb; *Opera Omnia*, II.869ff., cited by Croll and Clemons, p. 446,
note 4). Lyly here turns the image to praise of Elizabeth. Indeed, the *Euphues*
image occurs in a long passage of tribute (II.206ff.) to Queen Elizabeth as 'a
glass for all princes to behold', 'endued with mercy, patience, and moderation', 'adorned with singular beauty and chastity', and the like (II.208–9).
The speaker celebrates Elizabeth's overthrow of her treacherous enemies, as
in the suppression of the Northern Rebellion on behalf of Mary Stuart and
the Catholic conspiracy that Oxford purportedly exposed shortly before
Christmas in 1580 (Le Comte, *Endymion in England*, p. 82). See Introduction, pp. 30–2.

147. *fact*] deed.

150–1. *bees . . . harmony*] Compare *Campaspe*, II.ii.86–7: 'There is no sur-
feit so dangerous as that of honey' (taken from Erasmus, *Parabolae*, 237, and
Pliny, XXI.44, LCL, VI.214–15, as Hunter observes in his note), and *Sappho and
Phao*, II.iv.34–5: 'Bees that die with honey are buried with harmony.' The
notion that 'the bee is often hurt with its own honey' is proverbial (Dent
B204). See also Dent H560, 'Too much honey cloys the stomach', derived in
Hunter's estimation from Proverbs xxv.27. Lyly's plays and *Euphues* are full
of fables about bees (e.g. *Sappho and Phao*, Prologue at Blackfriars, 1–2, The
Prologue at the Court, 2–3, IV.iv.19–21, *Euphues*, I.221, 24–5, I.224, 10–11,
and I.314, 19–20), artfully mythologised with reference to Pliny (XI.19),
Bartholomew (Berthelet) XVIII.xii.347–9, and the like. See also III.iv.154 and
note in this play.

153. *dieted*] fed in a particular way, regulated as to diet (*OED, diet,* v. 1–2).

fall into a deadly surfeit or into his former sleep. See this
also be proclaimed: that whosoever will discover this
practice shall have of Cynthia infinite thanks and no small
rewards.

>   *Exit, [attended by her courtly entourage.*
>   *Floscula, Endymion, and Eumenides remain.]*

Floscula. Ah, Endymion, none so joyful as Floscula of thy   160
restoring!

Eumenides. Yes, Floscula, let Eumenides be somewhat glad-
der, and do not that wrong to the settled friendship of a
man as to compare it with the light affection of a
woman.—Ah, my dear friend Endymion, suffer me to die   165
with gazing at thee!

Endymion. Eumenides, thy friendship is immortal and not to
be conceived, and thy good will, Floscula, better than I
have deserved. But let us all wait on Cynthia. I marvel
Semele speaketh not a word.   170

Eumenides. Because if she do she loseth her tongue.

Endymion. But how prospereth your love?

Eumenides. I never yet spake word since your sleep.

Endymion. I doubt not but your affection is old and your
appetite cold.   175

Eumenides. No, Endymion, thine hath made it stronger, and

---

156. sleep] *No paragraph as in Dilke; Q introduces a new paragraph
here.*   159.1–2. S.D. *Exit, [attended . . . remain] This ed.; Exit / Q;* Exeunt all
except ENDYMION, EUMENIDES, FLOSCULA *and* SEMELE / *Baker.*

157–8. *discover this practice*] disclose this conspiracy.

159.1–2. Exit . . . remain] Baker's suggestion that Semele remains also
onstage, though conceivable, is rendered implausible by the fact that she is
not reconciled to Eumenides until v.iv.205 ff. Endymion's 'I marvel Semele
speaketh not a word' (ll. 169–70) would seem to refer not to her as silently
present but to her silence throughout the previous part of the scene. The
entire dialogue between Endymion and Eumenides (ll. 172–9) about
Eumenides's chances of prospering in Semele's love would seem tactless if
said in her presence.

163–5. *do not . . . woman*] Compare III.iv.129–50, where Geron exalts
friendship over love.

167–8. *not to be conceived*] (*a*) not capable of being understood (*b*) not
having any beginning.

169. *wait on*] attend.

176. *thine*] my affection for you (strengthened by your affection for me).

177. *sparks grown to flames*] This proverbial idea (Dent S714) occurs also in
Sappho and Phao, III.iii.106.

fancies] amorous inclinations; imaginings about love.

now are my sparks grown to flames and my fancies almost
to frenzies. But let us follow, and within we will debate all
this matter at large.   *Exeunt.*

Actus Quintus, Scaena Secunda

[*Enter*] SIR TOPHAS [*and*] EPITON.

Tophas. Epi, love hath jostled my liberty from the wall and
    taken the upper hand of my reason.

Epiton. Let me then trip up the heels of your affection and
    thrust your good will into the gutter.

Tophas. No, Epi, love is a lord of misrule, and keepeth Christ-   5
    mas in my corpse.

Epiton. No doubt there is good cheer. What dishes of delight
    doth his lordship feast you withal?

Tophas. First, with a great platter of plum-porridge of pleas-
    ure, wherein is stewed the mutton of mistrust.   10

1. jostled] *Q* (*iustled*).   6. corpse] *Q* (*corps*).

---

179. S.D. Exeunt] Perhaps the lunary bank, with its tree, is concealed by
means of a curtain until it is needed again in v.iv.

    1. *jostled . . . wall*] To be jostled from the wall is to be forced out as a
weakling into the gutter, as Epiton says in ll. 3–4. Compare *Rom.*, I.i.12–18—
though, as that same passage shows, and as the proverb attests, the weakest
are often 'thrust to the wall', i.e. jostled to the wall side rather than the gutter
side (Dent w15 and 185). In *Midas*, too, Petulus perceives that Licio is
'driven to the wall' (I.ii.73). A play title (*The Weakest Goeth to the Wall, c.*
1599–1600) attests to the currency of the saying.

    2. *taken the upper hand*] A conventional metaphor (Dent h95).

    3–4. *Let . . . gutter*] Epiton jestingly proposes to be rough with Tophas's
affection—his lust—and his *good will*—his loving attachment—since they are
disabling his reason.

    5–6. *lord of misrule . . . Christmas*] The *Gesta Grayorum*, written in 1594 by
Francis Bacon, Thomas Campion, and others to be put on by the gentlemen
of Gray's Inn, abundantly illustrates the old custom of electing a Lord of
Misrule to preside over festivities of the long Christmas season, with plays,
masques, processions, mock ceremonials, saturnalian inversions of authority,
carnival excess in eating and drinking, and the like.

    6. *corpse*] body.

    9. *plum-porridge*] The nursery rhyme of 'Little Jack Horner' attests to the
presence of plums in 'Christmas pie'. Stewed prunes have a bawdy connotation; see next note. Plum porridge dates from this passage in Lyly, according
to *OED*, plum pottage in 1573, plum pudding not until 1711.

    10. *stewed . . . mistrust*] Stewing and mutton are repeatedly associated with
prostitutes and their houses ('stews'), where stewed prunes might be served;

Epiton. Excellent love-lap!

Tophas. Then cometh a pie of patience, a hen of honey, a
goose of gall, a capon of care, and many other viands,
some sweet and some sour, which proveth love to be as it
was said of in old years: *dulce venenum.*   15

Epiton. A brave banquet!

Tophas. But Epi, I pray thee feel on my chin; something
pricketh me. What dost thou feel or see?

Epiton. [*Examining his chin*] There are three or four little
hairs.   20

Tophas. I pray thee call it my beard. How shall I be troubled
when this young spring shall grow to a great wood!

Epiton. O, sir, your chin is but a quiller yet. You will be most
majestical when it is full fledge. But I marvel that you love
Dipsas, that old crone.   25

Tophas. *Agnosco veteris vestigia flamma*, I love the smoke of an
old fire.

Epiton. Why, she is so cold that no fire can thaw her thoughts.

Tophas. It is an old goose, Epi, that will eat no oats; old kine
will kick, old rats gnaw cheese, and old sacks will have   30

---

19. S.D.] *This ed.*

see, for example, *TGV*, I.i.97–9, and *Meas.*, II.i.90 ff. and III.ii.175. Tophas
complains that such pleasures are melting down his rationality into *mistrust*,
i.e. the suspicion and doubt that accompany debauchery.

11. *love-lap*] love-broth, love-portion—a meagre fare. Not in *OED* in this
form, but based evidently on *lap* (*OED*, sb.²) meaning liquid food for dogs,
hence any weak beverage or thin liquid food.

13. *goose, capon*] In addition to being food for feasts, both are associated
with foolishness. Compare *MND*, v.i.229–32 and *Cym.* II.i.24–5, where *capon*
or castrated rooster also connotes a lack of manliness.

15. dulce venenum] sweet poison—a truism about love (Dent P456.1).

16. *brave*] splendid (said sardonically).

22. *spring*] copse, grove of saplings (*OED*, sb.¹ 10).

23. *quiller*] a bird not fully fledged (l. 23); *OED*'s only citation in this sense.
Quill can refer to the whole feather.

26. Agnosco . . . flamma] I recognise the traces of an old fire (Virgil,
Aeneid, IV.23, LCL, I.398–9). Compare Berowne in *LLL*, v.ii.417–18: 'Yet I
have a trick / Of the old rage.' Lyly turns the reference to Dido's reawakened
desire into an expression of Tophas's interest in the 'old crone' Dipsas.

29. *It is . . . oats*] Proverbial (Dent G368); repeated from *Euphues*, II.133, 5–
6. *Old sacks . . . patching*, ll. 30–1, is similarly proverbial (Dent s8).

much patching. I prefer an old cony before a rabbit-
sucker, and an ancient hen before a young chicken
peeper.

Epiton. *Argumentum ab antiquitate.* [*Aside*] My master loveth
antique work.   35

Tophas. Give me a pippin that is withered like an old wife.

Epiton. Good, sir.

Tophas. Then *a contrario sequitur argumentum.* Give me a wife
that looks like an old pippin.

Epiton. [*Aside*] Nothing hath made my master a fool but flat   40
scholarship.

Tophas. Knowest thou not that old wine is best?

Epiton. Yes.

Tophas. And thou knowest that like will to like?

Epiton. Ay.   45

Tophas. And thou knowest that Venus loved the best wine?

Epiton. So.

34, 40. s.d.] *Baker.*

31–2. *old cony . . . rabbit-sucker*] Falstaff dares Prince Hal to 'hang me up
by the heels for a rabbit-sucker or a poulter's hare' in *1H4*, II.iv.431–2, shortly
after he has parodied Lyly's Euphuistic style in his florid analogy of 'the
camomile, the more it is trodden on the faster it grows', etc. (ll. 396 ff.). A
rabbit-sucker is a sucking rabbit, very young and hence a delicacy; a *cony* is a
rabbit, usually a mature one.

33. *peeper*] one that still peeps like a chick.

34. Argumentum ab antiquitate] an argument from ancient authorities.
Epiton's arch jest is that one who quotes old authorities—Virgil, Erasmus,
proverbial wisdom—is well suited to 'antique work' (l. 35), an old crone.

36. *pippin*] Pippins are numerous varieties of apples grown from seeds or
pips. Tophas seems to have in mind an apple like the applejohn. In *2H4*,
Prince Hal is reported to have set a dish of five applejohns before Falstaff and
to have departed with a ceremonious removal of his hat, saying, 'I will now
take my leave of these six dry, round, old, withered knights' (II.iv.4–8).
Withered fruit is often anatomically compared with a woman, especially an
older woman, and the pippin is often used in metaphors for the countenance,
like *pippin-faced* (*OED*, *pippin*, 4).

38. a contrario sequitur argumentum] from the contrary follows the proof,
the converse of the grammatical structure holds: If a pippin is withered like
an old woman (l. 36), then an old woman should look like a pippin. As
Epiton observes in the next speech, this 'scholarship' or logical demonstration is vapid and leads to an absurd conclusion.

40. *flat*] downright, plain.

41. *scholarship*] mastery of the argumentative terms of scholastic disputa-
tion.

44. *like will to like*] A commonplace expression meaning that people are

Tophas. Then I conclude that Venus was an old woman in an
old cup of wine. For, *est Venus in vinis, ignis in igne fuit.*

Epiton. O *lepidum caput,* O madcap master! You were worthy   50
to win Dipsas, were she as old again, for in your love you
have worn the nap of your wit quite off and made it
threadbare. But soft, who comes here?

[*Enter* SAMIAS *and* DARES.]

Tophas. My solicitors.

Samias. All hail, Sir Tophas! How feel you yourself?   55

Tophas. Stately in every joint, which the common people term
stiffness. Doth Dipsas stoop? Will she yield? Will she
bend?

Dares. O, sir, as much as you would wish, for her chin almost
toucheth her knees.   60

Epiton. Master, she is bent, I warrant you.

Tophas. What conditions doth she ask?

53.1. S.D.] *Placement as in Bond; after l. 54, Dilke; not in Q.*

---

attracted to their own kind; see next note.

49. est . . . fuit] Ovid's *Ars Amatoria,* 1.244 (LCL, pp. 28–9), reads, '*Et Venus in vinis ignis in igne fuit*', 'Venus [i.e. Love] in the wine has been fire in fire.' Tophas's fatuous syllogism is vitiated by a sliding definition of 'old'— a good thing in wines, but not (in Epiton's view) necessarily so in women. Tophas characteristically draws the terms of his syllogism from standard proverbial lore: 'Old friends and old wine are best' (Dent F755), and 'Like will to like' (L286). He constructs his syllogism badly as well: line 46 would seem to be the logical deduction combining the syllogistic propositions in ll. 42 and 44, thereby demonstrating that the best love (Venus) should love the best wine, but Tophas instead states this idea as though it were a third proposition leading to his conclusion in ll. 48–9.

50. O lepidum caput] O fine head, O witty mind! From Terence, *Adelphoe,* 966 (V.ix.9; LCL, II.320–1), or Plautus, *Miles Gloriosus,* 725 (LCL, III.198–9; Mustard). Epiton playfully mistranslates the phrase as 'madcap', punning on *caput* and *cap. Lepidus -a -um,* 'pleasant, agreeable', can have a negative connotation of 'effeminate' that adds to the wordplay.

51. *as old again*] twice as old as she is.

54. *solicitors*] Thopas engaged Samias and Dares at III.iii.158–9 to plead for him to Dipsas.

58. *bend*] yield. Dares plays upon the meaning 'bent over double' in ll. 59–60, and Epiton's *bent* in l. 61 may hint at other sorts of spiritual crookedness as well as 'determined, resolute'. *Stoop,* l. 57, yields a similar range of wordplay: 'submit', 'bend over with age', 'degrade oneself morally', and possibly 'descend swiftly on one's prey'.

59–60. *for her chin . . . knees*] Perhaps an aside (Baker).

Samias. She hath vowed she will never love any that hath not
a tooth in his head less than she.

Tophas. How many hath she?   65

Dares. One.

Epiton. That goeth hard, master, for then you must have
none.

Tophas. A small request, and agreeable to the gravity of her
years. What should a wise man do with his mouth full of   70
bones like a charnel house? The turtle true hath ne'er a
tooth.

Samias. [*Aside to Epiton*] Thy master is in a notable vein, that
will lose his teeth to be like a turtle.

Epiton. [*Aside to Samias*] Let him lose his tongue too, I care   75
not.

Dares. Nay, you must also have no nails, for she long since
hath cast hers.

Tophas. That I yield to. What a quiet life shall Dipsas and I
lead, when we can neither bite nor scratch! You may see,   80
youths, how age provides for peace.

Samias. [*Aside to Epiton and Dares*] How shall we do to make
him leave his love? For we never spake to her.

Dares. [*Aside to Samias*] Let me alone. [*To Sir Tophas*] She is

---

71. charnel] *Blount;* channel *Q.*   73, 75, 82. s.d.] *Baker, subst.*   74–5.
lose . . . lose] *Q* (loose . . . loose).   75. too] *Q* (to).   84. s.d. *Aside to
Samias . . . To Sir Tophas] Baker, subst.*

---

65. *How many hath she?*] Here begins another parody of the blazon, or
catalogue of the mistress's physical virtues, as at iii.iii.55–64 (see note there)
and at ll. 101–7 below. In *Midas,* the page Licio similarly undertakes to
'unfold every wrinkle of my mistress' disposition', praising her head 'as
round as a tennis ball', her parrot's tongue, her mole-like ears, and the like
(i.ii.19–87). See also *The Woman in the Moon,* i.i.113–17.

71. *charnel house*] a vault for the bones of the dead. Q's *channel house* is an
easy compositor's error. *OED* does not record *channel* as a variant spelling of
charnel.

71–2. *The turtle . . . tooth*] 'nothing in Pliny, nor Barth. Angl. [i.e.
Bartholomew (Berthelet)]. It sounds like a fragment of an old ballad'
(Bond). A *turtle* is a turtledove, a type of constant love. Like birds generally,
the turtledove lacks teeth in its beak; Lyly may simply have made up this
witticism.

78. *cast*] shed (*OED,* v. 20, generally applied to reptiles and caterpillars).

84. *Let me alone*] leave it to me.

a notable witch, and hath turned her maid Bagoa to an   85
aspen tree for bewraying her secrets.

Tophas. I honour her for her cunning, for now, when I am
weary of walking on two legs, what a pleasure may she do
me to turn me to some goodly ass and help me to four!

Dares. Nay then, I must tell you the truth: her husband Geron   90
is come home, who this fifty years hath had her to wife.

Tophas. What do I hear? Hath she an husband? Go to the
sexton and tell him Desire is dead, and will him to dig his
grave. Oh heavens, an husband? What death is agreeable
to my fortune?   95

Samias. Be not desperate, and we will help you to find a
young lady.

Tophas. I love no Grissels; they are so brittle they will crack
like glass, or so dainty that if they be touched they are
straight of the fashion of wax. *Animus maioribus instat*; I   100

---

93. sexton] *Blount;* Sexteene *Q.*

85–6. *to an aspen tree*] In Gascoigne's *Princely Pleasures at Kenilworth Castle*
(1576), Zabeta is reported to have converted Inconstancy into a poplar
'whose leaves move and shake with the least breath or blast' (in *The Complete
Works of George Gascoigne*, ed. John W. Cunliffe (Cambridge University
Press 1910), II.125; Bond).

86. *bewraying*] divulging.

89. *some goodly ass*] Comic metamorphoses of humans into asses by means
of enchantment are to be found, among others, in Apuleius's *Metamorphoses*
or *Golden Ass* (III.24 ff., LCL, I.168–75) and Shakespeare's *MND*. See *ass* at
I.iii.97 and 101 and III.iii.120.

94–5. *is agreeable to*] agrees with, befits (Baker), as at l. 69 above.

98. *Grissels*] i.e. tender and delicate persons. The term is perhaps derived
from the gristly nature of bones in infancy (though we tend to associate
gristly meat with toughness and age). *Brittle* also suggests young bones (or,
ambivalently, old bones). *OED* cites this present passage under *gristle*, sb. 3,
quoting several instances from Udall in 1553 to Richard Brome's *A Mad
Couple Well Matched* in 1637–39 ('Alas, y'are but a grissell, / Weak picking
meat', v.ii, in *The Dramatic Works of Richard Brome*, 3 vols (London: John
Pearson, 1873, rpt. AMS Press, 1966), I.92) and applied to both sexes ('I am
a grissell, and these spider fingers / Will never hold a sword', Philip
Massinger, *The Bondman*, I.ii.388–9, ed. B. T. Spencer (Princeton University
Press, 1932), p. 96). Quite possibly Lyly refers also to the young and patient
Griselda in Chaucer's *Clerk's Tale*.

100. *straight . . . wax*] quickly and easily pushed out of shape.

Animus maioribus instat] 'My spirit ventures greater themes' (Ovid, *Ars
Amatoria*, II.535, LCL, pp. 102–3). Tophas takes *maioribus* to be from *majores*,

desire old matrons. What a sight would it be to embrace
one whose hair were as orient as the pearl, whose teeth
shall be so pure a watchet that they shall stain the truest
turquoise, whose nose shall throw more beams from it
than the fiery carbuncle, whose eyes shall be environed   105
about with redness exceeding the deepest coral, and
whose lips might compare with silver for the paleness!
Such a one if you can help me to, I will by piecemeal
curtail my affections towards Dipsas and walk my swelling thoughts till they be cold.   110
Epiton. Wisely provided. How say you, my friends, will you
angle for my master's cause?

---

104. turquoise,] *Q* (Turkis ?).   109. curtail] *Q* (curtoll).

'ancestors', rather than from *maior, maiores*, the comparative of *magnus*,
'great, large'; and thus he arrives at 'old matrons' (l. 101).
    102. *orient*] lustrous, sparkling, as in *Woman in the Moon*, III.ii.9, with
overtones of the Far East and of the dawn. Tophas's comic affinity at ll. 101–
7 for assigning praising attributes to the wrong part of the body, in this
continuation of his blazon from ll. 65 ff. (see note there), is like that of Thisbe
lamenting the dead Pyramus in *MND*: 'These lily lips, / This cherry nose, /
These yellow cowslip cheeks' (v.i.327–9). Instead of gleaming hair, pale blue
teeth, fiery nose, red eyes, and pale lips, the woman should have gleaming
teeth, coral-red lips, pale blue eyes, etc.; the eyes, not the nose, should throw
forth beams. *Coral* is proverbially red (Dent c648.1).
    103. *watchet*] light blue.
    stain] (*a*) deprive of its lustre, disgrace, eclipse (*b*) discolour. The Lylyan
wordplay, of which Tophas may be unconscious, underscores the inap-
positeness of Tophas's blazon. Lyly uses the same wordplay in *Campaspe*,
I.i.14.
    104. *turquoise*] Q's *Turkis* is one of many spelling variants suggestive of a
precious stone found in the Middle East and deriving its name from
Turkestan.
    105. *fiery carbuncle*] Compare the comments on Bardolph's nose in *1H4*,
II.iv.311–22, *H5*, II.iii.39–43, etc.
    109. *curtail*] Q's *curtoll* is, according to *OED*, a spelling variant for *curtail*
(verb) and *curtal* (noun). Modernised spelling thus loses the potential wordplay on *curtal*, a small, dock-tailed horse—a term often used derisively to
connote either a nag or a whore (*OED, curtal*, sb. and a., 3d). The equine
image may lead into Tophas's speaking of his 'swelling thoughts' as a horse
he must now walk to cool it off after its recent exertions.
    111. *provided*] arranged for.
    112. *angle*] lay yourselves out, devise stratagems (*OED*, v.¹ 2). Epiton
speaks ambivalently as to whether these strategies will be on Tophas's behalf
or at his expense.

Samias. Most willingly.

Dares. If we speed him not shortly, I will burn my cap. We
   will serve him of the spades, and dig an old wife out of the   115
   grave that shall be answerable to his gravity.

Tophas. Youths, adieu. He that bringeth me first news shall
   possess mine inheritance.   [*Exit.*]

Dares. [*To Epiton*] What, is thy master landed?

Epiton. Know you not that my master is *liber tenens*?   120

Samias. What's that?

Epiton. A freeholder. But I will after him.

Samias. And we to hear what news of Endymion for the
   conclusion.   *Exeunt.*

Actus Quintus, Scaena Tertia

[*Enter*] PANELION [*and*] ZONTES.

Panelion. Who would have thought that Tellus, being so fair

---

118. s.d. *Exit*] Baker, *subst.; not in* Q.   119. s.d.] *This ed.*

114. *speed him not*] do not cause him to prosper. (But see previous note.)
my cap] betokening an apprentice's status. Burning one's cap is proverbial
in situations like this (Dent c65.11).

115. *serve . . . spades*] This proverbial-sounding locution, seemingly not in
the *OED*, may have an implication similar to 'serve him with the same sauce'
(*OED*, *serve*, 31d) or 'serve him right' (*OED*, 47b). 'To call a spade a spade'
in the sense of not mincing words dates from 1542 (*OED*, sb.¹ 2); the spade
in the pack of cards dates from 1598 (*OED*, sb.²), though the expression to
do something 'in spades' is considerably later. Possibly Dares is parodying
the idea of feudal service. He and his friends will dig around for Tophas, but
with a suggestion of letting him dig his own grave.

116. *grave . . . gravity*] As Bond notes, the dying Mercutio uses similar
wordplay in *Rom.*, III.i.97.

119. *landed*] (*a*) possessed of a landed estate (*b*) caught (continuing the
image of *angle* in l. 112 above).

120. liber tenens] freeholder, possessing land in fee-simple (for ever), fee-
tail (limited to a certain class of heirs), or for life—but said here in a way that
sounds perhaps to Samias like *libertine*. In the 'old' pronunciation ('liber-
teenens') it would sound very like.

122. *freeholder*] See the previous note; but the term had acquired slangy
and disparaging meanings by 1700 (*OED*, 2) and seems to be the vehicle here
for a joke at Thopas's expense—a freeloader or dissolute person in some way.

123–4. *for the conclusion*] to complete what we don't know—but with a
metatheatrical signal to the audience that the finale of the play will begin
shortly.

by nature, so honourable by birth, so wise by education,
would have entered into a mischief to the gods so odious,
to men so detestable, and to her friend so malicious?

Zontes. If Bagoa had not bewrayed it, how then should it have   5
come to light? But we see that gold and fair words are of
force to corrupt the strongest men, and therefore able to
work silly women like wax.

Panelion. I marvel what Cynthia will determine in this cause.

Zontes. I fear as in all causes: hear of it in justice and then   10
judge of it in mercy. For how can it be that she that is
unwilling to punish her deadliest foes with disgrace will
revenge injuries of her train with death?

Panelion. That old witch Dipsas, in a rage, having understood
her practice to be discovered, turned poor Bagoa to an   15
aspen tree. But let us make haste and bring Tellus before
Cynthia, for she was coming out after us.

Zontes. Let us go.   *Exeunt.*

---

5. *If . . . it*] At II.iii.54–61, Bagoa reveals her pity for Endymion and her
reluctance to carry out the enchantment of him under Dipsas's direction and
at Tellus's behest, thus establishing Bagoa's motive for giving away the secret
once she need no longer fear Dipsas's threat to turn her hair to adders and
her teeth to tongues if she tattles (II.iii.64–6). Cynthia has now presumably
offered Bagoa her protection.

6. *gold*] The play affords no evidence that Tellus turned against
Endymion as she did for financial gain, or that she bribed Dipsas and Bagoa
to carry out the enchantment. The sentiment here is general and sententious—and speciously misogynistic.

8. *work . . . wax*] This common proverbial idea appears also in *Mother
Bombie*, II.i.69, III.ii.1–2, and IV.i.82. *Silly* means 'foolish, innocent, defence-
less, weak'.

9. *marvel*] wonder, as also at III.ii.20, IV.i.1, V.i.169, and V.ii.24.
determine in this cause] decide in this case.

10. *I . . . causes*] The exasperation of Cynthia's courtiers that her clemency
will merely encourage further disobedience and conspiracy is not unlike the
impatience of Elizabeth's courtiers, who, throughout the early and mid
1580s, urged her to disarm the plots against her by executing Mary Queen of
Scots.

15. *practice to be discovered*] conspiracy to be divulged.

17. *coming out*] The phrase suggests that Cynthia is to enter in the play's
final scene as from her palace doors. See next note.

[SCENE 4]

[*Enter*] CYNTHIA, SEMELE, FLOSCULA, DIPSAS, ENDYMION,
EUMENIDES[, GERON, PYTHAGORAS, GYPTES, *and* SIR TOPHAS.
A tree stands by the lunary bank, as in IV.iii *and* V.i].

Cynthia. Dipsas, thy years are not so many as thy vices, yet
more in number than commonly nature doth afford or
justice should permit. Hast thou almost these fifty years
practised that detested wickedness of witchcraft? Wast
thou so simple as for to know the nature of simples, of all   5
creatures to be most sinful? Thou hast threatened to turn
my course awry and alter by thy damnable art the government that I now possess by the eternal gods. But know
thou, Dipsas, and let all the enchanters know, that
Cynthia, being placed for light on earth, is also protected   10
by the powers of heaven. Breathe out thou mayst words,

---

0. [SCENE 4] *This ed.; not marked as a new scene in* Q.   0.2. S.D.
GERON . . . SIR TOPHAS] *Baker; not in* Q.   0.3. S.D. *A tree. . . . v.i*] *This ed.*

0.1–3. [Enter . . . v.i] Q does not mark a scene here, and the action is
essentially continuous, in that Panelion's last words in v.iii prepare us for
Cynthia's entrance. Still, Panelion and Zontes do exit, and do not re-enter
until they bring Corsites and Tellus at l. 36.1–2. The marking of a new scene
is thus editorially defensible, even though in the theatre the distinction is
unobservable. The tree representing Bagoa would seem to be visible, as in
IV.iii and v.i, 'discovered' anew perhaps by drawing back a curtain. (Conceivably, this 'discovery' could occur later in this scene, at l. 291.) Panelion refers
in v.iii.16–17 to Dipsas's having turned Bagoa 'to an aspen tree', speaking as
though the tree is not present. It is now visibly an older tree than in IV.iii, one
that will be transformed back into Bagoa by Cynthia at l. 297.1.
    3. *almost these fifty years*] For a possible historical interpretation hearken-
ing back to Henry VIII's break with the Catholic Church in the 1530s, see
Introduction, p. 34. Lines 6–11 similarly may hint at Queen Elizabeth's
(Cynthia's) denunciations of Catholic conspiracy and her heaven-sent deliverance from such enemies.
    4–6. *Wast . . . sinful?*] Were you so foolish as to strive to know the nature
of magical drugs, you who were born to be the most sinful of creatures?
Simples, or drugs used in magic spells, are literally single substances, ingredi-
ents used in compounds; with wordplay on *simple*, foolish. (Daniel's emendation of *for* to *not* in l. 5 is also plausible.) *Creatures* in l. 6 may possibly refer
to herbs rather than to Dipsas, though *simples* are not ordinarily referred to
as *creatures*.

gather thou mayst herbs, find out thou mayst stones
agreeable to thine art, yet of no force to appal my heart,
in which courage is so rooted, and constant persuasion of
the mercy of the gods so grounded, that all thy witchcraft   15
I esteem as weak as the world doth thy case wretched.
This noble gentleman Geron, once thy husband but now
thy mortal hate, didst thou procure to live in a desert,
almost desperate. Endymion, the flower of my court and
the hope of succeeding time, hast thou bewitched by art   20
before thou wouldst suffer him to flourish by nature.

Dipsas. Madam, things past may be repented, not recalled.
There is nothing so wicked that I have not done, nor
anything so wished for as death. Yet among all the things
that I committed, there is nothing so much tormenteth   25
my rented and ransacked thoughts as that in the prime of
my husband's youth I divorced him by my devilish art, for
which, if to die might be amends, I would not live till
tomorrow. If to live and still be more miserable would
better content him, I would wish of all creatures to be   30
oldest and ugliest.

Geron. Dipsas, thou hast made this difference between me
and Endymion, that, being both young, thou hast caused
me to wake in melancholy, losing the joys of my youth,
and him to sleep, not remembering youth.   35

Cynthia. Stay, here cometh Tellus. We shall now know all.

---

34. losing] *Q* (loosing).

12–13. *stones . . . art*] special minerals suited to your magical skill.
13. *yet of no force*] yet all will be of no force.
18. *mortal*] deadly.
procure] bring about, contrive.
desert] an unhabited region, including forest-land. Also at l. 51.
22. *things past . . . recalled*] A proverbial sentiment (Dent T204) of which
Lyly is fond; it occurs in *Euphues*, II.74, 14–16 and in *Midas*, II.i.43 and
V.iii.70–1. In each instance a penitent figure (usually a male) begs forgiveness
of a virtuous woman, suggesting a recurring element in Lyly of what Robert
G. Hunter calls 'the comedy of forgiveness' (*Shakespeare and the Comedy of
Forgiveness*, New York: Columbia University Press, 1965). *Recalled* means
'brought back into being'.
26. *rented*] rent, torn, the past participle passive of 'rend'; compare
Euphues, II.17, 29, 'renting his clothes' (Bond).
33. *being both young*] when the two of us were young.
34. *wake*] remain awake.

Enter CORSITES [*and*] TELLUS, [*escorted by*] PANELION
[*and* ZONTES].

Corsites. [*To Tellus*] I would to Cynthia thou couldst make as
good an excuse in truth as to me thou hast done by wit.

Tellus. Truth shall be mine answer, and therefore I will not
study for an excuse.   40

Cynthia. Is it possible, Tellus, that so few years should harbour so many mischiefs? Thy swelling pride have I borne
because it is a thing that beauty maketh blameless, which,
the more it exceedeth fairness in measure, the more it
stretcheth itself in disdain. Thy devices against Corsites I   45
smile at, for that wits the sharper they are, the shrewder
they are. But this unacquainted and most unnatural practice with a vile enchantress against so noble a gentleman
as Endymion I abhor as a thing most malicious, and will
revenge as a deed most monstrous. And as for you,   50
Dipsas, I will send you into the desert amongst wild
beasts, and try whether you can cast lions, tigers, boars,
and bears into as dead a sleep as you did Endymion, or
turn them to trees as you have done Bagoa. But tell me,

36.1–2. S.D. [*escorted by*] PANELION [*and* ZONTES] Baker, *subst.; Panelion. &c.*
/ Q.   37. S.D.] *This ed.*

40. *study*] search, cast about, exert myself.

41. *so few years*] (*a*) so short a span of time (*b*) a person so young.

43. *maketh blameless*] excuses, mitigates. Cynthia will not censure what is
none the less a defect. Compare the proverb, 'Where beauty is there needs no
other plea' (Dent B177).

44. *exceedeth fairness in measure*] goes beyond the bounds of normal
beauty.

45. *stretcheth itself*] increases in size, swells, preens itself, like a peacock's
tail. Compare the proverb, 'Beauty may have fair leaves yet bitter fruit' (Dent
B173).

devices] plots.

46–7. *for that . . . shrewder they are*] i.e. since the more that people behave
cleverly the more mischievous they are likely to be, and since Corsites's
discomfiture at your hands is not undeserved.

47. *unacquainted*] unparalleled, as in *Sappho and Phao*, II.iv.1, *Gallathea*,
III.iv.58, and *Love's Metamorphosis*, I.ii.145.

47–8. *practice*] conspiracy. Compare I.ii.43, v.iii.15, and elsewhere.

52–4. *try whether . . . Bagoa*] Cynthia does not mean simply that Dipsas
can now practise her magical skills on animals, like Circe; she will be obliged
to defend her very life against wild beasts. Cynthia is speaking of a revenge

Tellus, what was the cause of this cruel part, far unfitting   55
thy sex, in which nothing should be but simpleness, and
much disagreeing from thy face, in which nothing seemed
to be but softness?

Tellus. Divine Cynthia, by whom I receive my life and am
content to end it, I can neither excuse my fault without   60
lying nor confess it without shame. Yet were it possible
that in so heavenly thoughts as yours there could fall such
earthly motions as mine, I would then hope, if not to be
pardoned without extreme punishment, yet to be heard
without great marvel.   65

Cynthia. Say on, Tellus. I cannot imagine anything that can
colour such a cruelty.

Tellus. Endymion, that Endymion, in the prime of his youth
so ravished my heart with love that to obtain my desires
I could not find means, nor to resist them reason. What   70
was she that favoured not Endymion, being young, wise,
honourable, and virtuous? Besides, what metal was she
made of, be she mortal, that is not affected with the spice,
nay infected with the poison, of that not-to-be-expressed

---

70. resist] *Bond;* resite *Q;* recite *Blount.*   70. What] *No paragraph as in
Dilke; Q introduces a new paragraph here; also at 6, 17, and 50 above and 91 and
115 below.*   72. metal] *Q (*mettall*).*

---

suitable to a 'monstrous' deed (l. 50), though again it is notable that she does
not plan to execute Tellus even in this moment of just anger.
  55. *part*] act, conduct.
  56. *simpleness*] innocence, humbleness, honesty. Compare l. 5 and note 4–6.
  63. *motions*] inward promptings, emotions (*OED*, 9), set opposite to
Cynthia's *thoughts*, l. 62, and with a further astronomical meaning of earthly
movement as under the influence of the heavenly spheres. The image alludes
to Cynthia's and Tellus's metaphorical names.
  67. *colour*] render plausible, represent in fair colours (*OED*, v. 3).
  70–2. *What . . . virtuous*] Lyly appears to have in mind Medea's explanation of her love for Jason: '*quid enim commisit Iason? / quem, nisi crudelem, non
tangat Iasonis aetas / et genus et virtus?*', 'For what has Jason done? Who that
is not heartless would not be moved by Jason's youth, his noble birth, his
manhood?' (Ovid, *Metamorphoses*, VII.25–7, LCL, I.344–5; Edge, 'Sources', pp.
179–80).
  71. *favoured*] loved.
  being] Endymion being.
  72. *metal*] Q's *mettall* embodies the common ambiguity of *metal*, substance, constituent matter, and *mettle*, temperament. They were originally
the same word, and variant spellings can catch all senses. Compare III.ii.28.

yet always-to-be-felt love, which breaketh the brains and   75
never bruiseth the brow, consumeth the heart and never
toucheth the skin, and maketh a deep wound to be felt
before any scar at all be seen? My heart, too tender to
withstand such a divine fury, yielded to love—madam, I
not without blushing confess, yielded to love.   80
Cynthia. A strange effect of love, to work such an extreme
hate. How say you, Endymion, all this was for love?
Endymion. I say, madam, then the gods send me a woman's
hate.
Cynthia. That were as bad, for then by contrary you should   85
never sleep. But on, Tellus, let us hear the end.
Tellus. Feeling a continual burning in all my bowels and a

---

76. bruiseth] *Q* (brooseth).   77–8. wound to be felt before any scar at all
be seen] *Bond, on the suggestion of P. A. Daniel;* skarre to be seene, before any
wounde at all be felt *Q.*   79–80. love—madam, I not without blushing
confess, yielded] *Bond;* Loue. Madame I not without blushing confesse,
yeelded *Q;* love, madam; I, not without blushing, confess, yielded *Dilke;*
love. Madam, I, not without blushing, confess I yielded *Baker.*

---

76. *bruiseth the brow*] hurts the forehead.
76–7. *consumeth . . . skin*] Tellus speaks of love as like lightning, which
proverbially bruises the tree but does not break the bark (Dent L280). Lyly
uses the proverb elsewhere, as in *Euphues,* II.75, 37–II.76, I.
77–8. *maketh . . . seen*] Bond's emendation from Q's 'maketh a deepe
skarre to be seene, before any wounde at all be felt' preserves the logic of
Tellus's series of contrasts between inner hurt and outward apparent health.
The inversion is a plausible compositorial error. Conceivably, Lyly was
making the point that it is more magical to make the scar appear *before* the
wound is felt, but the sequence here is about Tellus's falling in love rather
than about magic.
83–4. *then . . . hate*] i.e. if it was love that produced Tellus's vengefulness
towards me, I would prefer that she dislike me.
85–6. *you should never sleep*] i.e. you would never have a moment's peace—
the extreme opposite of your long sleep.
87. *bowels*] the internal organs generally, especially the heart; the bowels in
this sense are considered the seat of the tender emotions (*OED,* sb.¹ 3, 4).
The inward burning and bursting of almost every 'vein', the 'inward fire' and
the 'outward smoke', the flying of sparks and the 'scalding flames' (ll. 88–91),
all suggest volcanic activity, in an witty elaboration of the metaphor of the
earth (Tellus) rebelling against the heavens governed by Cynthia or the
moon. The metaphor is picked up again in the references to the 'fumes' of
'Etna' and to the 'Alps' in l. 98. See note at l. 63. The *bowels* are thus also,
in the conventional phrase, the *bowels* or inward regions of the earth. Lyly
also draws on proverbial wisdom: 'fire that's closest kept burns most of all'
(Dent F265) and 'there is no fire without some smoke' (Dent F282).

bursting almost in every vein, I could not smother the
inward fire, but it must needs be perceived by the outward smoke; and, by the flying abroad of divers sparks,   90
divers judged of my scalding flames. Endymion, as full of
art as wit, marking mine eyes (in which he might see
almost his own), my sighs (by which he might ever hear
his name sounded), aimed at my heart (in which he was
assured his person was imprinted), and by questions   95
wrung out that which was ready to burst out. When he
saw the depth of my affections, he swore that mine in
respect of his were as fumes to Etna, valleys to Alps, ants
to eagles, and nothing could be compared to my beauty
but his love and eternity. Thus drawing a smooth shoe   100
upon a crooked foot, he made me believe that (which all
of our sex willingly acknowledge) I was beautiful, and to
wonder (which indeed is a thing miraculous) that any of
his sex should be faithful.

Cynthia. Endymion, how will you clear yourself?   105
Endymion. Madam, by mine own accuser.

94–5. *my heart . . . imprinted*] For the Petrarchan conceit of the lover carrying the image of the beloved in his heart, see for example Shakespeare's
Sonnet 24, 'Mine eye hath played the painter and hath stelled / Thy beauty's
form in table of my heart'.

98. *Etna*] The eruptions of this famous volanic mountain in Sicily were
attributed in ancient mythology to Encedalus, one of the Giants who rose
against the gods and were imprisoned in the earth for their audacity;
Encedalus was imprisoned under Etna. The Cyclopes are also frequently
associated with Sicily. See Virgil, *Aeneid*, III.578–87 (LCL, I.386–7), and notes
at ll. 87 and 63.

98–9. *ants to eagles*] Compare Erasmus's adage *aquila non muscas captat*
(*Opera Omnia*, II.761e), which contrasts the eagle with the fly in terms of size
and power.

100–1. *a smooth . . . foot*] Compare *Euphues*, I.179, 27–I.180, 1:
'Demonydes must have a crooked shoe for his wry foot', making clear Lily's
aquaintance with the story of the crippled Damonidas who prayed that the
man who stole his boots 'might have feet which they would fit' (Plutarch,
Moralia, 'How a Young Man Should Study Poetry', *De. Aud. Poet.* 18D,
Chapter III, LCL, I.94–5; cited in Bond). Lyly reverses the image: the passage
in *Euphues* urges candour about unflattering details even in praiseworthy and
famous people, whereas Tellus's inverted maxim is about deceitful appearance. Compare also *Sappho and Phao*, 'a great shoe upon a little foot'
(I.iii.21–2), Erasmus's *Adagia*, II.566D (II.v.46 in vol. 33 of the Toronto
edition, p. 262) and II.861C, and Dent s366; and *Euphues*, II.7, 6.

103. *wonder*] marvel.

Cynthia. Well, Tellus, proceed, but briefly, lest, taking delight
   in uttering thy love, thou offend us with the length of it.
Tellus. I will, madam, quickly make an end of my love and my
   tale. Finding continual increase of my tormenting   110
   thoughts, and that the enjoying of my love made deeper
   wounds than the entering into it, I could find no means to
   ease my grief but to follow Endymion, and continually to
   have him in the object of mine eyes, who had me slave
   and subject to his love. But in the moment that I feared   115
   his falsehood, and fried myself most in mine affections, I
   found (ah, grief! even then I lost myself), I found him in
   most melancholy and desperate terms, cursing his stars,
   his state, the earth, the heavens, the world, and all for the
   love of—   120
Cynthia. Of whom? Tellus, speak boldly.
Tellus. Madam, I dare not utter for fear to offend.
Cynthia. Speak, I say. Who dare take offence if thou be commanded by Cynthia?
Tellus. For the love of Cynthia.   125
Cynthia. For my love, Tellus? That were strange. Endymion,
   is it true?
Endymion. In all things, madam. Tellus doth not speak false.
Cynthia. What will this breed to in the end? Well, Endymion,
   we shall hear all.   130
Tellus. I, seeing my hopes turned to mishaps, and a settled
   dissembling towards me, and an unmovable desire to
   Cynthia, forgetting both myself and my sex, fell unto this
   unnatural hate. For knowing your virtues, Cynthia, to be
   immortal, I could not have an imagination to withdraw   135

---

107. lest] *Q* (least).   128. madam. Tellus] *Q* (Madame. *Tellus); Madame,
Tellus *Dilke.*

111. *enjoying*] experiencing.
114. *in . . . eyes*] always before my eyes (*OED*, *object*, sb. 9, 'the presentation (of something) to the eye or perception', now obsolete; compare *Cor.*,
I.i.19–20). With wordplay on the antithesis of *object* and *subject*, l. 115.
116. *fried . . . affections*] A commonplace image, as in *Euphues*, I.205, 4–5:
'Lucilla, who now began to fry in the flames of love', etc. (Bond).
117–18. *found him . . . terms*] Tellus recalls their meeting at II.i.58–112.
129. *breed to*] develop into.
133. *unto*] into.
135–6. *I . . . him*] I didn't imagine I could possibly get him back.

him; and finding mine own affections unquenchable, I
could not carry the mind that any else should possess
what I had pursued. For though in majesty, beauty, virtue, and dignity I always humbled and yielded myself to
Cynthia, yet in affections I esteemed myself equal with   140
the goddesses, and all other creatures, according to their
states, with myself. For stars to their bigness have their
lights, and the sun hath no more. And little pitchers,
when they can hold no more, are as full as great vessels
that run over. Thus, madam, in all truth have I uttered   145
the unhappiness of my love and the cause of my hate,
yielding wholly to that divine judgement which never
erred for want of wisdom or envied for too much
partiality.

Cynthia. How say you, my lords, to this matter? But what say   150
you, Endymion, hath Tellus told truth?

Endymion. Madam, in all things, but in that she said I loved
her and swore to honour her.

Cynthia. Was there such a time whenas for my love thou didst
vow thyself to death, and in respect of it loathed thy life?   155
Speak, Endymion. I will not revenge it with hate.

---

151. truth] *Dilke;* troth *Q.*   154. whenas] *Q (*when as*).*

---

137. *carry the mind*] bear the thought.
140–2. *yet . . . myself*] Tellus tactfully sets her presumptuous rivalry with
Cynthia in the context of an idea of proportion in the universe: though she
is of lesser dignity than Cynthia, her *affections* or sexual passions are no less
strong, as is appropriate to her place in the great chain of being; and so too
with the passions of all other *creatures* below her, who have feelings as
powerful as hers according to their various *states* or capacities and conditions.
142. *to*] in proportion to. Compare Dent s826.01: 'Stars have their lights.'
152. *but*] except.
152–3. *but . . . honour her*] The evidence in the play seems to suggest that
Endymion did in fact promise love to Tellus. At I.ii.7–13, in Floscula's
presence, Tellus apostrophises Endymion by asking rhetorically, 'Were thy
oaths without number, thy kisses without measure, thy sighs without end,
forged to deceive a poor credulous virgin . . . ?' She complains furthermore
about his 'perjury'. When Endymion confesses in soliloquy (II.iii.12–18) that
Tellus has seemed beautiful to him, and even wise and honourable in her
way, he seems to admit a courtship that has now ended. Yet he protests in an
earlier soliloquy that his attentions to Tellus were 'but as a cloak for mine
affections' that others might not perceive his interest in Cynthia (II.i.25–9).
Even though Endymion's ardour may have been partly feigned, his answer in
this present scene to Cynthia would appear to be disingenuous.

Endymion. The time was, madam, and is, and ever shall be,
    that I honoured Your Highness above all the world; but
    to stretch it so far as to call it love, I never durst. There
    hath none pleased mine eye but Cynthia, none delighted   160
    mine ears but Cynthia, none possessed my heart but
    Cynthia. I have forsaken all other fortunes to follow
    Cynthia, and here I stand ready to die if it please Cynthia.
    Such a difference hath the gods set between our states
    that all must be duty, loyalty, and reverence; nothing,   165
    without it vouchsafe Your Highness, be termed love. My
    unspotted thoughts, my languishing body, my discon-
    tented life, let them obtain by princely favour that which
    to challenge they must not presume, only wishing of
    impossibilities; with imagination of which I will spend my 170
    spirits, and to myself, that no creature may hear, softly
    call it love. And if any urge to utter what I whisper, then
    will I name it honour. From this sweet contemplation if I
    be not driven, I shall live of all men the most content,
    taking more pleasure in mine aged thoughts than ever I   175
    did in my youthful actions.
Cynthia. Endymion, this honourable respect of thine shall be
    christened 'love' in thee, and my reward for it 'favour'.

---

157. *was . . . be*] Endymion echoes The Book of Common Prayer: 'As it
was in the beginning, is now, and ever shall be'. (This is the congregation's
response to the *Gloria Patri*, 'Glory be to the Father, and to the Son, and to
the Holy Ghost', said for example after the recital of the Lord's Prayer during
Morning Prayer and Evening Prayer, according to the Standard Book of
1928.) Compare Lancelot Gobbo in *MV*, II.ii.81–2: 'your boy that was, your
son that is, your child that shall be'. An appropriate if slightly idolatrous way
to address a queen (Cynthia, or perhaps Elizabeth) as a deity.
    160–3. *Cynthia . . . Cynthia*] The poetic repetition of Cynthia's name at
the end of five phrases in succession, augmented by rhythmic effects of
repeated sound, length of phrase, and grammatical construction (isocolon
and parison), betrays in Endymion the rhetorical habits of a traditional lover.
    166. *without . . . Your Highness*] unless Your Highness would vouchsafe to
allow it.
    169. *challenge*] demand as a right, lay claim to.
    169–70. *only . . . impossibilities*] even though in my thoughts I may secretly
wish for something impossible.
    170–1. *spend my spirits*] expend my breath.
    172. *urge*] urge me.
    172–3. *then . . . honour*] then I will insist that my devotion is unspotted and
honourable.

Persevere, Endymion, in loving me, and I account more
strength in a true heart than in a walled city. I have   180
laboured to win all, and study to keep such as I have won;
but those that neither my favour can move to continue
constant, nor my offered benefits get to be faithful, the
gods shall either reduce to truth or revenge their treach-
eries with justice. Endymion, continue as thou hast be-   185
gun, and thou shalt find that Cynthia shineth not on thee
in vain.   [*Endymion's youthful looks are restored to him.*]
Endymion. Your Highness hath blessed me, and your words
have again restored my youth. Methinks I feel my joints
strong, and these mouldy hairs to moult, and all by your   190
virtue, Cynthia, into whose hands the balance that
weigheth time and fortune are committed.
Cynthia. What, young again? Then it is pity to punish Tellus.
Tellus. Ah, Endymion, now I know thee and ask pardon of
thee. Suffer me still to wish thee well.   195
Endymion. Tellus, Cynthia must command what she will.
Floscula. Endymion, I rejoice to see thee in thy former estate.
Endymion. Good Floscula, to thee also am I in my former
affections.
Eumenides. Endymion, the comfort of my life, how am I rav-   200

187. s.d.] *Bond, subst., conj. Dilke.*

179–80. *I account . . . walled city*] Cynthia's asseveration has a proverbial
ring: 'Men (men's love), not walls, make the city (prince) safe' (Dent M555).
184. *reduce to truth*] bring into order, obedience, reason, etc. (*OED, reduce,*
v. 19). The passage implies that Elizabeth's foes will find forgiveness if they
repent, and harsh vengeance if they do not. *Reduce* may also connote a
humbling or lowering of those who have been audacious.
187. s.d. Endymion's . . . to him] Some staging contrivances involving
removal of beard and white hair may be used here to create a visual effect, as
when Corsites is spotted at IV.iii.43 or when Endymion is transformed from
a sleeping youth to an aged man. See also the transformation of a 'tree' into
Bagoa at V.iv.297.1 below.
191. *virtue*] magical power; moral authority.
the balance] the emblem of Cynthia (and Elizabeth) as the embodiment of
justice.
192. *weigheth*] weighs as in a balance, one against the other.
194. *now I know thee*] Only with his youth restored can Tellus be sure who
Endymion is, though she must be aware of his apparent identity throughout
the scene; Cynthia repeatedly addresses Endymion by name (ll. 82, 105, 126,
151, 156) as Tellus relates her story.
195. *Suffer me still*] allow me after all I've done, and continually from now
on.

ished with a joy matchless, saving only the enjoying of my
mistress!

Cynthia. Endymion, you must now tell who Eumenides
shrineth for his saint.

Endymion. Semele, madam.   205

Cynthia. Semele, Eumenides? Is it Semele? The very wasp of
all women, whose tongue stingeth as much as an adder's
tooth?

Eumenides. It is Semele, Cynthia, the possessing of whose
love must only prolong my life.   210

Cynthia. Nay, sith Endymion is restored, we will have all
parties pleased. Semele, are you content after so long trial
of his faith, such rare secrecy, such unspotted love, to
take Eumenides?—Why speak you not? Not a word?

Endymion. Silence, madam, consents. That is most true.   215

Cynthia. It is true, Endymion. Eumenides, take Semele. Take
her, I say.

Eumenides. Humble thanks, madam. Now only do I begin to
live.

Semele. A hard choice, madam, either to be married if I say   220
nothing or to lose my tongue if I speak a word. Yet do I
rather choose to have my tongue cut out than my heart
distempered. I will not have him.

Cynthia. Speaks the parrot? She shall nod hereafter with
signs. Cut off her tongue, nay, her head, that, having a   225
servant of honourable birth, honest manners, and true
love, will not be persuaded!

203–4. *Endymion . . . saint*] Eumenides has insisted at v.i.19–20 that only
Endymion, once awakened, can reveal the secret of Eumenides's love.

206–8. *The . . . tooth*] More proverbial misogynistic wisdom from Cynthia
(compare ll. 85–6 and 224 and notes), alluding to the supposed waspishness
of women (Dent w76, *Shr.* II.i.209–18) and to the common idea that 'the
tongue is more venomous than a serpent's sting' (Dent T407).

209–10. *the possessing . . . life*] without whose love I can live no longer.

215. *Silence . . . consents*] A legal truism: Dent s446.

223. *distempered*] vexed, disordered, diseased.

224. *Speaks the parrot?*] Women are often accused in Renaissance literature of being parrot–like chatterers, as in *Midas*, I.ii.40: 'Well, she hath a
tongue of a parrot', in *Woman in the Moon*, I.i.116, and earlier in John
Skelton's *Speak, Parrot* (1521–22). See Dent P60 for other instances.

226. *servant*] wooer. In the typical Petrarchan love relationship, the male
wooer offers his duty to the woman whom he adores and serves, his *mistress*
(ll. 229–31).

Semele. He is no faithful lover, madam, for then would he
have asked his mistress.

Geron. Had he not been faithful, he had never seen into the   230
fountain, and so lost his friend and mistress.

Eumenides. Thine own thoughts, sweet Semele, witness
against thy words, for what hast thou found in my life but
love? And as yet what have I found in my love but
bitterness? Madam, pardon Semele, and let my tongue   235
ransom hers.

Cynthia. Thy tongue, Eumenides? What shouldst thou live,
wanting a tongue to blaze the beauty of Semele? Well,
Semele, I will not command love, for it cannot be enforced. Let me entreat it.   240

Semele. I am content Your Highness shall command, for now
only do I think Eumenides faithful, that is willing to lose
his tongue for my sake; yet loath, because it should do me
better service. Madam, I accept of Eumenides.

Cynthia. I thank you, Semele.   245

Eumenides. Ah, happy Eumenides, that hast a friend so faithful and a mistress so fair! With what sudden mischief will
the gods daunt this excess of joy? Sweet Semele, I live or
die as thou wilt.

229. *asked his mistress*] asked for Semele instead of Endymion at the
fountain. Compare v.i.16–17.

237. *What shouldst thou live*] how could you live. (Alternatively, by supply-
ing a comma after *What* that does not appear in Q, the phrase could mean,
'What, you mean you actually propose to live'.)

238. *wanting*] lacking.

blaze] proclaim (*OED*, v.² 2). See note on the *blazon*, the proclaiming of
one's mistress's excellences, at III.iii.55–64.

239–40. *it cannot be enforced*] Proverbial: 'Love cannot be compelled'
(Dent L499). Compare Hephestion's advice to Alexander in *Campaspe*,
II.ii.114–16.

243. *loath*] The term can apply to both Semele's and Eumenides's unwill-
ingness that he should lose his tongue and thus not be able to 'blaze' her
virtues.

248. *daunt*] vanquish, subdue. The idea that excess of joy can prove
ruinous is a familiar topic in Renaissance literature, as in Portia's plea that
love 'In measure rein thy joy' (*MV*, III.ii.111–14), and in Friar Lawrence's
adjuration that 'The sweetest honey / Is loathsome in his own deliciousness'
(*Rom.*, II.vi.11–12). The fate of the mythological Semele, consumed in a flash
of lightning for daring to be Jupiter's lover in his full presence, adds irony to
Eumenides's protestation here that he will 'live or die as thou wilt' (ll. 248–
9). See III.iv.101–4 and note.

Cynthia. What shall become of Tellus? Tellus, you know   250
Endymion is vowed to a service from which death cannot
remove him. Corsites casteth still a lovely look towards
you. How say you, will you have your Corsites and so
receive pardon for all that is past?

Tellus. Madam, most willingly.   255

Cynthia. But I cannot tell whether Corsites be agreed.

Corsites. Ay, madam, more happy to enjoy Tellus than the
monarchy of the world.

Eumenides. Why, she caused you to be pinched with fairies.

Corsites. Ay, but her fairness hath pinched my heart more   260
deeply.

Cynthia. Well, enjoy thy love. But what have you wrought in
the castle, Tellus?

Tellus. Only the picture of Endymion.

Cynthia. Then so much of Endymion as his picture cometh   265
to, possess and play withal.

Corsites. Ah, my sweet Tellus, my love shall be as thy beauty
is: matchless.

Cynthia. Now it resteth, Dipsas, that if thou wilt forswear that
vile art of enchanting, Geron hath promised again to   270
receive thee; otherwise, if thou be wedded to that wickedness, I must and will see it punished to the uttermost.

Dipsas. Madam, I renounce both substance and shadow of
that most horrible and hateful trade, vowing to the gods
continual penance and to Your Highness obedience.   275

Cynthia. How say you, Geron, will you admit her to your
wife?

---

252. look] *Blount;* lookes *Q.*   253. you. How say you, will you have] *Bond,
subst.;* you, how say you will haue *Q.*

---

252. *lovely*] loving.

265–6. *Then . . . withal*] On possible allegorical readings of this 'picture' of
Endymion that Tellus is allowed to keep, see Introduction, pp. 19–20, 28.

269. *resteth*] remains.

271. *wedded*] obstinately attached; with an obvious play on the primary
meaning, 'joined in wedlock'. Compare 'if thou be either so wicked that thou
wilt not, or so wedded that thou canst not abstain from their glances'
(*Euphues*, 1.255, 22–4, cited by *OED*, 3 as its earliest instance of this
meaning).

273. *substance and shadow*] A standard rhetorical antithesis (Dent s951 and
s951.11); compare *Gallathea*, III.iv.44 and *Love's Metamorphosis*, III.i.20.

Geron. Ay, with more joy than I did the first day, for nothing
could happen to make me happy but only her forsaking
that lewd and detestable course. Dipsas, I embrace thee.   280
Dipsas. And I thee, Geron, to whom I will hereafter recite the
cause of these my first follies.   [*They embrace.*]
Cynthia. Well, Endymion, nothing resteth now but that we
depart. Thou hast my favour, Tellus her friend,
Eumenides in paradise with his Semele, Geron contented   285
with Dipsas.
Tophas. Nay, soft. I cannot handsomely go to bed without
Bagoa.
Cynthia. Well, Sir Tophas, it may be there are more virtues in
me than myself knoweth of, for Endymion I awaked, and   290
at my words he waxed young. I will try whether I can turn
this tree again to thy true love.
Tophas. Turn her to a true love or false, so she be a wench I
care not.
Cynthia. Bagoa, Cynthia putteth an end to thy hard fortunes,   295

---

282. s.d.] *This ed.*

280. *lewd*] wicked.
287–8. *without Bagoa*] Tophas remains an absurd caricature to the very
end. While the others are united to their true loves or reconciled after years
of separation, Tophas is willing to settle for any woman now that he cannot
have Dipsas; she can be 'true love or false, so she be a wench' (l. 293). His
only response to Bagoa's being made human again is to curse her (l. 298).
292. *this tree*] See staging note at v.iv.0.1–3; the 'tree' seems to have been
visible throughout iv.iii and v.i as a young tree, then again in v.iv as an older
tree, perhaps 'discovered' next to the lunary bank on each occasion by the
opening of curtains. (Conceivably, in v.iv the 'discovery' is not made until
this present moment.) Bagoa's being transformed onstage from a tree into
human shape at l. 297.1 (her earlier transformation into a tree is offstage)
seems to have made use of a favourite theatrical device of Lyly; as Hunter
notes, Hebe in *Gallathea* is tied to a tree (v.ii), Gunophilus in *The Woman in
the Moon* is changed into a hawthorne at his final exit (v.i.272), and a tree in
Love's Metamorphosis contains a nymph, Fidelia, who cries out when the tree
is attacked with an axe (i.ii). 'Lyly seems to have acquired a trick tree at some
point in his career . . . All this would seem to imply a stage-tree with a hollow
trunk and with a door which opens to receive or eject an actor' (p. 110). The
Revels account for Christmas, New Year's tide, and Twelfth tide in 1573/4
(ed. Feuillerat, p. 203), mentions 'Lathes for the Hollo tree' as a property
(cited in Hunter, note 57, p. 359). There are other instances where *Endymion*
calls for similar *trompe l'oeil* effects, such as the spotting of Corsites (iv.iii.43
and note), Endymion's visible ageing, and then Endymion's restoration from
age to youth (v.iv.187. s.d. and note).

for, being turned to a tree for revealing a truth, I will
recover thee again if in my power be the effect of truth.

[*Bagoa regains her human shape.*]

Tophas. Bagoa? A bots upon thee!

Cynthia. Come my lords, let us in. You, Gyptes and Pythagoras, if you cannot content yourselves in our court to fall   300
from vain follies of philosophers to such virtues as are
here practised, you shall be entertained according to your
deserts, for Cynthia is no stepmother to strangers.

Pythagoras. I had rather in Cynthia's court spend ten years
than in Greece one hour.   305

Gyptes. And I choose rather to live by the sight of Cynthia
than by the possessing of all Egypt.

Cynthia. Then follow.

Eumenides. We all attend.   *Exeunt.*

The Epilogue

A man walking abroad, the wind and sun strove for
sovereignty; the one with his blast, the other with his
beams. The wind blew hard; the man wrapped his gar-

297.1. S.D.] *Baker, subst.*   300. cannot] *Q;* can *Bond.*

---

298. A *bots upon thee*] i.e. a plague upon you. *Bot* or *bott* is a parasitic
maggot afflicting the digestive organs of the horse; *botts* is sometimes used as
a singular noun for the disease. As an expression of execration (*OED, bot,* sb.
2), the first *OED* citation is in 1584.

300. *cannot*] The logic of Cynthia's speech would seem to require *can;* she
is offering to *entertain* or receive the wise men according to their deservings
if they will abandon the scholar's life and serve her. But *cannot* has its own
more threatening logic, that if the scholars cannot abandon vain learning to
practise virtue they deserve what they will get. In either case, the play ends
on a note of implied praise for Queen Elizabeth as the patron of an idealised
court, and accepts entire the capitulation of the philosopher into the
courtier—an issue at debate in *Euphues* (the university versus Athens),
Campaspe (where Alexander commands Plato, Aristotle, and other philosophers in I.iii to pay attention to courtly demands but finds in Diogenes a
more intractable critic), *Sappho and Phao* (Pandion versus Trachinus), and
other works.

303. *no stepmother*] Cynthia will not be niggardly and unsupporting.

1–9. *A man . . . coat*] This fable appears in *Euphues,* II.224, 7–15, where it
is given a notably different application: Euphues advises husbands that mild
words and gentle persuasions will prove more effective with their wives than
threats and blows, which will only stiffen opposition to male authority. The

ment about him harder. It blustered more strongly; he   5
then girt it fast to him. 'I cannot prevail', said the wind.
The sun casting her crystal beams began to warm the
man; he unloosed his gown. Yet it shined brighter; he
then put it off. 'I yield', said the wind, 'for if thou continue shining he will also put off his coat'.   10
  Dread sovereign, the malicious that seek to overthrow
us with threats do but stiffen our thoughts and make
them sturdier in storms. But if Your Highness vouchsafe
with your favourable beams to glance upon us, we shall
not only stoop, but with all humility lay both our hands   15
and hearts at Your Majesty's feet.

7. unloosed] Q (vnlosed).

fable and the domestic moral of it resemble Aesop's *Fables*, no. 65 (1665 ed.,
pp. 164–6), but are even more closely derived from the fourth fable of
Avienus, 'Of Phoebus and Boreas' (*Fabulae Aviani*, ed. Françoise Gaide
(Paris: Société d'Édition, 1980), pp. 81–2; Baker). Lyly's courtly application
here is original.
  10–15. *Dread . . . feet*] This argument—that the Queen can win unwaver-
ing loyalty by shining on her adoring petitioners, whereas the animosity of
malicious persons at court can only stiffen resentment—may suggest an
urging on Lyly's part that Oxford and English Catholics be reclaimed
through generous forgiveness rather than hounded into exile and opposition.
See Introduction, pp. 28–35. The statement here is contained in a conventional appeal for royal favour.
  14–15. *we shall . . . feet*] The performance at court ends with the speaker of
the Epilogue, and evidently the cast as well, kneeling before the Queen.
George Hunter points out in correspondence with me that two plays for
adult actors, *Mucedorus* (Epilogue) and *Locrine* (v.vi.202–3, ll. 2276–7 in the
MSR edition of 1908), similarly end with the actors kneeling to honour the
Queen, who is however spoken of as though not present. Whether
the practice was general on the public stage is hard to determine, since these
two plays are relatively early and could both have been Queen's Men plays.

Index

Page numbers refer to the Introduction and 'Characters in Order of Appearance'; act-scene-and-line numbers refer to the Commentary. An asterisk (*) preceding an entry indicates that the commentary note in this edition adds materially to the information given in the OED. Individual words appearing in various inflected forms are usually grouped under one form; phrases are indexed in the form in which they occur in the text. When a gloss is repeated in the annotations, only the initial occurrence is indexed.